D1482055

Index to Anthologies of Latin American Literature in English Translation

Edited and Compiled by
Juan R. Freudenthal
Patricia M. Freudenthal

G. K. HALL & CO., 70 LINCOLN STREET, BOSTON, MASS.

PQ
7087
.E5
F74
1977

Copyright © 1977 by Juan R. Freudenthal and Patricia M. Freudenthal

Library of Congress Cataloging in Publication Data

Freudenthal, Juan R
   Index to anthologies of Latin American literature in
English translation.

   Includes index.
   1. Latin American literature--Translations into
English--Indexes. 2. English literature--Translations
from Spanish--Indexes. 3. English literature--Transla-
tions from Portuguese--Indexes. I. Freudenthal,
Patricia M., joint author. II. Title.
Z1609.T7F74 [PQ7087.E5] 016.86'008   76-40964
ISBN 0-8161-7861-5

This publication is printed on permanent/durable acid-free paper
MANUFACTURED IN THE UNITED STATES OF AMERICA

With affection to

Heid, Ilse, Priscilla, Raquel,

and don Enrique.

Contents

Preface vii
  Purpose
  Scope
  Methodology
  Acknowledgments

Introduction xi
  Latin American Literature: Past and Present
  Contemporary Trends

Annotated Bibliography of Anthologies and Anthology Code . . . xvii

Index to Anthologies of Latin American Literature in
  English Translation 1

Translator Index 177

Geographic Index 185

Further Reading: Selected References 189

Preface

The purpose of this <u>Index</u> is to provide access to 116 anthologies
of Latin American literature in English translation, while identify-
ing 1122 Spanish-American and Brazilian authors representing 20 nations. We did not intend to confuse our readers by stating 1122 authors when our <u>Index</u> clearly enumerates 1128, but the Colombian writer
Miguel Ángel Osorio also published under the names of Ricardo Arenales and Porfirio Barba Jacob. Furthermore, Jorge Luis Borges wrote
together with Adolfo Bioy Casares under the pseudonym of Bustos Do-
mecq and Calvo, Lino Novas; Mirón, Salvador Díaz; and Nájera, Manuel
Gutierrez have additional works listed under their compound surname.
In all other cases we list works under one name only and use cross
references for pseudonyms, which are indicated by brackets.

Authors have been listed alphabetically, and the following information is provided for each one: dates when available, nationality,
English title of original work, translator, which is given in italic,
code for the anthology, and page in the anthology text. A Translator
<u>Index</u>, which identifies 415 translators, and a Geographic Index have
also been provided. To further facilitate the use of this <u>Index</u>, the
code is comprised of a shorthand version of personal names or titles
and follows--with few exceptions--the sequence of the "Annotated Bibliography of Anthologies and Anthology Code."

The need for more bibliographic tools dealing with Latin American
literature is apparent. The late 60s and first half of the 70s have
seen the appearance of several reference sources which ignore or pay
scant attention to Spanish-American and Brazilian literature. "Our
perception of Latin American literature has slowly been changing to
the point where it can be claimed, with a good measure of justifica-
tion, that it is the most living force in contemporary letters. The
word 'slowly' is needed when we consider the fate of this literature
in the 15th edition (1974) of the <u>Encyclopedia Britannica</u>. Only two
authors, Borges and Neruda, are accorded major articles in the Mac-
ropedia section, and the latter's discussion of 'Latin-American Literature in the 20th Century' does not even call for three full pages,
pages where brevity is not the soul of wit." (Philippe L. Poisson,
"Soundings in Modern Latin American Literature." Paper presented
July 24, 1974, for L.S. 413, Literature of the Humanities, Simmons

College, School of Library Science.) Also remiss in this particular
aspect are librarians, whose major task is to identify, organize and
disseminate information which reflects the cultural trends of our
times. For example, Books for College Libaries. A Core Collection
of 40,000 Titles, 2nd Edition, Volume II - Language and Literature
(Chicago, American Library Association, 1975), includes a few authors
--and almost no contemporary ones--representing ten Spanish-American
speaking nations out of a total of nineteen (if we include Puerto
Rico). Central America is dismissed with the mention of Nicaragua's
Rubén Darío and Guatemala's Miguel Ángel Asturias. No authors are
given for Bolivia, Paraguay, El Salvador, Costa Rica, Honduras, Re-
pública Dominicana, Puerto Rico, and Ecuador. This is certainly an
extraordinary omission if one considers that there are approximately
18 million Spanish-speaking people in the United States and that
25 million are predicted in the next few decades.

Scope

    This Index includes only Spanish-American and Brazilian authors
born during or after 1850. The first original and active literary
movement in Latin America--"modernismo" (Modernism)--owes its coa-
lescence to the authors born about the middle of the nineteenth century. Furthermore, the current interest in Latin American literary
expressions in the United States and other English-speaking nations
has focused more sharply on the modern and contemporary trends. It
was important that we consider the accessibility of the literature.
Several titles in our Index are out-of-print but all of them are
available in public, academic, or research libraries, and many can
still be purchased in bookstores or directly from the publisher.

    We have noticed that the criterion for the inclusion of authors
in the various anthologies here represented has varied according to
the background and interest of the editors and compilers. Some have
chosen "the best known of each generation" (which could also read as
"those writers whose output is published regularly or are anthologized more often"); other editors have preferred "quality of writing"
or "a balanced geographical representation   still others prefer "the
younger writers," "a national quota system," "a political bias," or
"a very subjective choice of this editor." Lennox Robinson, the anthologist of Irish poetry once remarked: "Did any anthologist satis-
fy anyone except the compiler?" In other words, an anthology be-
comes a kind of book for which no apology need ever be offered.

    It is regrettable that few women are represented in our Index,
but this is more the reflection of the anthology editors' choice than
the lack of women writers in Latin America.

    We have included in this Index most of the anthologies listed
in the Engber (1970), Levine (1970) and Shaw (1976) bibliographies
(see "Further Reading: Selected References"), but searched further,
trying also to identify journals which have devoted special issues to

Preface

Latin American literature in translation, such as The Massachusetts Review, TriQuarterly, Mundus Artium, Chicago Review, The Drama Review, Delos, etc.

In a few instances we have included pieces written originally in English because they represent the contemporary Latin American experience--particularly the Puerto Rican experience--in the United States.

Methodology

No single source exists which can be considered an "authority" on Latin American author names, dates and country of origin. Therefore we consulted not only some of the best-known literary histories and reference tools written in English, Spanish, and Portuguese, but we also checked the printed library catalogs of the Latin American Library at the University of Florida Libraries; the Latin American collection at the University of Texas, Austin; the Catalog of the Latin American Library, Tulane University Library; The Author and Subject Catalogues of the Canning House Library, London; the National Union Catalogue (including the available volumes of the Pre-1956 Imprints); and the Handbook of Latin American Studies.

Author dates varied from anthology to anthology. In several cases, dates proved totally elusive. On this subject, Willis Knapp Jones once observed that "...biography, like bibliography, is sometimes treated casually in Latin America. Lack of records or carelessness in keeping them is further complicated by whimsy. With two birth dates to choose from, I consulted the family of one writer. Her husband and her son each sent me another." (Willis Knapp Jones. Spanish-American Literature in Translation since 1888, p. viii).

While checking each anthology, we found that there existed some discrepancies between information given in the table of contents and in the text. In such cases we used the information given in the text. If translators were not mentioned and further reference sources or personal correspondence did not clarify the matter, we preferred to indicate "no translator" (no tr.) instead of guessing and thus provide erroneous information.

Acknowledgments

The editors of this Index owe much to the initial interest, research, and effort of Jeffrey Katz who, together with Juan R. Freudenthal, compiled a "Preliminary Index to Anthologized Contemporary Latin American Literature in Translation." (Papers. 20th SALALM. Bogotá, Colombia, June 1975. SALALM Secretariat, University of Massachusetts Library, Amherst, Mass. 54pp). Jeffrey Katz was also of great assistance in the preparation of the present volume.

Special thanks for their help and advice to: Margaret M. Schneider, our research assistant par excellence; David T. Buton, Margarita Anderson-Imbert and Vivian Sachs (Harvard University); Jane Garner and Laura Gutiérrez Witt (The University of Texas, Austin); Boyd Edmonston and Cathy Mark (Simmons College, Boston); Vai Read (Pan American Society of New England); Irene Zimmerman (University of Florida, Gainesville); Joan Stockard (Wellesley College); Bradley A. Shaw (Kansas State University); and Judith A. Ceven, our expert typist. Many courtesies were extended to us at the Harvard College Library and the Pan American Society of New England. Our appreciation to the Emily Hollowell Research Fund, Simmons College.

Introduction

> Political boundaries are of geographical
> but not poetic importance.

The vast portions of land south of the United States, commonly
known as Latin America, form a political, social and cultural struc-
ture which--with very few exceptions--owes its singularity to its
spiritual ties with Spain and Portugal. Although sharp social and
cultural contrasts among the Latin American nations do exist, the
Spanish language is a formidable link which has helped to overcome
many differences. Latin American literature, despite its very dis-
tinctive voices, proclaims in unison a literary wealth which ignores
political and geographic boundaries.

After 1810, when the struggle for political independence from
Spain began, literature became a derivative and imitative form strong-
ly influenced by Spanish and French writing. Literary originality
did not go beyond a popularization of the notion of the "noble savage"--a romantic movement which focused on such issues as individual
freedom and social reform. A need to reject Spanish tradition led
also to a literature which dealt with native themes. Probably the
best example of this period is José Hernández's Martín Fierro (1872),
a paean in honor of the gaucho.

The development of modern Latin American literature springs from
the modernista movement, which roughly spans the period between the
late 1880's and the 1930's. The Nicaraguan Rubén Darío (1867-1916)
is considered the focal point of this new literary school which led
"...to the discovery of the emotional life made by the romantics, the
almost professional awareness of what literature and its latest fash-
ions are...the pride of belonging to an Hispanic American generation
which, for the first time, is able to specialize in art."[1] Modernism
emphasized art for art's sake rather than didacticism. It sought to
emphasize its own experience and vision, although it continued to be
influenced by the French Parnassian group and by French symbolist
poetry.

LATIN AMERICAN LITERATURE IN ENGLISH TRANSLATION

By the time Latin American literature reached European and North American shores during the late 1920's, a vigorous regionalist novel developed. Its basic themes were played against the background of the Argentinian pampa, the Venezuelan plains, the Andean mountains, the villages of revolutionary Mexico or the jungle of Brazil. In essence, this literature was concerned more with nature than with the social and cultural realities of city life. Writers sought to present exotic materials to the urban dwellers.

It is only after World War II that Latin American literature became markedly introspective. Experiments with all types of literary modes, including stream-of-consciousness, forced writers to explore the inner regions of the heart and to probe the depths of the human psyche. Latin America was no longer isolated from the rest of the world. It had become part of the "global village." The new literary themes dealt with the problems of myth and reality, temporal rearrangements, the psychological dynamics and political complexities of society, rural and urban; in essence the problems of a slowly developing society in a rapidly changing world.

The so-called "boom of the Latin American novel" after World War II was caused primarily by the influx of exiled Spanish publishers and writers and by the population shifts from rural to major urban areas in Latin America. These changes fomented new educational needs and contributed to the creation of new school and public libraries. The Uruguayan literary critic Emir Rodríguez Monegal further suggests that World War II, having caused the interruption of the importation of European novels into Latin America, gave new impetus to the regional narrative by forcing "...the reading public to turn its eyes toward 'indigenous' writers..."[2] Other developments which brought about a literary Renaissance in Latin America during the 50's and 60's were the emergence of a new generation of readers, the creation of prestigious national and international literary contests, and the appearance of new, well edited journals including Siempre, in Mexico; Mundo Nuevo, in Paris; Primera Plana, in Argentina; and Revista, in Cuba.

Contemporary Trends

> "Latin America is today a continent that is changing its skin, that is becoming the subject rather than the object of history."[3]

Some United States literary critics and pessimists have suggested that when the North American novel lost its vitality and died of boredom--what else happened after Faulkner?--our publishers "discovered" the Latin American writers. Of course, the word "discovered" reveals the ignorance surrounding the powerful literary tradition south of the United States border, which includes, among many others, that worthy Nobel Prize contender, Jorge Luis Borges, celebrant of the mystery that is life, short-story writer, poet, translator and librarian, who has led millions of us into the deep seas which underlie our existence and has influenced contemporary narrative, the theatre of the absurd, and the cinema. Other "discoveries" are Pablo Neruda and Gabriel García Márquez, who have been translated into numerous languages; the Brazilian Vinícius de Moraes, who provided the script for Marcel Camus' film Black Orpheus; and the Argentinian Julio Cortázar, whose short story was the basis for Antonioni's film Blow Up. Suddenly, a new energy, a fresh, mythical breeze has come from the pampas, the cordilleras, the favelas, and the capitales. Three Nobel Prizes for Literature have been awarded to Latin American writers, yet very few individuals could identify them. Thomas Mann exclaims to Hermann Hesse, in a letter dated November 5, 1945: "Who on earth is the Chilean lady who has been awarded the Nobel Prize for literature this year? That I call roaming far afield when the good would have been so much closer at hand."[4] Edmund Wilson, the U. S. literary critic par excellence, gave his nod of approval to Latin American literature only late in his life.

Latin American literature has been slow in reaching the English-speaking market, particularly in the United States and Canada. In this regard we owe a great debt to teachers, quixotic editors and translators, who have instilled a love for Latin American literature in several generations of students. Indicative of the interest in Hispanic-American literature were a few isolated breakthroughs such as the translation and publication by Farrar & Rinehart of the Peruvian Ciro Alegría's Broad and Alien is the World (El mundo es ancho y ajeno), in 1941, and Alfred and Blanche Knopf's interest in and support of Latin American authors. In 1960, the Spanish edition of LIFE sponsored a literary contest and gave its first prize to that unforgettable story by the Argentinian Marco Denevi, Rosa at 10 O'Clock (Rosaura a las diez). In 1962, the Brazilian Jorge Amado's Gabriela, Clove and Cinnamon (Gabriela, cravo e canela), published by Alfred Knopf, became the first Latin American novel to make the best seller lists and the Book-of-the-Month Club selection. In 1966, the Instituto Nacional de Cultura y Bellas Artes of Venezuela instituted the "Rómulo Gallegos" Literary Prize, a distinguished award which was first bestowed upon the Peruvian Mario Vargas Llosa for his novel The Green House (La casa verde). In 1967, Gregory Rabassa won the National Book Award for his translation of Julio Cortázar's Hopscotch. Probably one of the most effective bridges between Latin American literature and the English speaking people have been translators like Rabassa, who have given us not only superb examples of the art of translation, but an almost perfect mirror of the Latin American soul. Also, in 1967, Gabriel García Márquez's One Hundred Years of Solitude (Cien años de soledad) won world acclaim after its first appearance in Buenos Aires and was translated into English, also by Gregory Rabassa, in 1970. Moreover, the Colombian writer's novel was on the New York Times best seller list for weeks.

It can be said with confidence that the early seventies mark a watershed for Latin American literature in translation, not only because excellent translators were available, but because more U. S. publishing houses became interested in sponsoring Latin American writers never before published in English. A wider audience in the United States is beginning to read the long-ignored giants: Borges, Carpentier, Vargas Llosa, Fuentes, Cortázar, Lezama Lima, Paz, Denevi, Onetti, Neruda, Sarduy, Puig, Cabrera Infante, Asturias, Donoso, Rulfo, Guimarães Rosa, Lispector, Bioy-Casares, Roa Bastos and many others. And a new generation is already pushing up behind them. The impact and influence of this literary avalanche cannot be assessed at this point, but it is safe to conclude that Latin American writers are here to stay. In spite of the fact that translations of most of their works are still infrequent, and good translations are even rarer, the Latin American writer has infiltrated the mass market and now walks proudly through the front door of most United States school, public and academic libraries.

Works of Latin American poets, playwrights, essayists, short story writers, and novelists are being translated and distributed, not only by established publishing houses but by alternative, underground and third world presses as well. Recognition of Latin American authors has also been furthered by the pioneering work of such non-profit organizations as the Center for Inter-American Relations, founded in 1967 and located in New York; the conferences on Octavio Paz, Nicolás Guillén, Jorge Luis Borges and Gabriel García Márquez, sponsored by the University of Oklahoma; and journals such as Books Abroad, Review, TriQuarterly, Mundus Artium, The Drama Review, which occasionally have devoted issues to Latin American literature; and the book reviews which now appear regularly in the literary sections of such well-known newspapers and magazines as The New York Times Book Review, The New York Review of Books, Times Literary Supplement, or Saturday Review. Perhaps most important is the fact that colleges and universities in the United States are offering a plethora of courses dealing with Latin American literature, and particularly, courses of literature in English translation.

As we read the hundreds of essays on the "boom" of the Latin American narrative, we cannot but hope that Enrique Anderson-Imbert's assertion that "the effective contributions of Spanish-American literature to international literature are minimal"[5] will be a truism of the past. Given the cultural interest, given a good translation, and given a fair chance in the promotional competition of the mass market, Latin American literature may have an opportunity not only to entertain and influence, but to inspire new literary movements.

---

[1] Enrique Anderson-Imbert, Spanish-American Literature. A History, Vol. 1, 1492-1910, (2nd ed., Detroit: Wayne State University, 1969), 311.

INTRODUCTION

²Mario Vargas Llosa, "The Latin American Novel Today: Introduction," <u>Books Abroad</u>, XLIV (Winter 1970), 11.

³Ibid., 12.

⁴Anni Carlson and Volker Michels, eds., <u>The Hesse/Mann Letters</u>, (New York: Harper & Row, 1975), 99.

⁵Enrique Anderson-Imbert, <u>op. cit</u>., 15.

Annotated Bibliography of Anthologies and Anthology Code

AHER   AHERN, MAUREEN and TIPTON, DAVID, eds. <u>Peru. The New Poetry</u>. London: London Magazine Editions, 1970. 128p.
    Includes eleven contemporary Peruvian poets. Introduction by David Tipton (pp. 8-11); "Statements and Comments on the Situation of the Writer in Peru" (pp. 115-126) consisting of four short essays translated by David Tipton; brief biographical notes.

ARC   ARCINIEGAS, GERMÁN. <u>The Green Continent. A Comprehensive View of Latin America by Its Leading Writers</u>. Selected and edited by Germán Arciniegas. Translated from the Spanish by Harriet de Onís and others. New York: Alfred A. Knopf, 1944. 533p.
    Thirty-two authors from the southern half of the hemisphere write about Latin America. The introduction by Germán Arciniegas, "Our Little Big World," is an excellent essay on the diversity of the cultural, social and geographical landscape of Latin America. Brief bio-bibliographical notes (pp. 523-533).

BABI   BABÍN, MARÍA TERESA and STEINER, STAN, eds. <u>Borinquen. An Anthology of Puerto Rican Literature</u>. New York: Alfred A. Knopf, 1974. 516p.
    Seventy-three Puerto Rican authors are included. Extensive introduction by María Teresa Babín, pp. xi-xxvi. "Our anthology...is the first attempt to offer in English a representative selection of important Puerto Rican poetry and prose writings from the sixteenth century to the present day." Also some poetry, fiction and non-fiction (Mass, psalms, church rituals) written in English by Puerto Ricans living in the United States. Most translations by Dr. Barry Luby, a few by José Nieto. Brief comments about the authors, pp. 481-506.

BANN   BANN, STEPHEN, ed. <u>Concrete Poetry. An International Anthology</u>. London: London Magazine Editions, 1967. 195p.
    Worldwide compilation of concrete poetry, including seven Brazilian poets. Introduction by Stephen Bann, pp. 7-27.

BECK   BECK, CLAUDIA and CARRANZA, SYLVIA, eds. Cuban Poetry 1959-1966. Havana, Cuba: Book Institute, 1967. 788p.
     Forty Cuban authors who published between 1959 and 1966 and "only the poems of authors of several generations who have had at least one book published in those years." Brief foreword by Heberto Padilla and Luis Suardíaz. Biographical sketches and photographs.

BENE   BENEDETTI, MARIO, ed. Unstill Life. An Introduction to the Spanish Poetry of Latin America. Translated by Darwin J. Flakoll and Claribel Alegría. Illustrated by Antonio Frasconi. New York: Harcourt, Brace & World, Inc., 1969. 127p.
     Twenty-three works written by poets from Nicaragua, Argentina, Chile, Uruguay, Cuba, Mexico, Peru, El Salvador, and Ecuador. Bio-bibliographical notes precede each poet's work. The oldest poet represented is Rubén Darío (1867-1916).

BENS   BENSON, RACHEL, trans. Nine Latinamerican Poets. New York: Cypress Books, 1968. 359p.
     Works by nine Spanish-speaking poets; each preceded by a bio-bibliographical note.

BIER   BIERSTADT, EDWARD HALE, ed. Three Plays of the Argentine. Translated from the Spanish by Jacob S. Fassett, Jr. New York: Duffield and Company, 1920. 148p.
     Includes "Juan Moreira" by Silverio Manco, "Santos Vega" by Luis Bayon Herrera, and "The Witches' Mountain" by Julio Sánchez Gardel. Introduction by Edward Hale Bierstadt, pp. xi-xlii.

BISH   BISHOP, ELIZABETH and BRASIL, EMANUEL, eds. An Anthology of Twentieth-Century Brazilian Poetry. Middletown, Connecticut: Wesleyan University Press, 1972. 181p. (Also available in paperback.)
     "Anthology consisting of selections from the work of fourteen poets of the modern generation and of the post-war generation of 1945...Inevitably, it is more representative of the editors' personal tastes than all-inclusive." A detailed table of contents and a bibliography of the most important works by each author is included, plus brief notes on editors and translators. Some poems appeared originally in The New Yorker, The Hudson Review, and Shenandoah.

BLAC   BLACKWELL, ALICE STONE. Some Spanish-American Poets. Translated by Alice Stone Blackwell. With an Introduction and Notes by Isaac Goldberg, Ph.D. New York and London: D. Appleton and Company, 1929. 559p.
     Eighty-one poets from nineteen countries, most of them born after 1850. This vast anthology encompasses more than 200 poems in translation accompanied by the original in Spanish. An appendix includes explanatory notes on terms which appear in the title or text of many of the poems.

BLY   BLY, ROBERT, ed. <u>Neruda and Vallejo: Selected Poems</u>. Boston: Beacon Press, 1971. 269p.
     Contains an interview with Pablo Neruda by Robert Bly, which took place in New York on June 12, 1966 (pp. 156-164).

BOLD   BOLD, ALAN, ed. <u>The Penguin Book of Socialist Verse</u>. Baltimore: Penguin Books, 1970. 550p.
     "Poems in this anthology fall into two main categories, (1) poems written by socialist poets aimed at extending the reader's consciousness of socialism; (2) poems not necessarily by socialists, but likely to appeal to socialists and to reinforce the assumptions of socialism because they examine events so radically." (p. 59.) The book begins with Marx's contemporary and friend, Heinrich Heine (1797-1856). The following Spanish-speaking poets from Latin America are included: Rubén Darío (Nicaragua), César Vallejo (Peru), Pablo Neruda (Chile), Nicanor Parra (Chile), Ernesto Che Guevara (Argentina), Pablo Armando Fernández (Cuba), Fayad Jamís (Cuba), Fernando Gordillo Cervantes (Nicaragua), Javier Heraud (Peru). Brief biographical sketches, index of poem titles and index of first lines.

BRAY   BRAYMER, NAN and LOWENFELS, LILLIAN, trans. <u>Modern Poetry from Spain and Latin America</u>. New York: Corinth Books, 1964. 63p.
     Includes four Latin American poets: Enoch Cancino Casahonda, Nicolás Guillén, Salomón de la Selva, and César Vallejo. These translations also appeared in the June 1964 issue of <u>The Literary Review</u>, Farleigh Dickinson University, Teaneck, N. J.

CARA   CARACCIOLO-TREJO, ENRIQUE. <u>The Penguin Book of Latin American Verse</u>. Baltimore: Penguin Books, 1971. 425p. Paperback.
     Contains the works of poets from fourteen Latin American countries (including Brazil), from 1800 to the late 1960's. The book includes an appendix by E. Caracciolo-Trejo entitled "An Explanatory Guide to Movements in Latin-American Poetry," (pp. 395-409); brief sketches and dates of the poets included; an index of first lines; an index of titles; and an alphabetical index· of poets identified by country and dates.

CARB   CARBALLIDO, EMILIO. <u>The Golden Thread and Other Plays</u>. Translated by Margaret Sayers Peden. Austin: University of Texas Press, 1970. 237p.
     Five plays and a Trilogy by "Mexico's most talented and successful playwright." Carballido published his first play, "The Intermediate Zone," in 1948. An introduction by Margaret Sayers Peden briefly surveys the theatre scene in Mexico and Carballido's <u>oeuvre</u> (pp. ix-xvii).

CARP   CARPENTIER, HORTENSE and BROF, JANET, eds. Doors and Mirrors. Fiction and Poetry from Spanish-America 1920-1970. New York: Grossman Publishers, 1972. 454p.
This anthology includes forty-four writers from fourteen countries. "The sequence of stories and poems reflects the editors' preference for a certain reading experience, and is only roughly chronological." The book also contains an introduction by Angel Rama and an epilogue by the Peruvian writer Mario Vargas Llosa, entitled "Literature is Fire," on accepting the 1967 "Rómulo Gallegos Prize" for his novel The Green House (pp. 430-435). Brief biographical notes and an index to translators are also included.

CARZ   CARRANZA, SYLVIA and CAZABON, MARÍA JUANA. Cuban Short Stories 1959-1966. Havana, Cuba: Book Institute, 1967. 229p.
A sample "...of the most dissimilar examples of the different literary trends that have emerged since 1959...the coherence within this diversity reflects...the human and universal characteristics of this universal, human age represented by the Revolution." (p. 7). Twenty-four Cuban authors are represented, with each contribution preceded by biographical data, a photo of the author, and several illustrations by Cuban artists. A glossary is also included.

CHI   Chicago Review. "Latin-American Writing. Essays, Fiction, Bilingual Poetry." Volume 27, Number 2, Autumn 1975. 171p.

COEL   COELHO, SALDANHA. (Coelho Pinto, José Saldanha da Gama). Contistas brasileiros. New Brazilian Short Stories. Selected by Coelho Saldanha. [Rio de Janeiro]: Revista Branca [1957]. 238p.
A selection of short stories translated by Rod W. Horton.

COH-1   COHEN, JOHN MICHAEL. Latin American Writing Today. Baltimore: Penguin Books, 1967. 267p. Paperback.
Selection of short stories and poems from thirty-two contemporary authors. Also contains a brief introduction and overview of Latin American literature up to 1964 and biographical notes on authors. Some of the poetry in this volume has appeared in Translation, The Southern Review, Atlanta, Peacock, Times Literary Supplement.

COH-2   COHEN, JOHN MICHAEL, ed. The Penguin Book of Spanish Verse. Rev. ed. Baltimore: Penguin Books, 1960. 472p. Paperback.
Anthology devoted to the Spanish-speaking poets from Spain and Latin America, embracing their writings from the 12th to the 20th century. This revised edition of the original 1956 version includes eighteen poets from the southern hemisphere. Each poem is followed by a plain prose English translation and the book also contains an index to first lines.

COH-3   COHEN, JOHN MICHAEL, ed. Writers in the New Cuba. Balti-
           more: Penguin Books, 1967. 191p. Paperback
             Poems and short stories by 23 contemporary Cuban intellec-
           tuals, including extracts from Fidel Castro's "Words to the
           Intellectuals," June 1961. "Except one or two poems, every-
           thing in this book has been written since 1959, the year of
           the Cuban revolution...everything has been chosen for its
           literary merit...I have drawn nothing from the expatriates
           since my purpose is to represent those who have said Yes to
           the new state of things." (Introduction by J. M. Cohen).

COLE   COLECCHIA, FRANCESCA and MATAS, JULIO, eds. Selected Latin
           American One-Act Plays. Edited and translated by Francesca
           Colecchia and Julio Matas. Pittsburgh, Pa.: University of
           Pittsburgh Press, 1973. 204p.
             One-act plays representing ten authors from Mexico, Argen-
           tina, Guatemala, Colombia, Cuba, Venezuela, and Chile, "...
           giving preference to those works which demand simple, yet
           imaginative stage production...Topics range from the exis-
           tential dilemma of modern man to social comment and political
           satire." Brief introduction on the Latin American theatre.
           Bio-bibliographical notes for each author.

COLF   COLFORD, WILLIAM EDWARD, ed. and trans. Classic Tales from
           Spanish America. Great Neck., N. Y.: Barron's Educational
           Series [1962]. 210p.
             A collection of twenty-one Spanish-American short stories
           in English translation. Each story is preceded by a short
           biographical sketch and a commentary on the author's work.

COUL   COULTHARD, GEORGE ROBERT, ed. Caribbean Literature. An An-
           thology. London: University of London Press Ltd., 1966.
           128p.
             Spanish-speaking poets represented in this work: Enrique
           Serpa (Cuba), Nicolás Guillén (Cuba), René Marqués (Puerto
           Rico), and Luis Palés Matos (Puerto Rico). Introduction:
           pp. 7-12.

CRAI   CRAIG, G. DUNDAS. The Modernist Trend in Spanish-American
           Poetry. A Collection of Representative Poems of the Modern-
           ist Movement and the Reaction. Translated into English
           Verse with A Commentary, by G. Dundas Craig. Berkeley, Cal-
           ifornia: University of California Press, 1934. 347p.
             Includes twenty Latin American poets. The book contains
           an introduction entitled "The Modernist Trend in Spanish-
           American Poetry" (pp. 1-29). Part III of the book is devot-
           ed to important critical essays for each author represented
           (pp. 251-339), and an historical, critical, and poetical
           bibliography (pp. 341-347).

CRAN   CRANFILL, THOMAS MABRY, ed. The Muse in Mexico. A Mid-
Century Miscellany. George D. Schade, translation editor.
Austin: University of Texas Press, 1959. 177p.
   Published as a supplement to The Texas Quarterly, Volume 2,
Number 1, this "miscellany" represents fiction, verse, pho-
tography and drawings by almost fifty Mexican artists, in-
cluding Juan José Arreola's "Five Fables" with illustrations
by Kelly Fearing. Translations by William Carlos Williams,
Donald Demarest, Denise Levertov, Eloïse Roach, Paul Black-
burn, Lysander Kemp.

DELOS. A Journal on & of Translations. Published by the
National Translation Center, Austin Texas. (DELOS, vols. 1-
6, was published between 1968 and 1971).

DEL-68   DELOS, Volume 1, Number 2, 1968, pp. 122-125. Includes five
poems by Octavio Paz, the original and the translation given.

DEL-70   DELOS, Volume 2, Number 5, 1970, pp. 170-175. Miguel Theft,
a short story by Carlos Drummond de Andrade, translated by
Robert Stock.

DORN   DORN, EDWARD and BROTHERSTON, GORDON, trans. Our Word.
Guerrilla Poems from Latin America. Palabra de guerrillero
Poesía guerrillera de Latinoamerica. New York: Grossman
Publishers in Association with Cape Goliard, London, 1968.
   With few exceptions, most poems by these ten Latin Ameri-
can poets appear in this anthology for the first time.
First edition, unpaged.

DOWN   DOWNES, LEONARD S., trans. An Introduction to Modern Brazilian Poetry. [São Paulo] Clube de Poesia do Brasil (Poetry Club of Brazil), 1954. 86p.
   Fifty Brazilian poets, from Manuel Bandeira (1886-1968) to
Cyro Pimentel (b. 1926). Includes forty-eight portraits of
the authors.

DR   The Drama Review. Volume 14, Number 2, Winter 1970. 244p.
   Joanne Pottlitzer is special editor of this issue devoted
to critical commentaries and short plays or excerpts from
plays. It features two perceptive introductions: Joanne
Pottlitzer's "Theatre of a Forgotten Continent," and Richard
Schechner's "Conformists in the Heart." Articles on the New
Cuban Theatre, theatre in Chile, Argentina, Brazil, Vene-
zuela, and Colombia, plus "A Selected Bibliography on Latin
American Theatre," (books, articles, plays in translation,
and bibliographies).

EVER   Evergreen Review. Volume 2, Number 7, Winter 1959. 256p.
   This issue presents "...a selective cross section of re-
cent work by the younger generation of Mexican painters,
poets, and prose writers."

FIFE   FIFE, AUSTIN E., ed. Latin American Interlude. Volume XIII, February 1966. Monograph series published by Utah State University Press, Logan, Utah.

Includes a section on Hispanic-American lyrics translated by the editor himself (pp. 48-69), representing a total of eight Latin American poets born after 1850.

FIG   FIGUEROA, JOHN. Caribbean Voices. Selected by John Figueroa. (Combined edition). Washington: Robert B. Luce Co., Inc., 1971.

This hardbound collection mainly of poetry combines both volumes of Caribbean Voices, selected by the Jamaican John Figueroa. Volume I is subtitled "Dreams and Visions," 119p.; Volume II is subtitled "The Blue Horizons," 228p. Both volumes include introductions, brief essays, bibliographies, and indices to authors, titles and first lines.

FITT   FITTS, DUDLEY, ed. Anthology of Contemporary Latin-American Poetry. Norfolk, Conn.: A New Directions Book, 1942, 1947. 677p.

Represents ninety-five Latin American authors who have written in Spanish, Portuguese, and French. Includes biographical and bibliographical notes for each author, a general index to translated poems (Spanish and English versions), an index of names and a list of the seventeen translators.

FLAK   FLAKOLL, DARWIN J. and ALEGRÍA, CLARIBEL. New Voices of Hispanic America. An Anthology. Edited, translated and with an Introduction by Darwin J. Flakoll and Claribel Alegría. Boston: Beacon Press, 1962. 226p.

Anthology of poems and short stories "by a new generation of writers from Hispanic America...Leading critics, editors of literary magazines, writers and professors of Latin American literature were asked to name their choices for inclusion in this volume; the nominees were then requested to submit their books or manuscripts for study and to suggest further nominations from their own generation." Selection restricted to 17 Spanish-speaking countries of Latin America and to those writers born in 1914 or later.

FLOR-1   FLORES, ANGEL, ed. An Anthology of Spanish Poetry from Garcilaso to García Lorca.. In English translation with Spanish originals. Garden City, New York: Anchor Books, Doubleday & Company, Inc., 1961. 516p. Paperback.

Includes a good poetic selection from the oeuvre of the Nicaraguan Rubén Darío (1867-1916) and Chile's Nobel Prize winner Gabriela Mistral (1889-1957).

FLOR-2   FLORES, ANGEL and POORE, DUDLEY. Fiesta in November. Stories from Latin America selected and edited by Angel Flores
and Dudley Poore. With an introduction by Katherine Ann
Porter. Boston: Houghton Mifflin Company, 1942. 608p.
  Eighteen writers from 10 Latin American nations: Argentina, Ecuador, Peru, Colombia, Venezuela, Mexico, Brazil,
Uruguay, Bolivia, and Chile.

FLOR-3   FLORES, ANGEL. Great Spanish Short Stories. Selected and
introduced by Angel Flores. New York: Dell Publishing Co.,
Inc., 1962. 304p. Paperback.
  A survey of four centuries of Spanish literature, it includes two Mexicans, two Argentinians, and one Colombian author. Each short story is preceded by a brief biographical
and critical introduction.

FLOR-4   FLORES, ANGEL, ed. Spanish Stories. Cuentos Españoles.
New York: Bantam Books, Inc., 1960. 339p. Paperback.
  Bilingual textbook edition which contains works by the
following Latin American authors: Horacio Quiroga (Uruguay), Benito Lynch (Argentina), and Jorge Luis Borges (Argentina). The book also includes Notes, Questionnaire, and
Vocabulary.

FRA-J   FRANCO, JEAN, ed. Short Stories in Spanish. Cuentos hispánicos. Baltimore, Maryland: Penguin Books, 1966. (Re-
printed 1968). 204p. Paperback.
  Includes eight short stories (original Spanish with English translation facing the page), seven from Spanish America, one from Spain. Also included: Introduction (pp. 7-11),
Biographical Notes on Authors, Notes on Spanish Texts.

FRAN   FRANK, WALDO, ed. Tales from the Argentine. Translated
from the Spanish by Anita Brenner. Illustrations by Morde-
cai Gorelik. New York: Farrar & Rinehart, 1930. 268p.
  Foreword by Waldo Frank, pp. ix-xvi.

FUEN   FUENTES, CARLOS; DONOSO, JOSÉ; and SARDUY, SEVERO, eds.
Triple Cross. New York: E. P. Dutton & Co., Inc., 1972.
329p.
  Contains three novellas: Carlos Fuentes' "Holy Place"
(Zona sagrada), José Donoso's "Hell Has No Limits" (El lugar
sin límites), and Severo Sarduy's "From Cuba with a Song"
(De donde son los cantantes). Translators are Suzanne Jill
Levine and Hallie D. Taylor.

GAN   GANNON, PATRICIO and MANNING, HUGO. Argentine Anthology of
Modern Verse. Edited with a preface by Patricio Gannon.
Buenos Aires: [Francisco A. Colombo] 1942. 77p.
  Fifteen Argentine poets, a bilingual anthology, which
spans from Leopoldo Lugones (1874-1938) to Roberto Ledesma
(1901-   ).

Annotated Bibliography of Anthologies and Anthology Code

GARR   GARRIGUE, JEAN. <u>Translations by American Poets</u>. Athens:
Ohio University Press, 1970. 371p.
    The Latin American poets represented are: João Cabral de
Melo Neto and Carlos Drummond de Andrade (Brazil), Julio
Cortázar (Argentina), Nicolás Guillén (Cuba), Jorge Carrera
Andrade (Ecuador), Julio Herrera y Reissig (Uruguay), César
Vallejo (Peru), Marco Antonio Montes de Oca (Mexico).

GOLD-1   GOLDBERG, ISAAC. <u>Brazilian Tales</u>. Translated from the Portuguese with an introduction by Isaac Goldberg. Boston:
The Four Seas Company, 1921. 135p.
    Only three authors in this anthology were born after 1850.

GOLD-2   GOLDBERG, ISAAC. <u>Mexican Poetry</u>. <u>An Anthology</u>. Edited,
with Introduction and Notes by Isaac Goldberg. Girard,
Kansas: Haldeman-Julius Company, 1925 (Little Blue Book
No. 810). 64p.

GRO   GROSSMAN, WILLIAM L. <u>Modern Brazilian Short Stories</u>.
Translated with an Introduction by William L. Grossman.
Berkeley and Los Angeles: University of California Press,
1967. 167p.
    Seventeen short stories by seventeen Brazilian writers,
all of which fall within the "modernist movement," which
dominated Brazilian literature between 1922 and 1945. Brief
bio-bibliographical notes for each author.

HAH   HAHNER, JUNE E., ed. <u>Women in Latin American History</u>.
<u>Their Lives and Views</u>. University of California, Los Ange-
les: UCLA Latin American Center Publications, 1976. 181p.
Paperback.
    This book presents "...the lives and views of women of
different Latin American countries and socio-economic condi-
tions from colonial times to the present..." An introduction "...analyzes the current state of knowledge concerning
the role of women in Latin America."

HAR67-2 <u>Haravec</u>. A Literary Magazine from Peru. Number 2, March
1967.
    A bilingual magazine published quarterly by the editors in
Lima, Peru, with co-editors from Latin America, England and
the United States. <u>Jarawiq</u> or <u>harawek</u> is a Quechua word
which designates a minstrel.

HAR67-3 <u>Haravec</u>. A Literary Magazine from Peru. Number 3, July
1967.

HAR67-4 <u>Haravec</u>. A Literary Magazine from Peru. Number 4, December
1967.

HAR68-5 <u>Haravec</u>. A Literary Magazine from Peru. Number 5, September 1968.

HAYDN   HAYDN, HIRAM and COURNOS, JOHN, eds. <u>A World of Great Stories</u>. New York: Crown Publishers, 1947. 950p.
   Short stories by authors from all over the world, limited to the twentieth century. The Latin American section (pp. 860-950) includes thirteen writers from Chile, Ecuador, Bolivia, Colombia, Mexico, Peru, Argentina, Cuba, Uruguay, Venezuela, and Brazil.

HAYS   HAYS, H. R., ed. <u>12 Spanish American Poets. An Anthology</u>. New Haven: Yale University Press, 1943. 336p.
   Authors from Mexico, Colombia, Chile, Cuba, Argentina, Ecuador, Peru, and Venezuela. Includes a lengthy introduction (pp. 1-21), a bibliography (pp. 329-332), and indices to English and Spanish Titles.

HOW-1   HOWES, BARBARA, ed. <u>The Eye of the Heart. Short Stories from Latin America</u>. Indianapolis/New York: The Bobbs-Merrill Company, Inc., 1973. 415p. Paperback.
   Forty-one writers and 42 short stories (two by Clarice Lispector) appear in chronological order, from Machado de Assis' "The Psychiatrist," originally published in 1882, to Mario Vargas Llosa's "Sunday, Sunday." Brief biographies of the authors and notes on translation.

HOW-2   HOWES, BARBARA, ed. <u>From the Green Antilles. Writings of the Caribbean</u>. New York: The Macmillan Company, 1966. 368p.
   The book is divided into four main sections, all preceded by a brief introduction: English, French, Spanish, Dutch. This anthology contains 11 Spanish-speaking authors from Cuba, Dominican Republic, and Puerto Rico. Also includes a general introduction by Barbara Howes (pp. xi-xvi) and biographical notes for the authors (pp. 363-368).

HUGH   HUGHES, LANGSTON and BONTEMPS, ARNA, eds. <u>The Poetry of the Negro 1746-1949</u>. New York: Doubleday & Company, Inc., 1949. 429p.
   "The common thread...is the Negro's experience in the Western world." This anthology includes authors from the Caribbean, such as the Cubans Regino Pedroso and Nicolás Guillén.

JOHN   JOHNSON, MILDRED E. <u>Swan, Cygnets, and Owl. An Anthology of Modernist Poetry in Spanish America</u>. Translations by Mildred E. Johnson. Columbia, Missouri: The University of Missouri Studies, 1956. (The University of Missouri Studies. Volume XXIX). 199p.
   Introductory essay on Modernism by J. S. Brushwood, pp. 1-33.

JONE-1   JONES, WILLIS KNAPP. Men and Angels. Three South American
          Comedies. Translated and with an Introduction by Willis
          Knapp Jones. Foreword by J. Cary Davis. Carbondale:
          Southern Illinois University Press, 1970. 191p.
              "The Fate of Chipí González," by José María Rivarola Matto,
          of Paraguay; "Man of the Century," by Miguel Frank, from
          Chile; and "The Quack Doctor," by Juan Fernando Camilo
          Darthes and Carlos S. Damel, from Argentina. "Each play
          presents a picture of contemporary society in each region...
          they are strictly meant to be entertaining..." Also includ-
          ed in this volume, a survey of the Spanish American Theater,
          with emphasis on Mexico, Paraguay, Chile and Argentina
          (pp. xiii-xlvi), and an important "Checklist of Translations
          of Spanish American Plays," pp. 181-191. This checklist is
          arranged alphabetically by countries and names of dramatists.
          Several of the works listed here have not been published and
          are filed in manuscript form in the repositories indicated.
          Includes sources for Argentina, Bolivia, Chile, Colombia,
          Cuba, Ecuador, Guatemala, Mexico, New Mexico, Nicaragua,
          Peru, Philippines, Puerto Rico, Uruguay, and Venezuela.

JONE-2   JONES, WILLIS KNAPP, ed. Spanish-American Literature in
          Translation: A Selection of Prose, Poetry and Drama Before
          1888. Volume I. New York: Frederick Ungar Publishing Co.,
          1966. 356p.
              Introduction, pp. 1-20. A reading list for "readers who
          want to become acquainted with other examples of Latin
          American literature before 1888," (pp. 345-351). Index of
          Authors and Major Works.

JONE-3   JONES, WILLIS KNAPP, ed. Spanish-American Literature in
          Translation: A Selection of Prose, Poetry, and Drama Since
          1888. Volume II. New York: Frederick Ungar Publishing Co.,
          1963. 469p.
              Introduction, pp. 1-18. A reading list, pp. 465-466. In-
          dex of Authors and Major Works.

JONE-4   JONES, WILLIS KNAPP. Short Plays of the Southern Americas.
          California: Stanford University, 1944. (Issued in Limited
          Edition by the Dramatists' Alliance of Stanford University.
          Coester Series II). 106p.
              Eight brief plays "by writers of Chile, Cuba, Argentina,
          Ecuador, Mexico, Uruguay, Colombia, and Peru: translated by
          Willis Knapp Jones, of Miami University, Oxford, Ohio, in
          collaboration with his students Frances Heitsman, Jean
          Jameson, and Marian Ferguson." A brief introductory note
          precedes each play.

KAI   KAIDEN, NINA; SOTO, PEDRO JUAN; and VLADIMIR, ANDREW, eds.
Puerto Rico. La Nueva Vida. The New Life. New York: Renaissance Editions, 1966. n.p.
    Along with a selection of poems and prose works in trans-
lation, this work includes black and white and color plates
by several important Puerto Rican artists.

LAWA   LAWAETZ, GUDIE, ed. Spanish Short Stories. Volume 2.
Cuentos hispánicos: Tomo 2. Baltimore, Maryland: Penguin
Books, 1972. 214p. Paperback.
    Short stories from Spain and Spanish America. Original
text in Spanish accompanied by the English translation. Includes an introduction (pp. 7-8), biographical notes on the
authors (pp. 201-207), and notes on the Spanish text.

LIEB   LIEBER, MAXIM and WILLIAMS, BLANCHE COLTON, eds. Great Stories of All Nations. New York: Brentano's, 1927. 1121p.
    Includes stories from the following Latin American coun-
tries: Brazil, Argentina, Mexico, Santo Domingo, and Chile.
Brief biographical notes.

LIT-1   Literature in Latin America. Washington, D. C.: Pan American Union, 1950. (Club and Study Fine Art Series.) 112p.
    In general, this selection of prose and poetry represents
excerpts from the Bulletin of the Pan American Union (1893-
1948) and Américas, the monthly magazine. Brief biographical notes on authors are given. Appendices: Additional
Notes on Authors, Selected List of English Translations and
Histories of Latin American Literature.

LIT-2   The Literature of Latin America. Volume I of the Series on
Literature-Art-Music. Revised edition. Washington, D. C.:
Pan American Union, 1944. 64p.
    Contains translations of the literature of the republics
of Latin America: 22 prose works, 28 poems.

LOW   LOWENFELS, WALTER, ed. For Neruda, For Chile. An International Anthology. Boston: Beacon Press, 1975. 249p. Paperback.
    "Dozens of people, publications, and organizations through-
out the world helped to gather and select the contents."
Includes poems, essays, tributes, speeches, etc., in memory
of Pablo Neruda, Chilean Nobel Prize for Literature in 1971,
by such artists as Louis Aragon, Miguel Angel Asturias, Rafael Alberti, Muriel Rukeyser, Matilde Urrutia Neruda (wife
of Neruda), Allen Ginsberg, Salvador Allende, Evgenii Yevtu-
shenko, Beatriz Allende (daughter of the late Chilean Presi-
dent), etc.

LUZU   LUZURIAGA, GERARDO and RUDDER, ROBERT S. The Orgy: Modern
One-Act Plays from Latin America. Edited and translated by
Gerardo Luzuriaga and Robert S. Rudder. University of Cali-
fornia, Los Angeles: UCLA Latin American Center, 1974.
(Latin American Studies. Volume 25.) 180p. Paperback.
  Modern Latin American theatre "which may be utilized by
theatre and experimental drama groups." Represented are:
Enrique Buenaventura (Colombia, 2 plays), Osvaldo Dragún
(Argentina, 2 plays), José Martínez Queirolo (Ecuador,
1 play), Marco Denevi (Argentina, 2 plays), Alvaro Menén
Desleal (El Salvador), Alberto Adellach (Argentina), Carlos
Solórzano (born in Guatemala in 1922 but has lived in Mexico
since 1939), and Jorge Díaz Gutiérrez (born in Rosario, Ar-
gentina, 1930, but naturalized Chilean).

MANC   MANCINI, PAT McNEES, ed. Contemporary Latin American Short
Stories. Greenwich, Connecticut: A Fawcett Premier Book,
1974. 479p. Paperback.
  Thirty-five Latin American authors are represented. Long
bio-bibliographies precede each story. Includes a selected
reading list composed of a Reference and Criticism section
("Only general works are listed here. Every library should
have them, and some are in paperback"), Short Story Anthologies section and A Basic Collection of Novels section.

MARQ   MÁRQUEZ, ROBERT, ed. Latin American Revolutionary Poetry.
A Bilingual Anthology. New York: Monthly Review Press,
1974. 505p.
  Introduction by Robert Márquez. Poems are preceded by
brief bio-bibliographical notes on each writer.

MR   The Massachusetts Review. Volume 15, nos. 1-2, Winter-
Spring 1975. 332p.
  This issue edited by Robert Márquez, includes stories,
drama, essays, poems and works of art from Latin America and
the Caribbean. The general title for this issue is taken
from the important essay by the Cuban Roberto Fernández Retamar, "Caliban. Notes Toward a Discussion of Culture in
Our America," (pp. 7-72).

MATI   MATILLA, ALFREDO and SILÉN, IVÁN, eds. The Puerto Rican
Poets. New York: Bantam Books, Inc., August 1972. 238p.
Paperback.
  Twenty-three Puerto Rican poets "...that express the full
range of the Puerto Rican experience in New York...Part I
includes the works of poets before 1955. Part II groups
three major poets, most of whose work was completed before
1960: Luis Palés Matos (1898-1959), Julia de Burgos (1914-
1953), and Hugo Margenat (1934-1957). Part III includes
representative work of poets who have written since Hugo
Margenat. The book includes a prologue, bibliographies and

(MATILLA, ALFREDO and SILÉN, IVÁN, eds.)
dates for each author. Also included is some poetry written
in English by Puerto Ricans and translated into Spanish by
Ángel Luis Méndez.

MERT   MERTON, THOMAS. Emblems of a Season of Fury. [Norfolk,
        Conn.: J. Laughlin, 1963.] 149p. Paperback.
            The following Latin American authors are represented: Pab-
        lo Antonio Cuadra, Alfonso Cortes, and Ernesto Cardenal, from
        Nicaragua; Jorge Carrera Andrade, from Ecuador; and César
        Vallejo, from Peru.

MILL   MILLER, JAMES E. JR.; O'NEAL, ROBERT: and McDONNELL, HELEN M.,
        eds. From Spain and the Americas. Literature in Translation.
        Glenview, Illinois: Scott, Foresman and Company, 1970. 420p.
            Anthology prepared especially for use in the classroom; con-
        tains 21 authors from Latin America. Angel Flores, in his
        introduction (pp. 9-16), gives a brief overview of the lit-
        erature since the turn of the century. Also included: Dis-
        cussion Questions, Biographies of Authors, Pronunciation
        Key, Index to Authors and Titles, and Index of Translators.

MU-69   Mundus Artium. A Journal of International Literature and
        the Arts. Volume III, no. 1, Winter 1969. 152p.
            "Special Spanish-American Poetry Issue" published by the
        Department of English, Ohio University, Athens, Ohio. Con-
        tains the works of 19 Latin American poets and photo repro-
        ductions of paintings and sculptures of various Latin Ameri-
        can artists. Includes also Sergio Mondragón's "Opening,"
        (pp. 8-9), Octavio Paz's "What Does Poetry Mean?" (pp. 10-
        12), and Ramón Xirau's "Introduction to Contemporary Spanish-
        American Poetry," (pp. 13-27). Notes on contributors
        (pp. 140-145), Important Spanish-American Journals (pp. 146-
        147).

MU-70   Mundus Artium. A Journal of International Literature and
        the Arts. Volume III, no. 3, Summer 1970. 124p.
            "Special Latin American Fiction Issue," which includes 14
        Latin American writers. Emir Rodríguez Monegal's essay "A
        Revolutionary Writing," states that "...in a short span of
        ten years, Latin American narrative has become one of the
        most widely read and discussed of this century," (pp. 6-11).
        Notes on contributors, pp. 116-119.

MU-73   Mundus Artium. A Journal of International Literature and
        the Arts. Volume VI, no. 2, 1973. 180p.
            Entitled "Contemporary Venezuelan Poetry," it also includes
        essays, and photos of paintings, sculptures, and ink drawings.
        Of importance is Juan Liscano's article entitled "A Profile
        of Venezuelan Poetry," (pp. 8-15). Notes on contributors,
        pp. 168-173.

Annotated Bibliography of Anthologies and Anthology Code

MU-74   Mundus Artium. A Journal of International Literature and
the Arts. Volume VII, no. 2, 1974. 160p.
    An "International Women's Issue," includes several Latin
American representatives. Notes on contributors, pp. 152-
156.

NEI   NEISTEIN, JOSÉ, ed. Poesia Brasileira Moderna. A Bilingual
Anthology. Washington, D. C.: Brazilian-American Cultural
Institute, Inc., 1972. 207p.
    Nineteen Brazilian poets "...represented at length, by a
different number of poems." Introduction on modern Brazilian poetry by José Neistein, pp. iii-xii. Translations by
Manoel Cardozo. Includes bio-bibliographical notes for each
author and a very basic bibliography on page 204.

NIST   NIST, JOHN. Modern Brazilian Poetry. An Anthology. Translated and edited, with the help of Yolanda Leite, by John
Nist. Bloomington: Indiana University Press, 1962. 175p.
    Anthology comprised of 12 leading Brazilian poets of the
first half of the twentieth century. The introduction
(pp. 11-16) gives an overview of Modernism vs. Parnassian
poetry. Biographical notes for authors, pp. 169-175.

OLIV   OLIVER, WILLIAM I. Voices of Change in the Spanish American
Theater. An Anthology Edited and Translated by William I.
Oliver. Austin: University of Texas Press, 1971. 294p.
    Six Spanish-American playwrights: Emilio Carballido (Me-
xico), Griselda Gambaro (Argentina), Carlos Maggi (Uruguay),
Enrique Buenaventura (Colombia), Luisa Josefina Hernández
(Mexico), and Sergio Vodánovic (Chile). Excellent introduc-
tion by the editor, pp. ix-xviii. "Aim of this anthology is
to present a selection of plays that are representative of a
new spirit and of societal pressures and changes in Spanish
American culture."

ONIS-1   ONÍS, HARRIET DE. The Golden Land. An Anthology of Latin
American Folklore in Literature. Selected, Edited, and
Translated by Harriet de Onís. New York: Alfred A. Knopf,
1948. 395p.
    Forty-nine writers encompassing four hundred years of lit-
erary traditions. In her preface (p. vii), the editor
writes: "My purpose has been to show how persistent the influence of Latin American folklore in its literature has
been...how it has served as a source of inspiration...Folk-
lore is used in its broadest sense, including myths and
legends out of America's remote past, tales of African, Indian, or European origin..."

ONIS-2   ONÍS, HARRIET DE, ed. Spanish Stories and Tales. New York:
Alfred A. Knopf, 1954. 270p.
    Includes Spanish as well as Latin American authors and an
introduction entitled "The Spanish Short Story," pp. v-xi.

PAZ-1   PAZ, OCTAVIO. Anthology of Mexican Poetry. Compiled by Oc-
         tavio Paz. Translated by Samuel Beckett. Preface by C. M.
         Bowra. Bloomington: Indiana University Press, 1958. 213p.
           This anthology of the works of 36 Mexican authors covers
         the period 1521-1910 and omits living writers. The book in-
         cludes C. M. Bowra's "Poetry and Tradition," (pp. 9-21), Oc-
         tavio Paz's "Introduction to the History of Mexican Poetry,"
         (pp. 23-44), and a foreword, also by Octavio Paz. Good bio-
         bibliographical notes on the writers represented in this an-
         thology, pp. 199-213.

PAZ-2   PAZ, OCTAVIO and STRAND, MARK, eds. New Poetry of Mexico.
         Selected, with notes, by Octavio Paz, Alí Chumacero, José
         Emilio Pacheco, and Homero Aridjis. Bilingual edition edit-
         ed by Mark Strand. New York: E. P. Dutton & Co. Inc., 1970.
         224p.
           Includes Octavio Paz's introduction to the Mexican edition
         of this anthology, which includes 42 poets (pp. 11-17), and
         a preface by Mark Strand discussing the preparation of the
         American edition, which includes only 24 Mexican poets
         (pp. 19-21). "...What is being offered the American reader
         is a view of relatively recent Mexican poetry, not a close
         look at a handful of poets." Contains index of authors,
         first lines-Spanish, and first lines-English.

PELL   PELLICER, CARLOS. 3 Spanish American Poets. Pellicer, Ne-
         ruda, Andrade. Translated by Lloyd Mallan, Mary and C. V.
         Wicker, and Joseph Leonard Grucci. Albuquerque, New Mexico:
         Swallow & Critchlow, 1942. 73p.

PLAY   Plays of the Southern Americas. Issued by the Dramatists'
         Alliance. Stanford University, 1942. 74p.
           Includes La Gringa ("The Foreign Girl") by the Uruguayan
         Florencio Sánchez (46 pages); Las Convulsiones ("My Poor
         Nerves") by the Colombian Luis Vargas Tejada (19 pages); and
         Cabrerita, by the Chilean A. Acevedo Hernández (9 pages).

POOR   POOR, AGNES BLAKE. Pan American Poems. An Anthology. Bos-
         ton: The Gorham Press, 1918. 80p.
           Preface by Agnes Blake Poor, pp. 5-9.

PRIZE   Prize Stories from Latin America. Winners of the LIFE EN
         ESPAÑOL Literary Contest. Garden City, N. Y.: Doubleday &
         Company, Inc., 1963. 398p.
           Eleven stories from five Latin American nations including
         the three main prizes, plus eight stories which won Honor-
         able Mention. Marco Denevi (Argentina), Carlos Martínez
         Moreno (Uruguay), Alfonso Echeverría (Chile), Tomás Mojarro
         (Mexico), Laura del Castillo (Argentina), Faustino González-
         Aller (Cuba), Carlos Rozas Larraín (Chile), Haroldo Pedro
         Conti (Argentina), Juan Carlos Onetti (Uruguay), Ramón
         Ferreira López (Cuba), Rolando Venturini (Argentina).

RES   RESNICK, SEYMOUR. Spanish-American Poetry. A Bilingual Selection. Irvington-on-Hudson, N. Y.: Harvey House, Inc.,
1964. 96p.
      Includes poetry from the 16th century on. Illustrated by
Anne Marie Jauss.

RUIZ   RUIZ DEL VIZO, HORTENSIA. Black Poetry of the Americas. (A
Bilingual Anthology). Miami, Florida: Ediciones Universal,
1972. 176p.
      Main emphasis on black poetry from Latin America and the
Caribbean, less on the French West Indies and Guyana poets.
All the poems have been translated by the editor.

SANCH   SÁNCHEZ, FLORENCIO. Representative Plays of Florencio Sánchez. Translated from the Spanish by Willis Knapp Jones.
Washington, D. C.: Pan American Union, 1961. 326p.
      Eleven plays by "the first important Latin American drama-
tist," the Uruguayan Florencio Sánchez, 1875-1910. This
playwright lived most of his life in Buenos Aires. The book
also includes a brief bibliography about Sánchez and an introduction on the Argentinian theatre during the turn of the
century, by Ruth Richardson.

SHA   SHAND, WILLIAM. Contemporary Argentine Poetry. An anthology compiled and translated by William Shand. Introduction
by Aldo Pellegrini. Buenos Aires: Fundación Argentina para
la Poesía, 1969. 275p.
      A total of 107 poets are represented in this vast antholo-
gy. The first, Juan L. Ortiz, was born in 1897, the last,
Leopoldo José Bartolomé, born in 1942. Brief bibliographies
precede each author's poems.

SHAY   SHAY, FRANK. Twenty-five Short Plays. International.
Selected and edited by Frank Shay. New York: D. Appleton
and Company, 1926. 381p.
      Represented in this anthology are the works of Cuba's José
Antonio Ramos, When Love Dies. A Worldly Comedy (pp. 123-
146), and Mexico's Teresa Farias de Issasi, The Sentence of
Death. A Play (pp. 273-281).

      The Sixties. Published occasionally by the Sixties Press,
Odin House, Madison, Minnesota. The issues listed below
have been edited by Robert Bly.

SIX60-4 Number 4 (Fall 1960).

SIX62-6 Number 6 (Spring 1962).

SIX64-7 Number 7 (Winter 1964).

STAR   STARR, FREDERICK. <u>Readings from Modern Mexican Authors</u>. Chicago: The Open Court Publishing Company, 1904. 420p.
Includes twenty-seven Mexican authors born after 1850.

TARN   TARN, NATHANIEL, ed. <u>Con Cuba. An Anthology of Cuban Poetry of the Last Sixty Years</u>. Cape Goliard Press, London: In Association with Grossman Publishers; New York: 1969. 143p.
Thirty Cuban poets are included in this anthology, from Félix Pita Rodríguez, born in 1909, to Eduardo Lolo, born in 1945. Many of the selections presented in this book appeared originally in <u>El Corno Emplumado</u> (Mexico, No. 23), an issue devoted exclusively to Cuba.

TORR   TORRES-RÍOSECO, ARTURO, ed. <u>Short Stories of Latin America</u>. Translators: Zoila Nelken and Rosalie Torres-Ríoseco. New York: Las Americas Publishing Co., 1963. 203p.
Includes 14 authors from Peru, Chile, Argentina, Cuba, Mexico, Ecuador, and Uruguay. Lino Novas Calvo and Francisco Ayala were both born in Spain but produced all their <u>oeuvre</u> in Latin America. Brief bio-bibliographical notes for each writer (pp. 199-203).

TOWN   TOWNSEND, FRANCIS E. <u>Quisqueya. A Panoramic Anthology of Dominican Verse</u>. Prefaced, Introduced, Arranged, and Anglicized by Francis E. Townsend. Second edition. Ciudad Trujillo, R. D.: Editora del Caribe, C. por A., 1954. 101p.
First edition published in 1947.

TRAN   <u>Translations from Hispanic Poets</u>. New York: Printed by Order of the Trustees, Hispanic Society of America, 1938. 271p.
Includes 29 Latin American authors born after 1850 and representing Argentina, Brazil, Chile, Colombia, Costa Rica, Cuba, Mexico, Nicaragua, Peru, Uruguay, Venezuela. Index of authors.

TRE   TREND, J. B. <u>Modern Poetry from Brasil</u>. Cambridge, Great Britain: [R. I. Severs, Ltd.], 1955. 32p.
Anthology which includes six Brazilian poets: Ribeiro Couto, Manuel Bandeira, Mário de Andrade, Cecilia Meireles, Augusto Frederico Schmidt, and Jorge de Lima.

TRI-13   <u>TriQuarterly</u>. Volume 13/14, Fall/Winter 1968/69. 510p. Published in the Fall, Winter, and Spring at Northwestern University, Evanston, Illinois.
Issue devoted to contemporary Latin American literature, co-edited by José Donoso, the Chilean writer, in cooperation with the Center for Inter-American Relations, New York, and the National Translation Center, Austin, Texas. Essays by Octavio Paz: "A Literature of Foundations" (pp. 7-12), Emir Rodríguez Monegal: "The New Latin American Novelists" (pp. 13-32), and Fabio Lucas: "Cultural Aspects of Brazil-

ian Literature" (pp. 33-53). Also published in hardback by
E. P. Dutton & Co. Inc., 496p., in 1969. Co-edited by José
Donoso and William Henkin, it includes 74 contributors of
poetry, short stories, extracts from novels and critical
essays.

TRI-15   TriQuarterly. Volume 15, Spring 1969.
      This issue carries a supplement to contemporary Latin Amer-
ican literature which appeared in the preceding volume of
TriQuarterly. Includes an essay on Jorge Luis Borges by
María Esther Vázquez (pp. 245-257), Richard Gott's "Intellectuals & Politics in Latin America" (pp. 258-263), plus
additional works in translation.

UND   UNDERWOOD, EDNA WORTHLEY, trans. Anthology of Mexican Poets
From the Earliest Times to the Present Day. Portland, Maine:
The Mosher Press, 1932. 332p.
      Foreword by Edna Worthley Underwood, pp. xxiii-xxxiii.

USIG   USIGLI, RODOLFO. Two Plays: Crown of Light. One of These
Days. Translated by Thomas Bledsoe. Introduction by Willis
Knapp Jones. Foreword by J. Cary Davis. Carbondale and Ed-
wardsville: Southern Illinois University Press, 1971.
234p.
      Crown of Light. An antihistorical comedy in three acts
(pp. 2-107); and One of These Days..., a nonpolitical fan-
tasy in three acts, (pp. 110-234). Jones writes about Usigli in his introduction, pp. xiv-xxii, written in 1970.

WALS   WALSH, THOMAS. Hispanic Anthology. Collected and arranged
by Thomas Walsh. New York: G. P. Putnam's Sons, 1920.
779p.
      Includes Latin American poets from Mexico, Cuba, Puerto
Rico, Brazil, Colombia, Santo Domingo, Nicaragua, Venezuela,
Argentina, Peru, Uruguay, Chile, Honduras. Author index
provided.

WILL-1   WILLIAMS, EMMETT, ed. An Anthology of Concrete Poetry. New
York: Something Else Press, Inc., 1967. 342p.
      All Latin American concrete poets represented in this in-
ternational anthology are Brazilians. Brief bio-bibliographies for each author. Concrete poetry "...a return to the
poem as picture: to the Calligrammes of Apollinaire, the
mouse's tail in Alice, the permutational poems of the caba-
lists, the anagrams of the early Christian monks, the
carmina figurata of the Greek Bucolic poets..."

WILL-2   WILLIAMS, MILLER. Chile; An Anthology of New Writing. Selected and Edited by Miller Williams. The Kent State University Press, 1968. (n.p.)
      Poems, two short stories and one play by 13 Chilean au-
thors. It also contains illustrations by Nemesio Antúnez
and Cecilia Bruna.

WOOD   WOODYARD, GEORGE, ed. <u>The Modern Stage in Latin America</u>:
<u>Six Plays. An Anthology</u>. New York: E. P. Dutton & Co.
Inc., 1971. 331p. Paperback.
    Introduction by George Woodyard, pp. ix-xx. "The selec-
tion is small...chosen as the best and most representative
examples of current themes and techniques." René Marqués
(Puerto Rico), Alfredo Dias Gomes (Brazil), Osvaldo Dragún
(Argentina), Jorge Díaz (Chile), José Triana (Cuba), Emilio
Carballido (Mexico).

YATE   YATES, DONALD A., ed. <u>Latin Blood. The Best Crime and De-
tective Stories of South America</u>. New York: Herder and
Herder, 1972. 224p.
    Fifteen mystery writers: from Chile, several from Argen-
tina, others from Mexico and Colombia. Brief critical notes
on the works selected. Introduction by Donald A. Yates,
pp. xi-xv.

YOU   <u>Young Poetry of the Americas</u>. Volume I. Washington, D. C.:
Pan American Union [1967]. 116p. Paperback.
    Includes poets from Argentina, Brazil, Chile, Costa Rica,
Ecuador, El Salvador, Haiti, Mexico, Panama, and Uruguay.

Index to Anthologies of Latin American Literature in English Translation

1   ABRIL, XAVIER (1903-   ) Peru
    Poetry
    Elegy To The Invented Woman. *M. Lee*. FITT, 405.
    Elegy To The Lost And Already Blurred By Time. *B. Castellón*.
        FITT, 403.
    Exaltation of Elementary Materials. *H. R. Hays*. FITT, 407.
    Nocturne. *H. R. Hays*. FITT, 407.

2   ACCIOLI, JOÃO (1912-   ) Brazil
    Poetry
    The Song Of Tomorrow. *L. S. Downes*. DOWN, 54.

3   ACCIOLY, BRENO (1921-1966) Brazil
    Fiction
    João Urso. *R. P. Joscelyne*. COH-1, 235.
    The Needles. *R. W. Horton*. COEL, 45.

4   ACEVEDO DÍAZ, EDUARDO (1851-1921) Uruguay
    Fiction
    The Prairie Fire (from: Soledad). *W. K. Jones*. JONE-3,
        233.

5   ACEVEDO HERNÁNDEZ, ANTONIO (1886-1962) Chile
    Drama
    Cabrerita. *W. E. Bailey*. PLAY, 1.
    Chañarcillo (Excerpt). *D. Davis & K. Booher*. JONE-3, 412.

6   ACUÑA, MANUEL (1849-1873) Mexico
    Poetry
    Withered Pages XV. *I. Goldberg*. GOLD-2, 16.

7   [ADÁN, MARTÍN pseud.] (1908-   ) Peru
    FUENTE BENAVIDES, RAFAEL DE LA
    Poetry
    Nativity. *M. Lee*. FITT, 489.
    Stentato in ischerzo. *J. Hill*. CARA, 341.
    Stenza tempo. Afrettando ad libitum. *J. Hill*. CARA, 342.

1

8 ADELLACH, ALBERTO (1933–) Argentina
   Drama
   March. *G. Luzuriaga & R. Rudder.* LUZU, 127.

9 ADOUM, JORGE ENRIQUE (1926–) Ecuador
   Poetry
   Farewell And No. *D. J. Flakoll & C. Alegría.* BENE, 109.
   Medals And Promotion. *R. Márquez & E. Randall.* MARQ, 235.
   Pastology. *R. Márquez.* MARQ, 241.
   Drama
   The Sun Trampled Beneath the Horses' Hooves. *D. A. McMurray & R. Márquez.* MR, 285.

10 AGOSTINI, VÍCTOR (1908–) Cuba
   Fiction
   Rebirth. no tr. CARZ, 43.

11 AGRAIT, GUSTAVO (1909–) Puerto Rico
   Poetry
   Find. *B. Luby.* BABI, 283.

12 AGÜERO, LUIS (1938–) Cuba
   Fiction
   One Friday the thirteenth. no tr. CARZ, 167.
   Santa Rita's Holy Water. *J. M. Cohen.* COH-3, 167.

13 AGÜEROS, JACK (   ) Puerto Rico
   Poetry
   Canción del Tecato. Originally Engl. BABI, 451.
   El Apatético. Originally Engl. BABI, 452.

14 AGÜEROS, VICTORIANO (1854–?) Mexico
   Other
   Criticism of the New School of Mexican Writers (Essay).
      F. Starr. STAR, 222.
   Peon y Contreras and his Romances Dramaticos (Essay).
      F. Starr. STAR, 225.
   The Day of the Dead (Essay). *F. Starr.* STAR, 218.
   The Student at Home (Essay). *F. Starr.* STAR, 220.

15 AGUIAR, ENRIQUE (1890–1947) Dominican Republic
   Poetry
   Ass, Patient Ass. *F. E. Townsend.* TOWN, 38.

16 AGUILAR, MARCO (1944–) Costa Rica
   Poetry
   Nocturne To The Light. *A. Edwards.* YOU, 47.

17 AGUILERA MALTA, DEMETRIO (1905–) Ecuador
   Fiction
   Don Goyo. *E. E. Perkins.* FLOR-2, 120.
   The Virgin Island (Excerpt). *W. K. Jones.* JONE-3, 204.

18   AGUIRRE, ISIDORA (1919-   ) Chile
     Drama
     The Three Pascualas (Excerpt). *W. K. Jones.* JONE-3, 423.

19   AGUIRRE, RAÚL GUSTAVO (1927-   ) Argentina
     Poetry
     And So... *T. Raworth.* CARA, 45.
     Reasons For Writing. *W. Shand.* SHA, 209.
     The Dancer In The "Cafe of the Moon." *W. Shand.* SHA, 210.
     The Day Of The Wretched One. *W. Shand.* SHA, 210.
     The Mutilated Man. *T. Raworth.* CARA, 45.
     The Triumph Of Letters. *W. Shand.* SHA, 211.

20   AGUSTÍN, JOSÉ (1944-   ) Mexico
     Fiction
     Mourning. *M. E. Ellsworth.* MANC, 463.

21   AGUSTÍN CONCEPCIÓN, J. (1906-   ) Dominican Republic
     Poetry
     Dreams of Glory. *F. E. Townsend.* TOWN, 77.

22   AGUSTINI, DELMIRA (1886-1914) Uruguay
     Poetry
     Another Race. *M. González.* CARA, 364.
     Nocturne. *M. E. Johnson.* JOHN, 147.
     Pale Evening. *M. E. Johnson.* JOHN, 143.
     The Intruder. *M. E. Johnson.* JOHN, 141.
     The Wings. *M. E. Johnson.* JOHN, 145.
     Your Love. *M. E. Johnson.* JOHN, 141.

AISEMBERG, ISAAC. See [EISEN, W. I. pseud.]

23   ALBÁN, LAUREANO (1942-   ) Costa Rica
     Poetry
     Caged. *A. Edwards.* YOU, 44.

24   ALBIZU CAMPOS, PEDRO (1891-1965) Puerto Rico
     Other
     Everybody Is Quiet But The Nationalistic Party (Speech).
        B. Luby. BABI, 250.

25   ALBORNO, PABLO (1877-?   ) Paraguay
     Other
     A Colonial Church in Paraguay (Essay). no tr. LIT-1, 79.
     A Colonial Church in Paraguay (Essay). no tr. LIT-2, 37.

26   ALCÂNTARA MACHADO, ANTÔNIO DE (1901-1935) Brazil
     Fiction
     Gaetaninho. *W. L. Grossman.* GRO, 71.

27 ALCIDES, RAFAEL (1933-   ) Cuba
    Poetry
    A Chronicle of Love (Fragment). *A. Boyer*. BECK, 555.
    A List Of Things Hands Can Do. *A. Kerrigan*. TARN, 75.
    'All That Winter, All That Spring.' *D. Gardner*. TARN, 73.
    Appreciation. *A. Boyer*. BECK, 545.
    The Case Of The Lady. *S. Carranza*. BECK, 551.
    The Hero. *A. Boyer*. BECK, 549.
    The Page. *A. Boyer*. BECK, 547.
    The Sign. *A. Boyer*. BECK, 543.
    'This Is Not A Letter To Be Opened.' *D. Gardner*. TARN, 73.

28 ALEGRÍA, CIRO (1909-1967) Peru
    Fiction
    A Small Place in the World (from: The Hungry Dogs).
      E. Schaefer. JONE-3, 199.
    Ayaymama (from: Broad and Alien Is the World). *H. de Onís*.
      ONIS-1, 254.
    The Hungry Dogs (Excerpt). *H. de Onís*. ARC, 45.
    The Stone and the Cross. *Z. Nelken*. TORR, 111.
    The Stone and the Cross. *Z. Nelken*. MILL, 126.

29 ALEGRÍA, RICARDO E. (1921-   ) Puerto Rico
    Other
    The Renegades (Folklore). *B. Luby*. BABI, 13.

30 ALFARO, RICARDO J. (1882-?   ) Panama
    Fiction
    The Liberator. no tr. LIT-2, 35.
    Other
    A Half Century of Pan Americanism (Essay). no tr. LIT-1,
      77.

31 ALFONSO, DOMINGO (1936-   ) Cuba
    Poetry
    A Biography of Little Reknown. *R. Llopis*. BECK, 599.
    A Love-Affair at Forty. *R. Llopis*. BECK, 607.
    Arte poética. *J. M. Cohen*. COH-3, 166.
    As Hard As Myself. *R. Llopis*. BECK, 613.
    Crossing the River. *R. Llopis*. BECK, 603.
    People Like Me. *S. Carranza*. BECK, 601.
    Poems of the Ordinary Man. *S. Carranza*. BECK, 609.
    Señor Julio Osorio. *R. Llopis*. BECK, 605.
    The Table. *R. Llopis*. BECK, 611.

32 ALLENDE, SALVADOR (1908-1973) Chile
    Other
    President Salvador Allende's Farewell Speech over Radio Ma-
      gallanes, September 11, 1973. *COFFLA*. LOW, 45.

4

33 [ALMAFUERTE pseud.] (1854-1917) Argentina
    PALACIOS, PEDRO B.
    Poetry
    Very Far Ahead. *A. S. Blackwell.* BLAC, 392.

34 ALMEIDA, GUILHERME DE (1890-1969) Brazil
    Poetry
    Dull Weather. *M. Cardozo.* NEI, 33.
    Nocturne. *L. S. Downes.* DOWN, 22.
    Poster. *L. S. Downes.* DOWN, 22.
    Rosamor, 8, 13, 14, 31. *M. Cardozo.* NEI, 35.
    Speed. *M. Cardozo.* NEI, 35.
    Vera Cruz! Land Of The True Cross! *M. Cardozo.* NEI, 31.

35 ALMEIDA, RENATO (1895-   ) Brazil
    Other
    Brazilian Music (Essay). no tr. LIT-1, 17.

36 ALONSO, DORA (1910-   ) Cuba
    Fiction
    The rat. no tr. CARZ, 89.

37 ALONSO, RODOLFO (1934-   ) Argentina
    Poetry
    River Banks. *W. Shand.* SHA, 261.
    The Girl Of The Canary Islands. *W. Shand.* SHA, 260.
    The Unhappy One. *W. Shand.* SHA, 261.
    The Waist Of The World. *W. Shand.* SHA, 259.

38 ALONSO ORTÍZ, RUBÉN (   ) Argentina
    Fiction
    The Hot Center of Thunder. *H. E. Francis.* MU-70, 67.

39 ALVARADO, RAFAEL (   ) Venezuela
    Drama
    From 7:15 to 8:00 The Entrance Is Through The Hoop.
      J. Pottlitzer. DR, 138.

    ALVARES, ROLANDO. See [VILLA, ALVARO DE pseud.]

40 ÁLVAREZ, JOSÉ SEFERINO (1858-1903) Argentina
    Fiction
    At Dusk (from: Un viaje al país de los matreros). no tr.
      LIT-2, 1.

41 ÁLVAREZ BARAGAÑO, JOSÉ (1932-1962) Cuba
    Poetry
    Eulogy to Death. *C. Beck.* BECK, 497.
    Fallen between the Marsh and the Sea. *C. Beck.* BECK, 501.
    From Revolutionary Poems. *S. Carranza.* BECK, 505.
    Illumination. *J. M. Cohen.* COH-3, 139.
    In the Pentagon. *C. Beck.* BECK, 507.

42 ÁLVAREZ BRAVO, ARMANDO (1938-   ) Cuba
Poetry
A Bit of Metaphysics. *C. Beck*. BECK, 681.
Anguish. *C. Beck*. BECK, 687.
Every Man to his Death. *C. Beck*. BECK, 685.
Narrow Gardens. *C. Beck*. BECK, 689.
On a Snapshot. *C. Beck*. BECK, 677.
The Boon. *C. Beck*. BECK, 691.
The Pilgrims. *C. Beck*. BECK, 693.
Those Gods. *C. Beck*. BECK, 683.

43 ÁLVAREZ HENAO, ENRIQUE (1871-1914) Colombia
Poetry
The Bee. *A. S. Blackwell*. BLAC, 418.

44 AMADO, JORGE (1912-   ) Brazil
Fiction
How Porciúncula the Mulatto Got the Corpse Off His Back.
    E. & M. Honig. HOW-1, 253.
Sea of The Dead   Yemanjá, Mistress Of The Seas And The
    Sails. *D. D. Walsh*. FLOR-2, 384.
Sweat. *L. C. Kaplan*. MANC, 115.

45 AMBROGI, ARTURO (1875-1936) El Salvador
Fiction
The Shade of the Wild Fig Tree. no tr. LIT-1, 50.
The Shade of the Wild Fig Tree. no tr. LIT-2, 23.

46 AMOR, GUADALUPE (1920-   ) Mexico
Fiction
My Mother's Bedroom (from: Yo soy mi casa). *D. Demarest*.
    EVER, 121.
The Small Drawing Room (Chapter from: Yo soy mi casa, her
    autobiographical novel). *D. Demarest*. CRAN, 56.

47 ANDERSON-IMBERT, ENRIQUE (1910-   ) Argentina
Fiction
The General Makes A Lovely Corpse. *D. Yates*. YATE, 151.

48 ANDRADE, MÁRIO DE (1893-1945) Brazil
Poetry
Aspiration. *J. Nist & Y. Leite*. NIST, 34.
At Forty. *L. S. Downes*. DOWN, 29.
Impromptu of the Dead Boy. *J. Nist & Y. Leite*. NIST, 33.
Improvisation of the Dead Boy. *R. Eberhart*. BISH, 21.
Meditation On The Tietê. *M. Cardozo*. NEI, 9.
Moment. *P. Standish*. CARA, 67.
Moment. *J. Nist & Y. Leite*. NIST, 37.
Moment. *J. Nist & Y. Leite*. NIST, 40.
Mother. *L. S. Downes*. DOWN, 28.
Night-Piece from Belo Horizonte. no tr. TRE, 6.
Poems Of The Negress V, VII. *M. Cardozo*. NEI, 7.

Poems of the Woman Friend (Excerpt). *J. Nist & Y. Leite*. NIST, 42.
Rola-Môça Mountains. *M. Cardozo*. NEI, 11.
Rondeau for You. *J. Nist & Y. Leite*. NIST, 41.
Song of the Corner. *J. Nist & Y. Leite*. NIST, 39.
Streets of My São Paulo. *J. Nist & Y. Leite*. NIST, 38.
That Man Who Walks All Alone. *J. Nist & Y. Leite*. NIST, 39.
The Flock. *P. Standish*. CARA, 68.
The Girl and the Goat. *J. Nist & Y. Leite*. NIST, 43.
The Khaki Lozenge (XVII). *M. Cardozo*. NEI, 5.
The Major's "coco." *M. Cardozo*. NEI, 3.
The Mountains of Rolling-Girl. *J. Nist & Y. Leite*. NIST, 36.
Variation on the Bad Friend. *J. Nist & Y. Leite*. NIST, 35.
Fiction
It Can Hurt Plenty. *W. L. Grossman*. GRO, 12.
Macunaíma (Excerpt). *H. de Onís*. ONIS-1, 391.

49 ANDRADE, OSWALD DE (1890–1953) Brazil
    (JOSÉ OSWALD DE SOUZA ANDRADE)
    Poetry
    Advertisement. *J. R. Longland*. BISH, 13.
    Bengaló. *M. Cardozo*. NEI, 23.
    Black-Out (from: "The Canticle of Canticles For Flute And Violão"). *M. Cardozo*. NEI, 21.
    Congonhas Do Campo. *M. Cardozo*. NEI, 23.
    Dowry (from: "Canticle of Canticles For Flute And Violão"). *M. Cardozo*. NEI, 19.
    Epitaph. *J. R. Longland*. BISH, 17.
    Epitaph No. 2 (from: "The Golden Beetle"). *M. Cardozo*. NEI, 17.
    Frontier (from: "The Golden Beetle"). *M. Cardozo*. NEI, 15.
    Funeral Procession. *J. R. Longland*. BISH, 15.
    Good Luck (from: "The Golden Beetle"). *M. Cardozo*. NEI, 17.
    Hierofante (from: "The Golden Beetle"). *M. Cardozo*. NEI, 15.
    Hymen (from: "The Canticle of Canticles for Flute and Violão"). *M. Cardozo*. NEI, 21.
    March (from: "The Canticle of Canticles For Flute And Violão"). *M. Cardozo*. NEI, 19.
    National Library. *J. R. Longland*. BISH, 11.
    Passionária. *M. Cardozo*. NEI, 25.
    Plebescite (from: "The Golden Beetle"). *M. Cardozo*. NEI, 17.
    Potted Music. *L. S. Downes*. DOWN, 23.
    The Diver's Suit (from: "The Golden Beetle"). *M. Cardozo*. NEI, 15.
    The Mistake Of The Portuguese. *L. S. Downes*. DOWN, 23.

50   ANDRADE RIVERA, GUSTAVO (1921-   ) Colombia
     Drama
     Remington 22. *F. Colecchia & J. Matas.* COLE, 69.

51   ÁNGEL SILVA, MEDARDO (1900-1929) Ecuador
     Poetry
     Nocturnal Detail. *M. & C. V. Wicker.* JONE-3, 103.
     The Sleeping Malecón. *W. K. Jones.* JONE-3, 103.

52   ANGUITA, EDUARDO (1914-   ) Chile
     Poetry
     Passage To The End. *L. Mallan.* FITT, 555.
     Service. *L. Mallan.* FITT, 553.
     The True Countenance. *D. Flakoll & C. Alegría.* FLAK, 191.

53   ANJOS, AUGUSTO DOS (   ) Brazil
     Poetry
     Energy. *E. Brown.* LIT-2, 17.

54   APARICIO, RAÚL (1913-   ) Cuba
     Fiction
     There were four of us. no tr. CARZ, 71.

55   APPLEYARD, JOSÉ-LUIS (1927-   ) Paraguay
     Poetry
     Colophon. *J. Upton.* TRI-13, 283.
     There is a place. *J. Upton.* TRI-13, 204.

56   ARANGO, ÁNGEL (1926-   ) Cuba
     Fiction
     The day New York reached heaven. no tr. CARZ, 125.

57   ARÁOZ ANZOÁTEGUI, RAÚL (1923-   ) Argentina
     Poetry
     In The Wood. *W. Shand.* SHA, 172.
     Poem Of The Road. *W. Shand.* SHA, 173.

58   ARAUJO SÁNCHEZ, FRANCISCO (1940?-   ) Ecuador
     Poetry
     Third Memory. *R. Connally.* YOU, 53.

59   ARAY, EDMUNDO (1936-   ) Venezuela
     Poetry
     I Read This To My Daughter. *R. Márquez.* MARQ, 505.
     Seven Fifty-Five. *E. Randall & R. Márquez.* MARQ, 501.
     Untitled. *E. Randall & R. Márquez.* MARQ, 499.

60   ARCE DE VÁZQUEZ, MARGOT (1904-   ) Puerto Rico
     Fiction
     The Puerto Rican Landscape. no tr. KAI, n.p.
     Other
     Hostos, Exemplary Patriot (Essay). *B. Luby.* BABI, 52.

8

61 ARCHANJO, NEIDE (   ) Brazil
    Poetry
    Canto I - Terúrica, 26. *M. Cardozo.* NEI, 177.
    Canto II - Onírica, I. *M. Cardozo.* NEI, 179.

62 ARCINIEGAS, GERMÁN (1900-   ) Colombia
    Other
    The Little Horses of Ráquira (Essay). no tr. LIT-1, 25.
    The Little Horses of Ráquira (from: America, Tierra firme).
       H. de Onís. ONIS-1, 225.

63 ARENAL, HUMBERTO (1926-   ) Cuba
    Fiction
    Mister Charles. *J. M. Cohen.* COH-3, 88.
    Mister Charles. no tr. CARZ, 95.

64 [ARENALES, RICARDO pseud.] (1883-1942) Colombia
    OSORIO, MIGUEL ÁNGEL
    Poetry
    Song of La Vida Profunda. *E. W. Underwood.* UND, 72.
    Stanzas. *E. W. Underwood.* UND, 72.
    The Lament of October. *E. W. Underwood.* UND, 71.

65 ARÉVALO MARTÍNEZ, RAFAEL (1884-?   ) Guatemala
    Poetry
    Clean Clothes. *M. Lee.* FITT, 497.
    Human Wolves. *A. S. Blackwell.* BLAC, 474.
    Las Imposibles (Excerpt). *W. Williams.* WALS, 729.
    Like The Cypresses. *M. E. Johnson.* JOHN, 177.
    My Sister. *A. S. Blackwell.* BLAC, 476.
    The Contemporary Sancho Panza. *W. Williams.* WALS, 731.
    The Men-Wolves. *M. E. Johnson.* JOHN, 177.
    The Wolf Men. *B. J. Johnson & W. K. Jones.* JONE-3, 285.
    Fiction
    The Man Who Resembled a Horse. *S. Toye & W. K. Jones.*
       JONE-3, 281.

66 ARGUEDAS, ALCIDES (1879-1941) Bolivia
    Fiction
    Race of Bronze (Excerpt). *H. de Onís.* ONIS-1, 231.
    The Funeral of the Indian (from: Race of Bronze).
       E. Turner. JONE-3, 187.
    Other
    Melgarejo (from: The Barbarous Chieftains). *H. de Onís.*
       ARC, 205.

67 ARGUEDAS, JOSÉ MARÍA (1911-1969) Peru
    Fiction
    Death Of The Arangos. *M. Shipman & M. Valencia.* HAR67-2,
       69.
    The Ayla. *H. St. Martin.* CARP, 174.
    Warma Kuyay (Puppy Love). *H. St. Martin.* HOW-1, 246.

68   ARGÜELLES BRINGAS, ROBERTO   (1875-1915)   Mexico
     Poetry
     Will. *E. W. Underwood.* UND, 109.

69   ARGÜELLO, LINO   (1886-1936)   Nicaragua
     Poetry
     A Day in the Country. *W. K. Jones.* JONE-3, 66.

70   ARGÜELLO BARRETO, SANTIAGO   (1872-1942)   Nicaragua
     Poetry
     The Eagle and the Dry Leaf. *A. S. Blackwell.* BLAC, 202.
     The Eagle and the Dry Leaf. *A. S. Blackwell.* JONE-3, 65.

71   ARIDJIS, HOMERO   (1940-   )   Mexico
     Poetry
     Before the Kingdom. *W. S. Merwin.* PAZ-2, 29.
     "I love your confusion..." *E. Randall.* TRI-13, 335.
     It's Your Name and It's Also October. *W. S. Merwin.*
       PAZ-2, 27.
     May her presence last. *E. Weinberger.* MU-69, 139.
     "Night dies on a crushed apple..." *E. Randall.* TRI-13, 335.
     Noon splits the riverbank. *E. Weinberger.* MU-69, 139.
     On this bridge where time moves immobile. *E. Weinberger.*
       MU-69, 135.
     Possess lady the bodies. *E. Weinberger.* MU-69, 137.
     Sometimes We Touch a Body. *W. S. Merwin.* PAZ-2, 25.
     The chant beneath the mist. *E. Weinberger.* MU-69, 137.
     The Hatching. no tr. YOU, 85.
     V. *E. Weinberger.* CHI, 127.
     XXIV. *E. Weinberger.* CHI, 129.

72   ARÍSTIDES, JULIO   (1921-   )   Argentina
     Poetry
     The Disproportionate One. *W. Shand.* SHA, 158.
     The Excavator. *W. Shand.* SHA, 159.

73   ARÍZAGA, CARLOS MANUEL   (1943?-   )   Ecuador
     Poetry
     Naiad. *R. Connally.* YOU, 55.

74   ARLT, ROBERTO   (1900-1942)   Argentina
     Fiction
     Esther Primavera. *N. T. di Giovanni.* CARP, 60.
     One Sunday Afternoon. *N. T. di Giovanni.* HOW-1, 123.
     Small-Time Property Owners. *M. J. Wilkie.* MANC, 123.

75   ARMANÍ, HORACIO   (1925-   )   Argentina
     Poetry
     Soliciting A Sign. *W. Shand.* SHA, 192.
     Victory Through The Dream. *W. Shand.* SHA, 191.

76 AROZARENA, MARCELINO (1912-   ) Cuba
   Poetry
   Caridá. *H. Ruiz del Vizo.* RUIZ, 41.

77 ARREGUI, MARIO (1917-   ) Uruguay
   Fiction
   The Cat. *G. McWhirter.* MU-70, 106.

78 ARREOLA, JUAN JOSÉ (1918-   ) Mexico
   Poetry
   Deer. *W. S. Merwin.* PAZ-2, 101.
   Elegy. *W. S. Merwin.* PAZ-2, 93.
   Metamorphosis. *W. S. Merwin.* PAZ-2, 103.
   Telemachus. *W. S. Merwin.* PAZ-2, 97.
   The Cave. *W. S. Merwin.* PAZ-2, 95.
   The Toad. *W. S. Merwin.* PAZ-2, 99.
   Fiction
   I'm Telling You the Truth. *G. B. Schade.* MANC, 199.
   The Prodigious Milligram. *D. Flakoll & C. Alegría.* FLAK,
      99.
   The switchman. *B. Belitt.* TRI-13, 185.
   The Switchman. *B. Belitt.* HOW-1, 303.
   Truly, I Tell You. *P. Blackburn.* CRAN, 44.
   Other
   Epithalamium. *L. Kemp.* EVER, 136.
   Freedom (Sketch). *L. Kemp.* EVER, 134.
   Gravity (Sketch). *L. Kemp.* EVER, 135.
   Insects (Sketch). *L. Kemp.* EVER, 135.
   Moles (Sketch). *L. Kemp.* EVER, 134.
   The Boa (Sketch). *L. Kemp.* EVER, 138.
   The Encounter (Sketch). *L. Kemp.* EVER, 137.
   The Hippopotamus (Fable). no tr. CRAN, 36.
   The Hyena (Fable). no tr. CRAN, 43.
   The Map of Lost Objects (Sketch). *L. Kemp.* EVER, 137.
   The Rhinoceros (Fable). no tr. CRAN, 41.
   The Sadly Feathered Hen and the Diamond (Fable). *G. Mendel-
      sohn.* CRAN, 38.
   The Seals. no tr. CRAN, 39.
   The Toad (Sketch). *L. Kemp.* EVER, 136.

79 ARRIAZA, ARMANDO (1903-   ) Chile
   Fiction
   Pilgrimage. *A. De Sola.* FLOR-2, 480.
   Pilgrimage. *A. De Sola.* MILL, 144.

80 ARRIETA, RAFAEL ALBERTO (1889-?   ) Argentina
   Poetry
   In An Abandoned Cemetery. *M. E. Johnson.* JOHN, 173.
   January Night... *M. Lee.* FITT, 477.
   Moment and soul. *P. Gannon.* GAN, 37.
   Rain. *A. J. McVan.* TRAN, 191.
   The Absent Voice. *M. E. Johnson.* JOHN, 171.

81   ARRIVÍ, FRANCISCO (1915-   ) Puerto Rico
Drama
Masquerade: Devil Masks. *R. E. Coulthard*. BABI, 165.

82   ARRUFAT, ANTÓN (1935-   ) Cuba
Poetry
Exile 1958. *C. Beck*. BECK, 623.
On One Who Came from the Spanish Civil War. *C. Beck*.
  BECK, 619.
Playa Girón. *C. Beck*. BECK, 617.
Requiem. *C. Beck*. BECK, 621.
Tempo I. *C. Beck*. BECK, 629.
The Erudite. *C. Beck*. BECK, 625.
The Keepsake. *C. Beck*. BECK, 627.
The Retelling. *C. Beck*. BECK, 631.
Fiction
The discovery. no tr. CARZ, 145.
The Discovery. *J. G. Brotherston*. COH-3, 100.

83   ARTECHE, MIGUEL (1926-   ) Chile
Poetry
Elegy For A Dead Boy. *M. Williams*. WILL-2, 9.
Epithalamium. *M. Williams*. WILL-2, 3.
Golf. *M. Williams*. WILL-2, 5.
Rain. *J. Upton*. TRI-13, 390.
Spinning. *M. Williams*. WILL-2, 5.
The cafe. *J. Upton*. TRI-13, 389.
The Cafe. *R. Connally*. YOU, 39.
The Idiot Child. *M. Williams*. WILL-2, 13.

84   ARTEL, JORGE (   ) Colombia
Poetry
I Am A Negro. *H. Ruiz de Vizo*. RUIZ, 96.
Mr. Davi. *H. Ruiz de Vizo*. RUIZ, 98.

85   ARZOLA, MARINA (1939-   ) Puerto Rico
Poetry
St. Petersburg - Before the Revolution of 1917. *M. Arri-
  llaga*. MATI, 129.
Weariness   Girl of the Pretty Feet. *M. Arrillaga*. MATI,
  129.

86   ASTURIAS, MIGUEL ÁNGEL (1899-1974) Guatemala
Poetry
Pablo Neruda Alive. *N. Braymer*. LOW, 8.
The Indians Come Down From Mixco. *D. D. Walsh*. FITT, 157.
Fiction
Legend of "El Cadejo." *H. St. Martin*. MANC, 71.
Strong wind (Excerpt). *G. Rabassa*. TRI-13, 393.
Tatuana's Tale. *P. Emigh & F. MacShane*. HOW-1, 118.
The Mirror Of Lida Sal. *H. R. Hays*. CARP, 84.

87   ATILES GARCÍA, GUILLERMO   (   ) Puerto Rico
     Poetry
     My shack. *G. Pando.* KAI, n.p.

88   AUGIER, ÁNGEL (1910-   ) Cuba
     Poetry
     Island at my Fingertips. *A. Boyer.* BECK, 93.

89   AVILÉS, JUAN (1905-   ) Puerto Rico
     Poetry
     The Coffee Plantation. *B. Luby.* BABI, 287.

90   AYALA GAUNA, VELMIRO (1905-   ) Argentina
     Fiction
     Early Morning Murder. *D. Yates.* YATE, 53.

91   AZAMBUJA, DARCY PEREIRA DE (1903-   ) Brazil
     Fiction
     At the Side of the Road. *W. L. Grossman.* GRO, 138.

92   AZCONA CRANWELL, ELIZABETH (1935-   ) Argentina
     Poetry
     The Absence. *W. Shand.* SHA, 263.
     When Love Sets Fire To Places. *W. Shand.* SHA, 262.

93   AZEREDO, RONALDO (1937-   ) Brazil
     Poetry
     body. *H. de Campos.* WILL-1, n.p.
     like the wind. *H. de Campos.* WILL-1, n.p.
     speed. no tr. BANN, 111.
     street(s)/sun. no tr. BANN, 112.
     sun/streets. *H. de Campos.* WILL-1, n.p.
     "tic tac." *H. de Campos.* WILL-1, n.p.
     up to/here. no tr. BANN, 114.
     Velocidade. no tr. WILL-1, n.p.
     west/east. no tr. BANN, 113.

94   AZUELA, MARIANO (1873-1952) Mexico
     Fiction
     The Underdogs (Excerpt). *E. Munguía, Jr.* JONE-3, 258.

95   BABÍN, MARÍA TERESA (1910-   ) Puerto Rico
     Fiction
     Puerto Rican Fancy. no tr. KAI, n.p.
     Other
     Symbols Of Borinquen (Essay). *B. Luby.* BABI, 139.
     The Hymn of Puerto Rico (Notes on Hymn). *M. T. Babín.*
       BABI, 82.

96 BAILEY, EDGAR (1919-   ) Argentina
    Poetry
    I Walk On The Earth. *W. Shand.* SHA, 140.
    The Modern Man. *W. Shand.* SHA, 139.
    Violence. *W. Shand.* SHA, 140.

97 BALLAGAS, EMILIO (1908-1954) Cuba
    Poetry
    María Belén Chacón Eligía. *H. Ruiz del Vizo.* RUIZ, 31.
    Nocturne. *J. Hill.* CARA, 206.
    Poem of Impatience. *J. Hill.* CARA, 207.
    Streetcall Of A Peddler. *H. Ruiz del Vizo.* RUIZ, 29.

98 BALSEIRO, JOSÉ A. (1900-   ) Puerto Rico
    Poetry
    The Black Trumpet. *B. Luby.* BABI, 178.

99 BAN, EVA (   ) Brazil
    Poetry
    In Memoriam Pablo Neruda (USA - 1973). no tr. LOW, 4.

100 BANCHS, ENRIQUE (1888-1968) Argentina
     Poetry
     A Little Song. *M. E. Johnson.* JOHN, 165.
     A Small Pain. *T. Raworth.* CARA, 20.
     Babbling. *W. K. Jones.* JONE-3, 155.
     Faltering Utterance. *G. D. Craig.* CRAI, 175.
     Sonnet LVII. *H. Manning.* GAN, 33.
     Sonnet LX. *P. Gannon.* GAN, 35.
     Stammering. *M. E. Johnson.* JOHN, 163.
     The Statue. *G. D. Craig.* CRAI, 177.
     The Tiger. *M. E. Johnson.* JOHN, 169.
     The Vow. *M. E. Johnson.* JOHN, 167.
     Thou gentle spirit.... *G. D. Craig.* CRAI, 181.
     Tiger. *E. du Gué Trapier.* TRAN, 190.
     Tiger (Iridescent Flanks). *E. du Gué Trapier.* JONE-3, 156.
     Veterrima Laurus. *T. Raworth.* CARA, 21.

101 BANDEIRA, ANTÓNIO RANGEL (1917-   ) Brazil
     Poetry
     The End Of The World. *L. S. Downes.* DOWN, 66.

102 BANDEIRA, MANUEL (1886-1968) Brazil
     (Manuel Carneiro de Souza Bandeira Filho)
     Poetry
     A Brazilian Tragedy. *M. Cardozo.* NEI, 53.
     A Moment In A Café. *M. Cardozo.* NEI, 49.
     Absolute Death. *J. Nist & Y. Leite.* NIST, 21.
     Absolute Death. *A. Levitin.* CHI, 51.
     Anthology. *J. R. Longland.* BISH, 5.
     Apple. *J. Nist & Y. Leite.* NIST, 22.
     Brazilian Tragedy. *E. Bishop.* BISH, 9.

14

Dead Bull. *A. Levitin.* CHI, 49.
Dead Of Night. *D. Poore.* FITT, 137.
Death. *M. Cardozo.* NEI, 51.
Evoking Recife. *M. Cardozo.* NEI, 55.
I Am Going Away to Pasargada. *J. Nist & Y. Leite.* NIST, 25.
I Don't Dance. no tr. TRE, 24.
"I Will Arise and Go Now...." no tr. TRE, 28.
I'm Going Away To Pasargadae. *M. Cardozo.* NEI, 49.
I'm Leaving For Pasárgada. *A. Levitin.* CHI, 53.
In Soapsuds Street. *D. Poore.* FITT, 131.
Last Song of the Dead End. *J. Nist & Y. Leite.* NIST, 26.
Lovely Lovely. *A. Levitin.* CHI, 47.
Moment in a Café. *J. Nist & Y. Leite.* NIST, 21.
Moment in a Café. no tr. TRE, 28.
Mozart In Heaven. *D. Poore.* FITT, 133.
My Last Poem. *E. Bishop.* BISH, 3.
Pneumothorax. *J. Nist & Y. Leite.* NIST, 20.
Poetica. *J. Nist & Y. Leite.* NIST, 19.
Poetics. *P. Standish.* CARA, 65.
Poetics. no tr. TRE, 22.
Profundamente. *J. Nist & Y. Leite.* NIST, 23.
Rondeau of the Little Horses. *R. Wilbur.* BISH, 7.
Roundel of the Little Horses. *J. Nist & Y. Leite.* NIST, 24.
Sacha and the Poet. no tr. TRE, 26.
Salute To Recife. *D. Poore.* FITT, 125.
Song Of The Wind And My Life. *L. S. Downes.* DOWN, 19.
Spiritual Wedding. *M. Cardozo.* NEI, 59.
Teresa. no tr. TRE, 26.
The Cactus. *D. Poore.* FITT, 135.
The Hammer. *P. Standish.* CARA, 64.
The Highway. *D. Poore.* FITT, 137.
The Morning Star. *L. S. Downes.* DOWN, 20.
The Morning Star. *M. Cardozo.* NEI, 47.
The Morning Star. *J. Nist & Y. Leite.* NIST, 28.
The Woods. *D. Poore.* FITT, 133.

103 BAÑUELOS, JUAN (1932-   ) Mexico
   Poetry
   A Gun, the Leaf That Moves the Entire Tree. *R. Márquez.*
     MARQ, 305.
   Dogs. *R. Márquez.* MARQ, 301.
   El habitante amoroso (Excerpt). *E. Randall.* TRI-13, 338.
   In Vietnam the Thorns Drip Clouds of Lambs. *R. Márquez.*
     MARQ, 299.

104 BAREIRO SAGUIER, RUBÉN (1930-   ) Paraguay
   Poetry
   Awakening. *J. Upton.* TRI-13, 287.
   Sea bed. *J. Upton.* TRI-13, 286.

105 BARNET, MIGUEL (1940-   ) Cuba
     Poetry
     Agatha. *R. F. Hardy*. BECK, 721.
     Ché. *R. F. Hardy*. BECK, 711.
     Christ. *R. F. Hardy*. BECK, 709.
     Epitaph. *R. F. Hardy*. BECK, 719.
     Epitaph. *L. Kearns*. TARN, 97.
     Errata. *R. F. Hardy*. BECK, 717.
     Errata. *L. Kearns*. TARN, 97.
     Errata. *M. Randall*. TRI-13, 151.
     My Country. *R. F. Hardy*. BECK, 707.
     Revolution. *R. F. Hardy*. BECK, 713.
     The absent friend. *M. Randall*. TRI-13, 150.
     The Sacred Family. *R. F. Hardy*. BECK, 723.
     The Visitors. *R. F. Hardy*. BECK, 715.

106 BARQUERO, EFRAÍN (1931-   ) Chile
     Poetry
     Dreams Run In Your Eyes. *M. Williams*. WILL-2, 21.
     Legacy of honey. *J. Upton*. TRI-13, 378.
     My Beloved Is Knitting. *M. Williams*. WILL-2, 17.
     The Barn. *R. Connally*. YOU, 35.
     The house. *J. Upton*. TRI-13, 379.
     The Inheritance. *M. Williams*. WILL-2, 19.
     XXI. *J. Upton*. TRI-13, 380.

107 BARRERA, CARLOS (1888-?   ) Mexico
     Poetry
     Longing. *E. W. Underwood*. UND, 129.

108 BARRIOS, EDUARDO (1884-1963) Chile
     Fiction
     Brother Ass. *R. S. Rose & F. Aguilera*. FLOR-2, 488.
     Brother Ass (Excerpt). *W. K. Jones*. JONE-3, 331.
     Like Sisters. *W. E. Colford*. COLF, 27.
     Drama
     For The Sake Of A Good Reputation. *W. K. Jones*. JONE-4, 1.

109 BARROSO, GUSTAVO (1888-?   ) Brazil
     Other
     The Cattle Drovers (from: Terras de sol). *H. de Onís*.
        ONIS-1, 366.

110 BARTOLOMÉ, LEOPOLDO JOSÉ (1942-   ) Argentina
     Poetry
     Death Of A Magus. no tr. YOU, 7.
     Poem Written In The Dust. *W. Shand*. SHA, 274.
     The Most Distant Land. *W. Shand*. SHA, 275.

111 BASADRE, JORGE (1903-　) Peru
　　Other
　　The National Library of Peru and Ricardo Palma (Essay).
　　　no tr. LIT-1, 81.

112 BAYLEY, EDGAR (1919-　) Argentina
　　Poetry
　　A Question of Time. *T. Raworth*. CARA, 39.
　　Of men and years. *P. Morgan*. TRI-13, 249.
　　Violence. *T. Raworth*. CARA, 40.

113 BAYÓN HERRERA, LUIS (　) Argentina
　　Drama
　　Santos Vega. *J. Fassett*. BIER, 22.

114 BAZIL, OSVALDO (1884-1946) Dominican Republic
　　Poetry
　　Idyl. *M. Lee*. LIT-2, 47.
　　Nocturne Petit. *F. E. Townsend*. TOWN, 22.

115 BEDREGAL DE CONITZER, YOLANDA (1916-　) Bolivia
　　Poetry
　　Facing My Portrait. *D. D. Walsh*. FITT, 499.

116 BELAVAL, EMILIO S. (1903-　) Puerto Rico
　　Fiction
　　Monsona Quintana's Purple Child (Excerpt). *P. Vallés*.
　　　KAI, n.p.
　　The Purple Child. *N. Vandemoer*. HOW-2, 280.

117 BELL, LINDOLF (　) Brazil
　　Poetry
　　A Poem After The Manner Of An Index Card. *M. Cardozo*.
　　　NEI, 171.
　　I. *M. Cardozo*. NEI, 173.
　　VI. *M. Cardozo*. NEI, 175.

118 BELLI, CARLOS GERMÁN (1927-　) Peru
　　Poetry
　　Instead of Sweet Humans. *T. Raworth*. CARA, 344.
　　O Hada Cibernética (Excerpt of 10 poems). *M. Ahern &*
　　　D. Tipton. AHER, 35.
　　O Hada Cibernética! (Excerpt of 20 poems). *C. Eshleman*.
　　　TRI-13, 216.
　　Oh Cybernetic Fairy!.... *T. Raworth*. CARA, 345.
　　Papa, Mama. *D. J. Flakoll & C. Alegría*. BENE, 115.
　　Poem. *T. Raworth*. CARA, 344.
　　Segregation. *M. Ahern*. AHER, 34.
　　Segregation no. 1. *M. A. Maurer*. TRI-15, 200.
　　"...so much heaven...." *M. A. Maurer & D. Tipton*. TRI-15,
　　　201.

(BELLI, CARLOS GERMÁN)
    Tongue-tied. *M. Ahern*. AHER, 39.
    Tongue-tied. *D. Tipton & M. A. Maurer*. TRI-15, 202.
    "Why have they moved me...?" *M. A. Maurer & D. Tipton*.
      TRI-15, 201.

119   BELTRÁN, NEFTALÍ (1916-   ) Mexico
    Poetry
    Wherever I Go.... no tr. CRAN, 101.

120   BENARÓS, LEON (1915-   ) Argentina
    Poetry
    The Standard-Bearer. *W. Shand*. SHA, 113.
    The Years Invade Us. *W. Shand*. SHA, 114.

121   BENDEZÚ, FRANCISCO (1928-   ) Peru
    Poetry
    Aim. *P. Pomposinni*. HAR68-5, 22.

122   BENEDETTI, MARIO (1920-   ) Uruguay
    Poetry
    Against Drawbridges. *E. Randall & R. Márquez*. MARQ, 461.
    Burning the Ships. *D. A. McMurray*. MARQ, 457.
    Frustrated Poems. *R. Connally*. YOU, 107.
    Holocaust. *D. A. McMurray*. MARQ, 455.
    Juan Angel's Birthday. *D. A. McMurray*. MR, 137.
    With Your Permission. *D. A. McMurray*. MARQ, 451.
    Fiction
    Gloria's Saturday. *D. Flakoll & C. Alegría*. FLAK, 121.
    Gloria's Saturday. *G. Woodruff*. MANC, 367.
    The Budget. *G. Brown*. FRA-J, 29.
    The Iriartes. *J. Franco*. COH-1, 143.

123   BEOLA, IGNACIO (1935-   ) Argentina
    Poetry
    "All different from other women...." no tr. YOU, 11.
    "The warrior's wives will dance...." no tr. YOU, 10.

124   BERMÚDEZ, FEDERICO (1884-1921) Dominican Republic
    Poetry
    Serenely Grey. *F. E. Townsend*. TOWN, 37.
    Symbol. *F. E. Townsend*. TOWN, 36.

125   BERMÚDEZ, MARÍA ELVIRA (1916-   ) Mexico
    Fiction
    The Puzzle of the Broken Watch. *D. Yates*. YATE, 95.

126   BERNAL, RAFAEL (1915-   ) Mexico
    Fiction
    Natural Causes. *W. E. Colford*. COLF, 155.

127 BERNÁRDEZ, FRANCISCO LUIS (1900-   ) Argentina
     Poetry
     The City Without Laura. *H. Manning.* GAN, 53.
     The Earth. *W. Shand.* SHA, 39.

128 BERNÁRDEZ, MANUEL (1867-1936) Uruguay
     Fiction
     Paid in Full. *H. de Onís.* ONIS-1, 179.

129 BETANCES, SAMUEL (   ) Puerto Rico
     Other
     Race And The Search For Identity (from: The Rican).
       Originally Engl. BABI, 426.

   BETANCOURT, JOSÉ. See [IVANOVITCH, DMITRI pseud.].

130 BIAGIONI, AMELIA (1916-   ) Argentina
     Poetry
     Each Day, Each Night. *W. Shand.* SHA, 121.
     Manifesto. *W. Shand.* SHA, 120.

131 BIETTI, OSCAR (1913?-   ) Argentina
     Poetry
     Ballad of the Dead Love. *H. E. Fish.* TRAN, 195.

132 BILAC, OLAVO (1865-1918) Brazil
     Poetry
     Caçador de Esmeraldas (Excerpt). *L. Elliott.* WALS, 572.
     In Extremis. *P. Standish.* CARA, 57.
     To a Poet. *P. Standish.* CARA, 58.
     Other
     An International City (from: A Defesa Nacional). no tr.
       LIT-2, 10.

133 BIOY CASARES, ADOLFO (1914-   ) Argentina
     (Also wrote with JORGE LUIS BORGES under pseud. of BUSTOS
     DOMECQ)
     Fiction
     A Letter About Emilia. *G. Woodruff.* MANC, 217.
     Miracles Cannot Be Recovered. *N. T. di Giovanni.* HOW-1,
       278.

134 BLANCO, ANDRÉS ELOY (1897-1955) Venezuela
     Poetry
     As Good As Bread. *M. González.* CARA, 386.
     Conversation under the Cypress Tree. *M. González.* CARA,
       387.

135 BLANCO, ANTONIO NICOLÁS (1887-1945) Puerto Rico
     Poetry
     Intimate Prayer. *M. Lee.* LIT-2, 57.

136 BLANCO, TOMÁS (1900-   ) Puerto Rico
Poetry
Unicorn On The Island. *P. Vallés.* KAI, n.p.
Fiction
The Child's Gifts: A Twelfth Night Tale. *H. de Onís.*
  HOW-2, 298.
Other
Serenade Of the Coquí (from: The Five Senses). *B. Luby.*
  BABI, 147.
The Five Senses (Excerpt). no tr. KAI, n.p.

137 BLANCO FOMBONA, RUFINO (1874-?) Venezuela
Poetry
A Little Messenger Dove. *A. S. Blackwell.* BLAC, 434.
At Parting. *M. Lee.* WALS, 617.
Escape. *M. Lee.* LIT-1, 96.
Escape. *M. Lee.* LIT-2, 50.
Invitation to Love. *A. S. Blackwell.* BLAC, 436.
The Flight of Psyche. *A. S. Blackwell.* BLAC, 434.
The Horse on the Shield. *J. Longland.* TRAN, 265.
The Inevitable. *A. S. Blackwell.* BLAC, 436.
Within the Heart. *A. S. Blackwell.* BLAC, 428.
Fiction
Redeemers of the Fatherland. *E. Schaefer.* JONE-3, 277.

138 BOAL, AUGUSTO (   ) Brazil
Other
The Joker System: An Experiment by the Arena Theatre of
  São Paulo (Essay). *J. Pottlitzer.* DR, 91.

139 BOMBAL, MARÍA-LUISA (1910-   ) Chile
Fiction
The Tree. *R. Torres-Ríoseco.* HOW-1, 225.
The Tree. *R. Torres-Ríoseco.* MANC, 233.
The Tree. *R. Torres-Ríoseco.* TORR, 83.

140 BOMFIM, PAULO (1927-   ) Brazil
Poetry
Hands. *J. Nist & Y. Leite.* NIST, 162.
Madness. *J. Nist & Y. Leite.* NIST, 163.
Reincarnation. *J. Nist & Y. Leite.* NIST, 163.
Tempest. *J. Nist & Y. Leite.* NIST, 161.
The Fourth Kingdom. *J. Nist & Y. Leite.* NIST, 162.
The Idea. *J. Nist & Y. Leite.* NIST, 164.
The Invention. *J. Nist & Y. Leite.* NIST, 165.
The Sea. *J. Nist & Y. Leite.* NIST, 161.
The Shadow. *J. Nist & Y. Leite.* NIST, 164.

141 BOPP, RAUL (1898-   ) Brazil
Poetry
Daughter Of The Jungle. *L. S. Downes.* DOWN, 37.

142   BORGES, JORGE LUIS   (1899-   ) Argentina
       (Also wrote with ADOLFO BIOY CASARES under pseud. of BUSTOS
       DOMECQ)
       <u>Poetry</u>
       A Day's Run. *H. R. Hays*. HAYS, 127.
       A Page to Commemorate C. Suárez, Victor at Junín. *A. Reid*.
          CARP, 105.
       A patio. *H. Manning*. GAN, 71.
       A Patio. *H. R. Hays*. HAYS, 121.
       A Patio. *M. E. Johnson*. JOHN, 185.
       A Patio. *W. K. Jones*. JONE-3, 162.
       A soldier under Lee (1862). *N. T. di Giovanni*. TRI-13,
          365.
       Afterglow. *N. T. di Giovanni*. MILL, 166.
       Amorous Anticipation. *T. Raworth*. CARA, 30.
       An Unknown Street. *G. D. Craig*. CRAI, 245.
       Benares. *H. R. Hays*. HAYS, 123.
       Butcher Shop. *H. R. Hays*. HAYS, 121.
       Butchershop. *W. K. Jones*. JONE-3, 163.
       Conjectural Poem. *T. Raworth*. CARA, 33.
       Edgar Allan Poe. *R. Howard & C. Rennert*. TRI-13, 366.
       Emanuel Swedenborg. *R. Howard & C. Rennert*. TRI-13, 363.
       General Quiroga drives in coach to death. *P. Gannon*. GAN,
          67.
       General Quiroga Goes to Death in a Coach. *H. de Onís*.
          ONIS-1, 222.
       General Quiroga Rides To Death In A Carriage. *H. R. Hays*.
          HAYS, 129.
       Hengest Cyning. *N. T. di Giovanni*. MILL, 165.
       Heraclitus. *W. Shand*. SHA, 34.
       Houses Like Angels. *R. S. Fitzgerald*. FITT, 69.
       James Joyce. *W. Shand*. SHA, 32.
       July Avenue. *H. R. Hays*. HAYS, 131.
       June 1968. *W. Shand*. SHA, 33.
       Late Afternoon. *C. M. Hutchings*. JONE-3, 162.
       Love's Priority. *R. S. Fitzgerald*. FITT, 67.
       Menaced. *C. Maurer*. CHI, 11.
       Natural Flow Of Memory. *H. R. Hays*. HAYS, 135.
       Parting. *W. S. Merwin*. CARP, 103.
       Patio. *R. S. Fitzgerald*. FITT, 69.
       Rafael Cansinos-Assens. *J. Hollander*. TRI-13, 363.
       Sepulchral Inscription. *R. S. Fitzgerald*. FITT, 65.
       Someone. *W. S. Merwin*. TRI-13, 364.
       The Cyclical Night. *T. Raworth*. CARA, 31.
       The Dagger. *N. T. di Giovanni*. MILL, 167.
       The Guitar. *G. D. Craig*. CRAI, 247.
       The Guitar. *M. E. Johnson*. JOHN, 183.
       The Night They Kept Vigil In The South. *R. S. Fitzgerald*.
          FITT, 71.
       The Recoleta. *H. R. Hays*. HAYS, 125.
       The sea. *J. Updike*. TRI-13, 365.

(BORGES, JORGE LUIS)
  The Stranger. *W. Shand.* SHA, 35.
  To A Coin. *W. Shand.* SHA, 36.
  To a coin. *N. T. di Giovanni.* TRI-13, 362.
  To a Saxon poet. *A. Reid.* TRI-13, 366.
  To A Saxon Poet. *N. T. di Giovanni.* CARP, 107.
  To Rafael Cansinos Assens. *R. S. Fitzgerald.* FITT, 65.
  To Rafael Casinos Assens. *W. K. Jones.* JONE-3, 161.
  Fiction
  Death and the Compass. *N. T. di Giovanni.* MANC, 135.
  Death and the Compass. *D. Yates.* YATE, 213.
  Delia Elena San Marco. *M. Boyer.* CARP, 110.
  Emma Zunz. *D. Yates.* FRA-J, 15.
  Rosendo's Tale. *N. T. di Giovanni & J. L. Borges.* MU-70,
    19.
  Street Corner Man. *N. T. di Giovanni & J. L. Borges.*
    MU-70, 12.
  The Aleph. *Z. Nelken.* TORR, 181.
  The Dead Man. *N. T. Giovanni & J. L. Borges.* CARP, 111.
  The Garden of Forking Paths. *H. Temple & R. Todd.* MILL,
    152.
  The Garden of Forking Paths. *D. A. Yates.* YATE, 17.
  The Garden of the Forking Paths. *D. A. Yates.* JONE-3, 343.
  The Handwriting Of God. *J. M. Cohen.* COH-1, 18.
  The intruder. *R. Christ & P. Cantatore.* TRI-13, 224.
  The Other Death. *N. T. di Giovanni.* HOW-1, 111.
  The Secret Miracle. *H. de Onís.* ONIS-2, 18.
  The Shape of the Sword. *A. Flores.* FLOR-3, 248.
  The Shape Of The Sword. no tr. FLOR-4, 227.

143 BORRERO DE LUJÁN, DULCE MARÍA (1883-1945) Cuba
    Poetry
    Song. *A. S. Blackwell.* BLAC, 494.
    The Singing Rose. *A. S. Blackwell.* BLAC, 490.

144 BOSCH, JUAN (1909-) Dominican Republic
    Fiction
    The Beautiful Soul of Don Damián. *L. Kemp.* HOW-1, 217.
    The Beautiful Soul Of Don Damián. *H. de Onís.* HOW-2, 231.
    Two Dollars Worth of Water. *H. de Onís.* MANC, 101.
    Two Dollars Worth of Water. *H. de Onís.* ONIS-1, 302.

145 BRAGA, EDGARD (1897-) Brazil
    Poetry
    "a poor play." *H. de Campos.* WILL-1, n.p.
    ballad/quiet/beloved/winged. no tr. BANN, 129.
    firefly. no tr. BANN, 126.
    island/bright/tranquil. no tr. BANN, 125.
    limit of the eye. *H. de Campos.* WILL-1, n.p.
    Ode XXXI. *L. S. Downes.* DOWN, 36.
    Ode XXI. *L. S. Downes.* DOWN, 36.

poem. *H. de Campos.* WILL-1, n.p.
poor (man)/plays/game. no tr. BANN, 127.
vocable. *H. de Campos.* WILL-1, n.p.
water/white/wild/deep/smooth/mare. no tr. BANN, 128.

146 BRANDY, CARLOS (1923-) Uruguay
Poetry
Long Is The Lost Shadow, We Must Walk. *R. Connally.* YOU,
109.
You Have A Name. *R. Connally.* YOU, 110.

147 BRANLY, ROBERTO (1930-) Cuba
Poetry
Drought. *S. Carranza.* BECK, 351.
Ejaculation for Antonio Machado. *S. Carranza.* BECK, 347.
Homage. *R. Llopis.* BECK, 343.
Reminiscence January, '61. *R. Llopis.* BECK, 345.

BRANNON BEERS, CARMEN. See [LARS, CLAUDIA pseud.]

148 BRANT, ALICE (1881?-?) Brazil
[MORLEY, HELENA pseud.]
Other
The Diary of "Helena Morley" (Excerpt). *E. Bishop.* HAH, 49.

149 BRASCHI, WILFREDO (1918-) Puerto Rico
Fiction
The Hunchback's Zeppelin. *B. Luby.* BABI, 360.

150 BRAVO, MARIO (1882-1944) Argentina
Poetry
Song of the General Strike. *A. S. Blackwell.* BLAC, 386.

151 BRENES MESÉN, ROBERTO (1874-1947) Costa Rica
Poetry
Condors' Eyes. *A. S. Blackwell.* BLAC, 480.

152 BRITO, MARIO DA SILVA (1916-) Brazil
Poetry
Intermezzo With Psychology. *L. S. Downes.* DOWN, 64.

153 BROWN, ROY (1946-) Puerto Rico
Other
Monon. *M. C. López & S. Steiner.* BABI, 401.
Old Bastions Of Borinqueños (Protest Song). *M. C. López &
S. Steiner.* BABI, 399.
Paco Márquez (Protest Song). *M. C. López & S. Steiner.*
BABI, 400.
The Mind Is A Sleeping Soul (Protest Song). *M. C. López &
S. Steiner.* BABI, 397.

154 BRUGHETTI, ROMUALDO (1912-   ) Argentina
   Poetry
   America. *W. Shand.* SHA, 106.
   Loud Laughter. *W. Shand.* SHA, 108.
   One World. *W. Shand.* SHA, 107.

155 BRULL, MARIANO (1891-   ) Cuba
   Poetry
   Interior. *R. Gill.* WALS, 759.
   To The Mountain. *R. Gill.* WALS, 760.

156 BRUNET, MARTA (1901-   ) Chile
   Fiction
   Francina. *M. Bauman.* JONE-3, 290.

157 BUENAVENTURA, ENRIQUE (1925-   ) Colombia
   Drama
   In the Right Hand of God the Father. *W. I. Oliver.* OLIV,
      171.
   The Orgy. *G. Luzuriaga & R. Rudder.* LUZU, 6.
   The Twisted State (one of seven vignettes from Documents of
      Hell). *J. Barba-Martin & L. E. Roberts.* DR, 157.
   Other
   Theatre & Culture (Essay). *J. Pottlitzer.* DR, 151.

158 BURGOS, JULIA DE (1914-1953) Puerto Rico
   Poetry
   Encounter Between the Man and the River. *M. Arrillaga.*
      MATI, 71.
   From the Bridge Martín Peña. *M. Arrillaga.* MATI, 65.
   My River's Rival. *M. Arrillaga.* MATI, 69.
   Nothing (Excerpt). no tr. KAI, n.p.
   Poem for My Death. *M. Arrillaga.* MATI, 75.
   Río Grande de Loíza. *B. Luby.* BABI, 279.
   Río Grande de Loíza. *M. Arrillaga.* MATI, 63.
   To Julia de Burgos. *M. Arrillaga.* MATI, 61.

159 BUSIGNANI, MARIO (1915-   ) Argentina
   Poetry
   Time Absorbed In Thought (Excerpts). *W. Shand.* SHA, 115.

160 BUSTAMANTE Y BALLIVIÁN, ENRIQUE (1884-1937) Peru
   Poetry
   Telegraph Pole. *M. Lee.* FITT, 141.

161 BUSTILLOS, JOSÉ MARÍA (1866-1899) Mexico
   Poetry
   The Cavern of Cicalo. *A. Fife.* FIFE, 33.

162   BUSTOS, MIGUEL ANGEL   (1932–   )   Argentina
      Poetry
      "Fragments" (Excerpt). *P. Morgan*. TRI-13, 252.
      Fragments 1, 2, 3, 4, 5, 8, 9, 11, 12, 14, 29, 42, 44, 45,
        46. *W. Shand*. SHA, 251.

163   BYRNE, BONIFACIO   (1861-1936)   Cuba
      Poetry
      The Spanish Tongue. *A. S. Blackwell*. BLAC, 498.

164   CABADA, JUAN DE LA   (1903–   )   Mexico
      Fiction
      Maria-The-Voice. *L. Kemp*. CRAN, 21.

165   CABAÑAS, ESTEBAN   (   )   Paraguay
      Poetry
      "The wind vacated." *J. Upton*. TRI-13, 280.

166   CABEZAS, MIGUEL   (   )   Chile
      Other
      Victor Jara Died Singing (Eyewitness account). *L. Veltfort*.
        LOW, 80.

167   CABRAL, MANUEL DEL   (1907–   )   Dominican Republic
      Poetry
      Meek Negro. *H. Ruiz del Vizo*. RUIZ, 109.
      Mulattoe. *F. E. Townsend*. TOWN, 24.
      Negro With Nothing In Your House. *H. Ruiz del Vizo*. RUIZ,
        110.
      On the Village Street. *F. E. Townsend*. TOWN, 23.

168   CABRAL DE MELO NETO, JOÃO   (1920–   )   Brazil
      Poetry
      A Knife All Blade. *G. Kinnell*. BISH, 155.
      A Knife Blade Only. *M. Cardozo*. NEI, 147.
      Cemetery in Pernambuco (Our Lady of Light). *J. Cooper*.
        BISH, 123.
      Cemetery in Pernambuco (St. Lawrence of the Woods).
        J. Cooper. BISH, 125.
      Daily Space. *W. S. Merwin*. BISH, 115.
      Education by Stone. *J. Wright*. BISH, 149.
      Fable Of An Architect. *A. Brown*. CHI, 93.
      Imitation of Water. *A. Brown*. BISH, 141.
      Inhabiting Time. *M. Cardozo*. NEI, 159.
      Only the Blade of a Knife. *J. Nist & Y. Leite*. NIST, 145.
      Poem. *W. S. Merwin*. BISH, 119.
      Quaderna. *M. Cardozo*. NEI, 149.
      River And/Or Well. *A. Brown*. CHI, 91.
      The Canefield and the Sea. *L. Simpson*. BISH, 153.
      The Clouds. *A. Brown*. BISH, 145.
      The Dancer. *P. Standish*. CARA, 97.

(CABRAL DE MELO NETO, JOÃO)
'The Death And Life Of A Severino' (Excerpt). *E. Bishop*.
    COH-1, 167.
"The Death and Life of a Severino" Parts I, II, XIV.
    E. Bishop. BISH, 127.
The Death And Life Of A Severino Sections I, II, XIV.
    E. Bishop. GARR, 11.
The Dog Without Feathers, I. *M. Cardozo*. NEI, 153.
The Drafted Vulture. *W. S. Merwin*. BISH, 161.
The Emptiness of Man. *G. Kinnell*. BISH, 159.
The End of the World. *J. Wright*. BISH, 121.
The Engineer. *L. S. Downes*. DOWN, 71.
The Life And Death Of Severino (Fragment) 3. *M. Cardozo*.
    NEI, 141.
The Man From Up-Country Talking. *W. S. Merwin*. BISH, 163.
The Sea and the Canefield. *L. Simpson*. BISH, 147.
The Word Silk. *P. Standish*. CARA, 95.
Two of the Festivals of Death. *W. S. Merwin*. BISH, 165.
Weaving the Morning. *G. Kinnell*. BISH, 151.
Windows. *J. Valentine*. BISH, 117.

169   CABRERA, LYDIA (1900-   ) Cuba
      <u>Fiction</u>
      Turtle's Horse. no tr. HOW-2, 275.
      Walo-Wila. no tr. HOW-2, 277.

170   CABRERA, RAFAEL (1884-?   ) Mexico
      <u>Poetry</u>
      Nihil. *A. S. Blackwell*. BLAC, 130.
      Nihil. *A. S. Blackwell*. GOLD-2, 62.
      Without Words. *A. S. Blackwell*. BLAC, 134.

171   CABRERA INFANTE, GUILLERMO (1929-   ) Cuba
      <u>Fiction</u>
      A Nest of Sparrows on the Awning. *S. J. Levine*. HOW-1,
          357.
      A Sparrow's Nest In The Awning. *J. M. Cohen*. COH-3, 150.
      Apocalypse In Wonderland. *D. Gardner & S. J. Levine*.
          MU-70, 98.
      At The Great 'Ecbo.' *J. G. Brotherston*. COH-1, 203.
      Nest, Door, Neighbors. *G. Cabrera Infante*. MANC, 385.

172   CADENAS, RAFAEL (1930-   ) Venezuela
      <u>Poetry</u>
      Bungalow. *E. Randall*. MU-73, 41.
      Combat. *E. Randall*. MU-73, 39.
      Defeat. *M. González*. CARA, 390.
      Defeat. *E. Randall*. MU-73, 35.
      Love. *E. Randall*. MU-73, 43.
      Old Kingdom. *E. Randall*. MU-73, 41.
      Satori. *E. Randall*. MU-73, 43.

173 CADILLA, CARMEN ALICIA (1908-   ) Puerto Rico
Poetry
Angelus. *D. Fitts.* FITT, 513.
Responsories. *D. Fitts.* FITT, 511.
Sad Air. *D. Fitts.* FITT, 511.
The Circus Tent. *G. Pando.* KAI, n.p.

174 CAIGNET, FÉLIX B. (   ) Cuba
Poetry
I Am A Bongo-Player. *H. Ruiz del Vizo.* RUIZ, 61.

175 CAJIGAS, BILLY (1944-   ) Puerto Rico
Poetry
Antilullaby. *D. Sánchez-Méndez.* MATI, 159.
Between Us. *D. Sánchez-Méndez.* MATI, 163.
Let There Be Copper! *D. Sánchez-Méndez.* MATI, 159.
Let's Suppose.... *D. Sánchez-Méndez.* MATI, 163.
Poor God. *D. Sánchez-Méndez.* MATI, 165.

176 CALDERÓN, ALFONSO (   )
Other
Thus It Is - If You Think It Is (Essay). *M. S. Peden.*
   TRI-13, 375.

177 CALVETTI, JORGE (1916-   ) Argentina
Poetry
In The Village. *W. Shand.* SHA, 123.
To Man. *W. Shand.* SHA, 122.

178 CALVILLO, MANUEL (1919-   ) Mexico
Poetry
Book of the Migrant. *P. Blackburn.* EVER, 153.

179 CALVO, CÉSAR (1940-   ) Peru
Poetry
Blind Oedipus. *M. A. Maurer.* HAR67-3, 45.
The poet's room. *D. Tipton.* TRI-13, 206.

180 CALVO, IGOR (   ) Peru
Poetry
A Fable. *R. Márquez.* MR, 234.

181 CALVO, LINO NOVÁS (1905-) Cuba
See also NOVÁS-CALVO, LINO
Fiction
"Allies" And "Germans." *H. de Onís.* HOW-2, 244.

182 CAMARILLA Y ROA DE PEREYRA, MARÍA ENRIQUETA (1875-?   )
Mexico
Poetry
Hail! *E. W. Underwood.* UND, 114.
Landscape. *E. W. Underwood.* UND, 112.

(CAMARILLA Y ROA DE PEREYRA, MARÍA ENRIQUETA)
The Forgotten Path. *E. W. Underwood.* UND, 111.
The Scissor's Grinder. *E. W. Underwood.* UND, 115.
To a Shadow. *E. W. Underwood.* UND, 113.

183 CAMBIER, ENRIQUE (   ) Dominican Republic
Poetry
Bucolic at Noontide. *F. E. Townsend.* TOWN, 83.

184 CAMÍN, ALFONSO (   ) Cuba
Poetry
Negro. *H. Ruiz del Vizo.* RUIZ, 23.

185 CAMPÍNS, ROLANDO (   ) Cuba
Poetry
Blessing The Sick Negro Boy. *H. Ruiz del Vizo.* RUIZ, 66.
Description Of Death. *H. Ruiz del Vizo.* RUIZ, 67.

186 CAMPOS, AUGUSTO DE (1931-   ) Brazil
Poetry
axis/eye/pole/fixed/flower/weight/ground. no tr. BANN, 102.
axis. *E. Morgan.* WILL-1, n.p.
City poem. no tr. BANN, 107.
'earthquake.' *H. de Campos.* WILL-1, n.p.
"eye for eye." *H. de Campos.* WILL-1, n.p.
"here are the lovers." *A. de Campos.* WILL-1, n.p.
one time, once upon a time. *E. Morgan.* WILL-1, n.p.
ovo. *H. de Campos.* WILL-1, n.p.
side of square/four/picture/quarter/square. no tr. BANN,
   104.
snail/to hollow out/hollows out/obstacle. no tr. BANN,
   105.
to put on the mask. *H. de Campos.* WILL-1, n.p.
with sound. *H. de Campos.* WILL-1, n.p.
without a number/mere/numberless. no tr. BANN, 103.

187 CAMPOS, EDUARDO (1923-   ) Brazil
Fiction
Harelip. *R. W. Horton.* COEL, 67.

188 CAMPOS, GEIR (1924-   ) Brazil
Poetry
Ballet. *L. S. Downes.* DOWN, 82.
Lullaby. *L. S. Downes.* DOWN, 82.

189 CAMPOS, HAROLDO DE (1929-   ) Brazil
Poetry
Arabesquing. *J. R. Longland.* CHI, 85.
crystal. *H. de Campos.* WILL-1, n.p.
crystal/hunger/form. no tr. BANN, 99.
fly/gold/dusk/silver/black/ordinary/indigo/blue/white/small.
   no tr. BANN, 101.

if/(a human being) is born. *H. de Campos.* WILL-1, n.p.
orange/sun/golden-yellow/fragrance/grief/tower. no tr.
  BANN, 100.
POEM. *E. Morgan.* WILL-1, n.p.
Proem. *E. Morgan.* WILL-1, n.p.
"si len cio." no tr. WILL-1, n.p.
"the ear's pavilion." *H. de Campos.* WILL-1, n.p.
white/red/1 staunch/mirror. no tr. BANN, 98.
white. *E. Morgan.* WILL-1, n.p.

190 CAMPOS, JOSÉ ANTONIO (1868-1930) Ecuador
    Fiction
    Mamerto's Mother-in-Law. no tr. JONE-3, 335.

191 CAMPOS, JOSÉ MARÍA MOREIRA (1914-   ) Brazil
    Fiction
    Afterglow. *R. W. Horton.* COEL, 157.

192 CAMPOS, PAULO MENDES (1922-   ) Brazil
    Poetry
    Rural. *L. S. Downes.* DOWN, 77.

193 CAMPOS, RUBÉN M. (1876-1945) Mexico
    Poetry
    Tropic Nocturnes. *E. W. Underwood.* UND, 105.

194 CAMPOS CERVERA, HERIB (1905-1953) Paraguay
    Poetry
    A Handful of Earth. *W. K. Jones.* JONE-3, 141.

195 CAMPS, DAVID (1937-   ) Cuba
    Fiction
    The mouse. no tr. CARZ, 225.

196 CANAL FEIJÓO, BERNARDO (1898-   ) Argentina
    Poetry
    Joy Of The Wind. *W. Shand.* SHA, 18.
    Plenitude. *W. Shand.* SHA, 19.
    Rough Whiteness Of Salines. *W. Shand.* SHA, 17.

197 CANALES, NEMESIO R. (1878-1923) Puerto Rico
    Other
    Riches And Poverty (from: Paliques). *B. Luby.* BABI, 123.

198 CANCELA, ARTURO (1892-   ) Argentina
    Fiction
    Life and Death of a Hero. *M. M. Lasley.* ONIS-2, 98.

199   CANCINO CASAHONDA, ENOCH (   ) Cuba
Poetry
Cuba. *N. Braymer & L. Lowenfels*. BRAY, 56.
My Lucky Day. *N. Braymer & L. Lowenfels*. BRAY, 56.
Rain. *N. Braymer & L. Lowenfels*. BRAY, 57.
The Drunkard. *N. Braymer & L. Lowenfels*. BRAY, 57.

200   CANDEGABE, NELLY (1927-   ) Argentina
Poetry
On The Boundary Of Mirrors (Excerpts). *W. Shand*. SHA, 212.

201   CANÉ, LUIS (1897-1957) Argentina
Poetry
Prayer For Each Awakening. *D. Fitts*. FITT, 505.

202   CANTÓN, WILBERTO L. (1923-   ) Mexico
Poetry
Island. *D. Fitts*. FITT, 175.
On Lake Llanquihue. *D. D. Walsh*. FITT, 175.

203   CANZANI D., ARIEL (1928-   ) Argentina
Poetry
I Am He Who Sings. *W. Shand*. SHA, 219.
Men With Faces Of Bread And Souls Of Bread. *W. Shand*. SHA, 218.
The Limit Of Fire. *W. Shand*. SHA, 220.

204   CARBALLIDO, EMILIO (1925-   ) Mexico
Fiction
The Empty Coffin. *J. Rechy*. CRAN, 70.
Drama
I Too Speak Of The Rose. *W. I. Oliver*. WOOD, 292.
The Clockmaker from Córdoba. *M. S. Peden*. CARB, 151.
The Day They Let the Lions Loose. *W. I. Oliver*. OLIV, 1.
The Glacier. *M. S. Peden*. CARB, 22.
The Golden Thread. *M. S. Peden*. CARB, 49.
The Intermediate Zone. *M. S. Peden*. CARB, 121.
The Mirror. *M. S. Peden*. CARB, 1.
The Time and the Place. *M. S. Peden*. CARB, 9.
The Wine Cellar. *M. S. Peden*. CARB, 34.
Theseus. *M. S. Peden*. CARB, 211.

205   CARDENAL, ERNESTO (1925-   ) Nicaragua
Poetry
Behind the monastery. *H. St. Martin*. CARP, 289.
Drake In The Southern Sea. no tr. MERT, 122.
Epitaph For The Tomb of Adolfo Báez Bone. *J. Brof*. CARP, 285.
Gethsemani, Ky. (Excerpts). no tr. MERT, 117.
Hora 0 (Excerpt). *D. D. Walsh*. CHI, 117.
It Is the Time for the Evening Service. *M. González*. CARA, 311.

Long legged aquatic insects skate. *P. Lamantia.* CARP, 291.

Prayer for Marilyn Monroe. *D. J. Flakoll & C. Alegría.* BENE, 95.

Psalm 5. *R. Márquez.* MARQ, 323.

Psalm 36. *R. Márquez.* MARQ, 319.

Psalm 48. *R. Márquez.* MARQ, 315.

Someone told me you were in love. *Q. Troupe & S. Mondragón.* CARP, 291.

Someone told me you were in love. *Q. Troupe & S. Mondragón.* MU-69, 78.

Spring has come with its smell of Nicaragua. *H. St. Martin.* CARP, 289.

suddenly at night, as upon demonic wings. *Q. Troupe & S. Mondragón.* MU-69, 79.

Three Epigrams. no tr. MERT, 116.

2 A.M. *J. Brof.* CARP, 287.

2 A.M. *E. González.* MU-69, 77.

Waking up to cannon shots. *J. Brof.* CARP, 285.

With Walker in Nicaragua. *D. Flakoll & C. Alegría.* FLAK, 25.

Zero Hour. *D. Gardner.* MARQ, 327.

206 CÁRDENAS, ROLANDO (1933–   ) Chile
Poetry
Tierra Del Fuego. *M. Williams.* WILL-2, 25.
Wharves. *M. Williams.* WILL-2, 27.

207 CARDONA PEÑA, ALFREDO (1917–   ) Costa Rica
Poetry
My Aunt Esther. *D. Flakoll & C. Alegría.* FLAK, 40.

208 CARDOSO, ONELIO JORGE (1914–   ) Cuba
Fiction
It's A Long Time Ago. *J. G. Brotherston.* COH-1, 251.
The Cat's Second Death. *J. G. Brotherston.* COH-3, 37.
The peacock. no tr. CARZ, 65.

209 CARDOZA Y ARAGÓN, LUIS (1904–   ) Guatemala
Poetry
Ballad Of Federico García Lorca. *D. D. Walsh.* FITT, 531.
Pablo Neruda. *H. McCord & D. McCord.* LOW, 130.
Song to Solitude. *J. Hill.* CARA, 237.

210 CARDOZO, JOAQUIM (1897–   ) Brazil
Poetry
Birds Of Prey. *L. S. Downes.* DOWN, 35.
Cemetery of Childhood. *E. Bishop.* BISH, 29.
Elegy for Maria Alves. *E. Bishop.* BISH, 33.

211   CARI, TERESA (   )   Brazil
     (Joint author. <u>See also</u> FABBRI, TECLA and LOPES, MARIA.)
     <u>Other</u>
     To the Young Seamstresses of São Paulo (Newspaper article).
     J. E. Hahner.   HAH, 114.

212   CARLINO, ALFREDO   (1932-   )   Argentina
     <u>Poetry</u>
     Biography Of A Suicide. *W. Shand.*   SHA, 254.
     The Immigrants. *W. Shand.*   SHA, 253.

213   CARNEIRO, ANDRÉ   (1922-   )   Brazil
     <u>Poetry</u>
     Water. *L. S. Downes.*   DOWN, 76.

214   CARPENTIER, ALEJO   (1904-   )   Cuba
     <u>Poetry</u>
     Liturgy. *H. Ruiz del Vizo.*   RUIZ, 44.
     <u>Fiction</u>
     Journey Back to the Source. *F. Partridge.*   MANC, 151.
     Journey To The Seed. *J. Franco.*   COH-1, 53.
     Like the Night. *F. Partridge.*   HOW-1, 135.
     Return To The Seed. *Z. Nelken.*   HOW-2, 286.
     Return to the Seed. *Z. Nelken.*   TORR, 95.
     The Fugitives. *H. St. Martin.*   CARP, 156.

215   CARRANZA, EDUARDO   (1913-   )   Colombia
     <u>Poetry</u>
     Sunday. *D. D. Walsh.*   FITT, 181.

216   CARRASQUILLA, TOMÁS   (1858-1941)   Colombia
     <u>Fiction</u>
     Simon Magus. *H. de Onís.*   ONIS-1, 146.

217   CARRERA ANDRADE, JORGE   (1903-   )   Ecuador
     <u>Poetry</u>
     A Man From Ecuador Beneath The Eiffel Tower. *T. Merton.*
       MILL, 137.
     A Man From Ecuador Beneath The Eiffel Tower. no tr.   MERT,
       131.
     Anonymous Speech. *H. R. Hays.*   HAYS, 153.
     Biography. *H. R. Hays.*   HAYS, 143.
     Biography For The Use Of The Birds. *D. D. Walsh.*   FITT, 19.
     Bulletin Of Bad Weather. *H. R. Hays.*   HAYS, 151.
     Cocoa Tree. no tr.   MERT, 129.
     Complete Image. *M. González.*   CARA, 233.
     Contemporary History (from: <u>Handbook Of Time 1935</u>).
       L. Mallan.   PELL, 60.
     Corpse Of Time: Dust (from: <u>Secret Land 1939</u>). *L. Mallan.*
       PELL, 70.
     Defence of Sunday. *M. González.*   CARA, 232.

Dining-Room Mirror. *H. R. Hays.* HAYS, 145.
Dust, Corpse Of Time. *H. R. Hays.* HAYS, 163.
Earthly Dwelling. *J. M. Cohen.* COH-2, 416.
Election Handbill Of Green. *H. R. Hays.* HAYS, 149.
Elegy for Abraham Valdelomar. *L. Mallan.* JONE-3, 106.
Elegy For Abraham Valdelomar (from: Three Random Poems
  1922-1927). *L. Mallan.* PELL, 52.
Gull And Solitude (from: Secret Land 1939). *L. Mallan.*
  PELL, 68.
Handbill For Green. *J. Igo.* MILL, 136.
Hydrographic Poem. *H. R. Hays.* HAYS, 155.
Ill Humor. *D. D. Walsh.* FITT, 13.
Indian Rebellion. *H. R. Hays.* HAYS, 151.
Islands Without Name (from: Secret Land 1939). *L. Mallan.*
  PELL, 66.
It Rained In The Night. *M. Lee.* FITT, 9.
Klare Von Reuter. *M. Lee.* FITT, 15.
Life Of The Crickett. *J. M. Brinnin.* GARR, 57.
Nameless Islands. *H. R. Hays.* HAYS, 165.
Nameless Neighborhood (from: Handbook Of Time 1935).
  L. Mallan. PELL, 61.
Northeast Wind (from: Secret Land 1939). *L. Mallan.* PELL,
  67.
Notes From A Parachutist. *J. M. Brinnin.* GARR, 59.
Notes of A Parachute Jumper. no tr. MERT, 133.
Nothing Belongs To Us. *H. R. Hays.* HAYS, 159.
Philosophy Of Smoke (from: Three Random Early Poems 1922-
  1927). *L. Mallan.* PELL, 51.
Poem Number 2 (from: Mined Territory). *L. Mallan.* PELL,
  72.
Poem Number 3 (from: Mined Territory). *L. Mallan.* PELL,
  72.
Reaping The Barley. *M. Lee.* FITT, 7.
Second Life Of My Mother. *M. Lee.* FITT, 15.
Second Life Of My Mother (from: Secret Land 1939).
  L. Mallan. PELL, 69.
Sierra. *M. Lee.* FITT, 3.
Sierra. *M. Lee.* JONE-3, 104.
Sketches Of Cities 1930. *L. Mallan.* PELL, 54.
Solitude Of The Cities (from: Handbook Of Time 1935).
  L. Mallan. PELL, 57.
Spring & Co. *R. O'Connell.* FITT, 3.
Stroke Of One. *M. Lee.* FITT, 13.
Sunday. *M. Lee.* FITT, 5.
Sunday. *M. Lee.* JONE-3, 105.
The Clock. *M. González.* CARA, 233.
The Guest. *M. Lee.* FITT, 11.
The Guest (from: Three Random Poems 1922-1927). *L. Mallan.*
  PELL, 53.
The Mirror's Mission. no tr. MERT, 132.
The Perfect Life. *D. Fitts.* FITT, 7.

(CARRERA ANDRADE, JORGE)
The Stranger. *H. R. Hays*. HAYS, 157.
The Weathercock Of The Cathedral Of Quito. *T. Merton*.
MILL, 139.
The Weathercock On The Cathedral Of Quito. no tr. MERT,
129.
Third Class (from: Handbook Of Time 1935). *L. Mallan*.
PELL, 58.
Vocation Of The Mirror. *M. Lee*. FITT, 11.
Vocation of the Mirror. *M. González*. CARA, 231.
Windy Weather. *H. R. Hays*. HAYS, 143.
Windy Weather. *J. M. Brinnin*. GARR, 55.
I (from: Poems Of Yesterday Morning 1935). *L. Mallan*.
PELL, 63.
II (from: Poems Of Yesterday Morning 1935). *L. Mallan*.
PELL, 63.
III (from: Poems Of Yesterday Morning 1935). *L. Mallan*.
PELL, 64.
IV. Anonymous Speech (from: Poems Of Yesterday Morning
1935). *L. Mallan*. PELL, 65.
V (from: Poems Of Yesterday Morning 1935). *L. Mallan*.
PELL, 65.

218   CARRILLO, FRANCISCO (1925-   ) Peru
Poetry
All Souls' Day. *M. Ahern & D. Tipton*. AHER, 25.
Composition 1. *M. Ahern & D. Tipton*. AHER, 22.
I Love My Country. *M. Ahern & D. Tipton*. AHER, 20.
Procession. *M. Ahern & D. Tipton*. AHER, 22.
Provincia. *M. Ahern & D. Tipton*. AHER, 24.
The Tannery. *M. Ahern & D. Tipton*. AHER, 21.

219   CARRIÓN, ALEJANDRO (1915-   ) Ecuador
Poetry
A Good Year. *D. Fitts*. FITT, 297.

220   CARRIÓN, BENJAMÍN (1898-   ) Ecuador
Other
Caxamarca (from: Atahuallpa). *H. de Onís*. ARC, 163.

221   CARTOSIO, EMMA DE (1924-   ) Argentina
Poetry
A Round. *W. Shand*. SHA, 202.
Examination. *W. Shand*. SHA, 204.

222   CARVALHO, MARIA JOSÉ DE (   ) Brazil
Poetry
Épura. *M. Cardozo*. NEI, 43.
On A Walk In The Park. *M. Cardozo*. NEI, 181.
The Heartland. *M. Cardozo*. NEI, 45.
The Market For Silver, Gold, and Emeralds. *M. Cardozo*.
NEI, 43.

223 CARVALHO, RONALD DE (1893-1935) Brazil
     <u>Poetry</u>
     Brazil. *D. Poore*. FITT, 147.
     Interior. *D. Poore*. FITT, 145.
     Midsummer Night's Dream. *L. S. Downes*. DOWN, 27.
     Trinidad Market. *D. Poore*. FITT, 145.

224 CARVALHO DA SILVA, DOMINGOS (1915-   ) Brazil
     <u>Poetry</u>
     A Bit of Flame. *J. Nist & Y. Leite*. NIST, 131.
     Apocalypse. *J. Nist & Y. Leite*. NIST, 139.
     Elegy for the Viaduct Suicides. *J. Nist & Y. Leite*. NIST,
       133.
     Explanation. *L. S. Downes*. DOWN, 62.
     Lyricism. *L. S. Downes*. DOWN, 63.
     Message. *J. Nist & Y. Leite*. NIST, 138.
     Tertiary Poem. *J. Nist & Y. Leite*. NIST, 135.
     The Pastor of Hyenas. *J. Nist & Y. Leite*. NIST, 137.
     The Unrevealed Rose. *J. Nist & Y. Leite*. NIST, 139.

225 CASAL, JULIÁN DEL (1863-1893) Cuba
     <u>Poetry</u>
     Afternoons of Rain. *J. Hill*. CARA, 197.
     Confidences. *T. Walsh*. JONE-3, 73.
     Confidences. *T. Walsh*. WALS, 568.
     Flowers. *W. K. Jones*. JONE-3, 73.
     My Loves - Sonnet A La Pompador. *R. Gill*. WALS, 567.
     Nihilism. *M. E. Johnson*. JOHN, 57.
     Pages From Life. *M. E. Johnson*. JOHN, 59.
     Pax Animae. *J. Hill*. CARA, 196.
     Scene in the Tropics. *R. M. Anderson*. TRAN, 219.
     The Friar. *T. Walsh*. JONE-3, 73.
     The Pearl. *T. Walsh*. WALS, 568.
     To My Mother. *J. Godoy*. WALS, 564.

226 CASASÚS, JOAQUÍN D. (   ) Mexico
     <u>Poetry</u>
     To an Unknown Woman. *E. W. Underwood*. UND, 136.

227 CASAUS, VÍCTOR (1944-   ) Cuba
     <u>Poetry</u>
     A Story. *A. Kerrigan*. TARN, 117.
     Advertisement. *A. Kerrigan*. TARN, 119.
     Epitaph For God. *A. Kerrigan*. TARN, 117.
     It so happens that we. *S. Stolkowska*. BECK, 769.
     Poem. *S. Stolkowska*. BECK, 773.
     Poetica. *S. Stolkowska*. BECK, 775.
     We Are. *S. Stolkowska*. BECK, 771.

228 CASEY, CALVERT (1923-   ) Cuba
Fiction
The Execution. *J. G. Brotherston*. COH-3, 12.
The Lucky Chance. *J. M. Cohen*. COH-3, 48.

229 CASTAÑEDA ARAGÓN, GREGORIO (1886-?   ) Colombia
Fiction
Castaways Of The Earth (Excerpt). *H. de Onís*. ARC, 100.

230 CASTELLANOS, JOAQUÍN (1861-1932) Argentina
Poetry
Columbus. *A. S. Blackwell*. BLAC, 378.

231 CASTELLANOS, ROSARIO (1925-   ) Mexico
Poetry
A Palm Tree. no tr. CRAN, 93.
First Elegy. *O. Senior-Ellis*. CRAN, 92.
Foreign Woman. *J. M. Cohen*. COH-1, 103.
Silence Concerning an Ancient Stone. no tr. CRAN, 94.
The Empty House. *D. Flakoll & C. Alegría*. FLAK, 119.

232 CASTELPOGGI, ATILIO JORGE (1919-   ) Argentina
Poetry
Office Chronicle. *W. Shand*. SHA, 142.
The Anonymous Trades. *W. Shand*. SHA, 141.

233 CASTILLA, MANUEL J. (1918-   ) Argentina
Poetry
Magnetic Stone. *W. Shand*. SHA, 132.
The Hills Of Angastaco. *W. Shand*. SHA, 131.

234 CASTILLO, ABELARDO (1935-   ) Argentina
Fiction
Ernesto's Mother. *A. Colbin*. MANC, 453.

235 CASTILLO, LAURA DEL (1927-   ) Argentina
Fiction
A Plum For Coco. *J. Rothenberg*. PRIZE, 147.

236 CASTILLO, OTTO RENÉ (1936-1967) Guatemala
Poetry
Apolitical Intellectuals. *M. Randall*. MARQ, 265.
Let's Start Walking. *E. Dorn & G. Brotherston*. DORN, n.p.
Report of an Injustice. *M. Randall & R. Márquez*. MARQ,
  255.
Revolution. *R. Márquez*. MARQ, 261.
Widowed of the World. *T. Reynolds*. MARQ, 271.

237 CASTILLO NÁJERA, FRANCISCO (1886-?   ) Mexico
Other
Sor Juana Inés de la Cruz (Essay). no tr. LIT-1, 61.

238   CASTRILLO, PRIMO (1896-)
     Poetry
     Pablo Neruda (Excerpt). *R. Weeks.* LOW, 32.

239   CASTRO, FIDEL (1926-) Cuba
     Other
     Extracts from 'Words to the Intellectuals', June 1961
       (Speech). no tr. COH-3, 183.

240   CASTRO, HÉCTOR DAVID (1894-) El Salvador
     Other
     San Salvador (Essay). no tr. LIT-1, 47.

241   CASTRO RÍOS, ANDRÉS (1942-) Puerto Rico
     Poetry
     Four Voices Of Puerto Rico. *B. Luby.* BABI, 309.

242   CASTRO SAAVEDRA, CARLOS (1924-) Colombia
     Poetry
     Cluster of children. *A. Alwan.* TRI-13, 411.
     The insides of horses. *A. Alwan.* TRI-13, 409.
     Wife America. *D. Flakoll & C. Alegría.* FLAK, 22.

243   CASTRO Z., ÓSCAR (1910-1947) Chile
     Poetry
     Responsory For García Lorca. *D. Fitts.* FITT, 527.
     Fiction
     Lucero. *H. Kurz.* HAYDN, 872.

244   CAVÂLCANTI BORGES, JOSÉ CARLOS (1910-) Brazil
     Fiction
     With God's Blessing, Mom. *W. L. Grossman.* GRO, 131.

245   CERVANTES, FRANCISCO (1938-) Mexico
     Poetry
     Mambrú. *M. Strand.* PAZ-2, 41.

246   CESELLI, JUAN JOSÉ (1909-) Argentina
     Poetry
     Paradise Disinterred. *W. Shand.* SHA, 92.
     Whilst The Rain Escapes With The Wind. *W. Shand.* SHA, 91.

247   CÉSPEDES, AUGUSTO (1904-) Bolivia
     Fiction
     The Well (from: <u>Sangre de Mestizos</u>). *H. de Onís.* ARC,
      483.
     The Well. *H. Kurz.* HAYDN, 882.

248   CHALBAUD, RAMÓN (1931-) Venezuela
     Drama
     The Forceps. *F. Colecchia & J. Matas.* COLE, 141.

249 CHAMIE, MÁRIO (1933-   ) Brazil
Poetry
Harvest. *F. P. Hebblethwaite.* YOU, 24.

250 CHAN-MARIN, CARLOS FRANCISCO (1922-   ) Panama
Poetry
"Here is my tongue...." no tr. YOU, 91.
"The Moon Went to Sea." no tr. YOU, 90.
"The Ships Go Down." no tr. YOU, 91.

251 CHASE, ALFONSO (1945-   ) Costa Rica
Poetry
"Feel with me...." *A. Edwards.* YOU, 49.

252 CHÁVEZ, EDGARDO (1934-   ) Peru
Poetry
Childhood. *C. A. de Lomellini.* HAR67-4, 67.

253 CHÁVEZ, MARCO FIDEL (   ) Cuba
Poetry
My Heart Stays In Shadow. *H. Ruiz del Vizo.* RUIZ, 105.

254 CHOCANO, JOSÉ SANTOS (1875-1934) Peru
Poetry
A Manifesto. *M. E. Johnson.* JOHN, 109.
A Protest. *A. S. Blackwell.* BLAC, 224.
A Queen's Breast. *A. S. Blackwell.* BLAC, 220.
A Queen's Breast. *A. S. Blackwell.* JONE-3, 111.
A Song Of The Road. *J. P. Rice.* WALS, 680.
Archaeology. *A. S. Blackwell.* BLAC, 206.
Blazon. *G. D. Craig.* CRAI, 131.
Coat of Arms. *W. K. Jones.* JONE-3, 108.
Cuacthemoc. *G. D. Craig.* CRAI, 133.
Eagles and Sparrows. *A. S. Blackwell.* BLAC, 222.
Horn of Plenty. *A. S. Blackwell.* BLAC, 208.
Horses of the Conquerors. *J. R. Wendell.* JONE-3, 109.
Horses of the Conquerors. *J. R. Wendell.* TRAN, 252.
Horses of the Conquistadores. *M. Lee.* LIT-1, 29.
Lightning. *A. S. Blackwell.* BLAC, 226.
Oda Selvaje. *J. P. Rice.* WALS, 672.
Sun and Moon. *A. S. Blackwell.* BLAC, 206.
Sun and Moon. *A. S. Blackwell.* WALS, 679.
The Alligator's Dream. *A. S. Blackwell.* BLAC, 212.
The Andes. *A. S. Blackwell.* BLAC, 210.
The Andes. *G. D. Craig.* CRAI, 133.
The Boa-Constrictor's Dream. *A. S. Blackwell.* BLAC, 212.
The Condor's Dream. *A. S. Blackwell.* BLAC, 214.
The Dream of the Cayman. *T. Raworth.* CARA, 317.
The Frozen Heights. *G. D. Craig.* CRAI, 131.
The Indian Flute. *A. S. Blackwell.* JONE-3, 111.
The Lark. *A. S. Blackwell.* BLAC, 224.
The Magnolia. *A. S. Blackwell.* BLAC, 208.

The Magnolia. *J. P. Rice*. WALS, 671.
The Mouths of the Orinoco. *A. S. Blackwell*. BLAC, 218.
The Orchids. *A. S. Blackwell*. BLAC, 214.
The Quena. *A. S. Blackwell*. BLAC, 216.
The Spirit Primeval. *I. S. Shepard*. LIT-2, 54.
The Straits of Magellan. *A. S. Blackwell*. BLAC, 218.
The Vision of the Condor. *T. Raworth*. CARA, 318.
The Volcanos. *A. S. Blackwell*. BLAC, 216.
The Windmills. *A. S. Blackwell*. BLAC, 222.
Three Notes of our Indigenous Spirit. *G. D. Craig*. CRAI, 135.
Who Knows? *M. E. Johnson*. RES, 74.

255   CHUMACERO, ALÍ (1918-   ) Mexico
Poetry
Dialogue with a Portrait. no tr. CRAN, 98.
Epitaph For A Virgin. *J. M. Cohen*. COH-1, 106.
Gravestone of man unknown. *J. M. Cohen*. COH-2, 438.
The Bastard Son. *D. Hoffman*. MU-73, 157.
The Sphere of the Dance. *D. Hoffman*. PAZ-2, 105.
The Wanderings Of The Tribe. *W. C. Williams*. EVER, 60.
The Widower's Monologue. *D. Hoffman*. MU-73, 155.
Widower's Monologue. *W. C. Williams*. EVER, 59.

256   CISNEROS, ANTONIO (1942-   ) Peru
Poetry
After the Battle of Ayacucho: a mother's testimony.
  D. Tipton. TRI-13, 200.
After The Battle Of Ayacucho - From A Soldier. *M. A. de
  Maurer & D. Tipton*. HAR68-5, 34.
Ancient Peru. *M. Ahern & D. Tipton*. AHER, 62.
Ancient Peru. *M. A. de Maurer & D. Tipton*. HAR68-5, 32.
Between the Quay of San Nicolás & the Sea. *D. Tipton*.
  AHER, 76.
Chronicle of Chapi, 1965. *W. Rowe*. MARQ, 379.
Chronicle of Lima. *M. Ahern & D. Tipton*. AHER, 73.
Description of a Plaza, a Monument & Allegories in Bronze.
  D. Tipton. AHER, 71.
From A Mother - Again. *M. A. de Maurer & D. Tipton*.
  HAR68-5, 34.
I'm getting out & going some 30 kilometres towards the
  coast. *M. Ahern & D. Tipton*. AHER, 80.
I'm Getting Out & Going Some 30 Kilometres Towards The
  Coast. *M. A. de Maurer & D. Tipton*. HAR68-5, 37.
In Memoriam. *W. Rowe*. MARQ, 375.
Karl Marx, died 1883 aged 65. *M. Ahern & D. Tipton*. AHER,
  72.
Karl Marx, Died 1883 Aged 65. *M. A. de Maurer & D. Tipton*.
  HAR68-5, 38.
Karl Marx Died 1883 Aged 65. *M. Ahern & D. Tipton*. MARQ,
  371.

(CISNEROS, ANTONIO)
Loneliness 2. *M. Ahern & D. Tipton.* AHER, 78.
Loneliness II. *M. A. Maurer.* TRI-13, 198.
On The Death Of The Bishop, Who Was Truly Of Your Ilk.
  M. A. de Maurer & D. Tipton. HAR68-5, 36.
Pachacamac. *D. Tipton.* AHER, 61.
Paracas. *M. Ahern & D. Tipton.* AHER, 61.
Paracas. *M. A. de Maurer & D. Tipton.* HAR68-5, 32.
Prayers of a Repentant Gentleman. *M. Ahern & D. Tipton.*
  AHER, 65.
Question of Time. *D. Tipton.* AHER, 64.
Question of time. *D. Tipton.* TRI-13, 197.
Tarma. *M. Ahern & D. Tipton.* AHER, 68.
Tarma. *J. Rothenberg.* HAR68-5, 33.
The Dead Conquerors. *M. Ahern & D. Tipton.* AHER, 63.
The Novice. *J. Rothenberg.* HAR68-5, 33.
The Skulls In Ayacucho Airport. *M. A. de Maurer & D. Tipton.*
  HAR68-5, 37.
The spider hangs too far from the ground. *R. Greenwell.*
  HAR67-2, 17.
Three Testimonies of Ayacucho. *M. Ahern & D. Tipton.* AHER,
  69.
Túpac Amaru Relegated. *D. Tipton.* AHER, 68.
Tupac Amaru relegated. *D. Tipton.* TRI-13, 199.
Women Of Tahiti Paul Gauguin. *J. Rothenberg.* HAR68-5, 35.
Workers of the Sun's Land. *M. Ahern & D. Tipton.* AHER, 62.
Workers Of The World For The Sun. *J. Rothenberg.* HAR68-5,
  35.
Other
On the Situation of the Writer in Peru (Essay). *D. Tipton.*
  AHER, 115.

257 CLAUDIO, EDWIN (   ) Puerto Rico
     Poetry
     A Boycott. Originally Engl. BABI, 450.
     Where Am I At? Originally Engl. BABI, 449.

258 CÓCARO, NICOLÁS (1926-   ) Argentina
     Poetry
     Joy. *W. Shand.* SHA, 205.
     The Dovecot. *W. Shand.* SHA, 205.
     To A Strange Animal Among Glaciers. *W. Shand.* SHA, 206.

259 COELHO, SALDANHA (1926-   ) Brazil
     (José Saldanha Da Gamma Coelho Pinto)
     Fiction
     Memory. *R. W. Horton.* COEL, 195.

260 COLÍN, EDUARDO (1880-1945) Mexico
     Poetry
     After the Rain. *E. W. Underwood.* UND, 120.

261 COLL Y TOSTE, CAYETANO (1850–1930) Puerto Rico
Fiction
The Pirate's Treasure. *W. E. Colford.* COLF, 189.
Other
Guanina (Folklore). *B. Luby.* BABI, 15.

262 COLLAZO, MIGUEL (1936–) Cuba
Fiction
The man who worshipped the Saturnians. no tr. CARZ, 133.

263 COLÓN, JESÚS ( ) Puerto Rico
Other
Grandma, Please Don't Come! (from: <u>A Puerto Rican in New
York</u>). Originally Engl. BABI, 410.

264 CONCEPCIÓN DE GRACIA, GILBERTO (1909–1968) Puerto Rico
Other
A Revolution Of Our People (Speech). *B. Luby.* BABI, 237.

265 CONDÉ, JOSÉ (1919–) Brazil
Fiction
The Dog. *R. W. Horton.* COEL, 111.

266 CONTARDO, LUIS FELIPE (1880–1921) Chile
Poetry
Evening. *A. S. Blackwell.* BLAC, 304.
Home Of Peace And Purity. *T. Walsh.* WALS, 708.
The Calling. *T. Walsh.* WALS, 709.

267 CONTI, HAROLDO PEDRO (1925–) Argentina
Fiction
The Cause. *J. Rothenberg.* PRIZE, 259.

268 CONTÍN AYBAR, PEDRO RENÉ (1910–) Dominican Republic
Poetry
Charon. *F. E. Townsend.* TOWN, 34.

269 CONTRERAS, FRANCISCO (1880–1932) Chile
Poetry
The Charm of the Rains. *A. S. Blackwell.* BLAC, 304.

270 CORCUERA, ARTURO (1935–) Peru
Poetry
Cowboy and Fable of Buffalo Bill. *R. Márquez.* MARQ, 393.
Fierce Wolf: A Fable. *R. Márquez.* MARQ, 391.
Tom and Jerry: A Fable. *R. Márquez.* MARQ, 389.

271 CÓRDOVA, ARMANDO ( ) Cuba
Poetry
Hip...Macua is hip. *H. Ruiz del Vizo.* RUIZ, 76.

272　CÓRODOVA ITURBURU, CAYETANO　(1899-　　)　Argentina
　　　Poetry
　　　Poem. *W. Shand.* SHA, 38.
　　　Where I Speak Of A Hand. *W. Shand.* SHA, 37.

273　CORONEL URTECHO, JOSÉ　(1906-　　)　Nicaragua
　　　Poetry
　　　Barbershop. *J. Brof.* CARP, 169.
　　　Ode to Rubén Darío　Finale (with whistle). *J. Brof.*
　　　　CARP, 171.
　　　San Carlos. *J. Brof.* CARP, 173.
　　　Self-Portrait. *J. Brof.* CARP, 169.
　　　Wooden Moon. *J. Brof.* CARP, 171.

274　CORRAL, JESÚS DEL　(1871-1931)　Colombia
　　　Fiction
　　　Cross Over, Sawyer! *H. Kurz.* HAYDN, 891.
　　　Cross Over, Sawyer! *H. Kurz.* MILL, 169.

275　CORRAL, SIMÓN　(1950?-　　)　Ecuador
　　　Poetry
　　　Growl. *R. Connally.* YOU, 58.

276　CORREA, ARNALDO　(1935-　　)　Cuba
　　　Fiction
　　　Gunners. no tr. CARZ, 201.

277　CORRETJER, JUAN ANTONIO　(1908-　　)　Puerto Rico
　　　Poetry
　　　But in Spite of Everything. *D. Sánchez-Méndez.* MATI, 23.
　　　Distances. *B. Luby.* BABI, 295.
　　　Great Days. *D. Sánchez-Méndez.* MATI, 25.
　　　Praise Atop the Ciales Tower (Excerpt). no tr. KAI, n.p.

278　CORTÁZAR, JULIO　(1914-　　)　Argentina
　　　Poetry
　　　Nocturne. *P. Blackburn.* GARR, 29.
　　　The Widow. *P. Blackburn.* GARR, 29.
　　　Fiction
　　　Bestiary. *J. Franco.* COH-1, 72.
　　　Clocks (from: Stories of Cronopios and Famas). *P. Black-*
　　　　burn. SIX62-6, 69.
　　　End of the Game. *P. Blackburn.* HOW-1, 262.
　　　Letter to a Young Lady in Paris. *P. Blackburn.* MANC, 177.
　　　Silvia. *G. Rabassa.* CARP, 370.
　　　The Disused Door. *P. Ulyatt.* LAWA, 181.
　　　The Gates of Heaven. *D. Flakoll & C. Alegría.* FLAK, 136.
　　　The Song Of The Cronopios (from: Stories of Cronopios and
　　　　Famas). *P. Blackburn.* SIX60-4, 64
　　　Travel (from: Stories of Cronopios and Famas). *P. Black-*
　　　　burn. SIX60-4, 63.
　　　Unusual occupations. *P. Blackburn.* TRI-15, 184.

279   CORTES, ALFONSO   (   )   Nicaragua
        Poetry
        Aegeus In Prison. no tr. MERT, 147.
        Air. no tr. MERT, 147.
        Great Prayer. no tr. MERT, 145.
        Space Song. no tr. MERT, 143.
        Sundown. no tr. MERT, 148.
        The Flower Of The Fruit. no tr. MERT, 144.
        The Three Sisters. no tr. MERT, 145.
        The Truth. no tr. MERT, 146.
        When You Point Your Finger. no tr. MERT, 148.

280   CORVALÁN, STELLA   (1929-   )   Chile
        Poetry
        Anxiety. *W. K. Jones.* JONE-3, 133.

281   COSTA DU RELS, ADOLFO   (1891-   )   Bolivia
        Fiction
        La Misqui-Simi. *E. Wallace.* FLOR-1, 458.

282   COSTANTINI, HUMBERTO   (1924-   )   Argentina
        Fiction
        In The Beginning. *N. T. di Giovanni.* HOW-1, 329.
        In The Beginning. *N. T. di Giovanni.* MU-70, 83.

283   COUSTÉ, ALBERTO   (1940-   )   Argentina
        Poetry
        The Difficult New Time. no tr. YOU, 4.

284   COUTO, RUI RIBEIRO   (1898-1963) Brazil
        Poetry
        The Invention of Brasilian Poetry. no tr. TRE, 4.
        Fiction
        The Bahian. *W. L. Grossman.* GRO, 93.

   CRUZ, EDDY DIAS DA. See [REBÊLO, MARQUES pseud.].

285   CUADRA, JOSÉ DE LA   (1903-   )   Ecuador
        Fiction
        Valley Heat. *H. Kurz.* HAYDN, 877.

286   CUADRA, PABLO ANTONIO   (1912-   )   Nicaragua
        Poetry
        Cup With A Jaguar For The Drinking Of Health. no tr. MERT,
          98.
        Lament Of A Maiden For The Warrior's Death. no tr. MERT,
          102.
        Meditation Before An Ancient Poem. *T. Merton.* MILL, 181.
        Pain Is An Eagle Clinging To Your Name. no tr. MERT, 100.
        The Birth Of The Sun. no tr. MERT, 98.
        The Birth Of The Sun. *T. Merton.* MILL, 180.

(CUADRA, PABLO ANTONIO)
The Despairing Man Draws A Serpent. no tr. MERT, 99.
The Eye Is A Dog Howling In The Distance. no tr. MERT, 101.
The Jaguar Myth. no tr. MERT, 96.
The Jaguar Myth. *T. Merton.* MILL, 178.
The Secret Of The Burning Stars. no tr. MERT, 99.
The Secret Of The Burning Stars. *T. Merton.* MILL, 182.
The World Is A Round Earthen-Ware Plate. no tr. MERT, 102.
Urn With A Political Profile. no tr. MERT, 101.

287   CUENCA, AGUSTÍN F.   (1850-1884) Mexico
Poetry
Prismatic Lights. *A. S. Blackwell.* BLAC, 162.
Prismatic Lights. *A. S. Blackwell.* GOLD-2, 17.
To Ch-. *A. B. Poor.* POOR, 59.

288   CUEVAS, JOSÉ LUIS   (1933-   ) Mexico
Other
The Cactus Curtain (An open letter on conformity in Mexican
   art). *L. Kemp.* EVER, 111.

289   CUNHA, EUCLYDES DA   (1866-1909) Brazil
Other
Antonio Conselheiro, the "Counselor" [from: Os Sertões (Re-
   bellion in the Backlands)]. *H. de Onís.* ONIS-1, 349.
Description of Antonio Conselheiro [from: Os Sertões (Re-
   bellion in the Backlands)]. *H. de Onís.* ARC, 432.

290   CUNHA, JUAN   (1910-   ) Uruguay
Poetry
At My Back. *R. Connally.* YOU, 111.
Landscape. *D. J. Flakoll & C. Alegría.* BENE, 65.
Sometimes Among Yellow Leaves. *R. Connally.* YOU, 111.

291   CUZA MALÉ, BELKIS   (1942-   ) Cuba
Poetry
An Ill-Fated Woman. *A. Boyer.* BECK, 751.
I Have Not Forgotten You. *S. Carranza.* BECK, 747.
Photogenic People. *R. Llopis.* BECK, 753.
Rimbaud and I. *A. Boyer.* BECK, 749.

292   DA COSTA E SILVA, ALBERTO   (1931-   ) Brazil
Poetry
The Empty Space. *F. P. Hebblethwaite.* YOU, 19.

293   DALTON, ROQUE   (1933-   ) El Salvador
Poetry
At the Bottom. *T. Reynolds.* CARP, 411.
Jail again, dark fruit. *T. Reynolds.* CARP, 409.
Karl Marx. *E. Randall.* MARQ, 249.
No, I Wasn't Always So Ugly. *R. Márquez.* MR, 276.
OAS. *R. Márquez.* MARQ, 247.

On Headaches. *R. Márquez.* MARQ, 245.
Some Nostalgias. *T. Reynolds.* CARP, 409.
Two Greek Guerrillas: An Old Man and a Traitor. *E. Randall.* MARQ, 251.

294 DAMASCENO, DARCY (1922–   ) Brazil
Poetry
Poem. *L. S. Downes.* DOWN, 75.

295 DAMEL, CARLOS SANTIAGO (1890-1959) Argentina
(Joint author. See also DARTHÉS, JUAN FERNANDO CAMILO)
Drama
The Quack Doctor. *W. K. Jones.* JONE-1, 3.
The Quack Doctor (Excerpt). *M. L. H. Delgado.* JONE-3, 400.

296 DARÍO, RUBÉN (1867-1916) Nicaragua
Poetry
A Shell. *A. S. Blackwell.* BLAC, 190.
A Song of Autumn in the Spring. *A. Fife.* FIFE, 61.
A Song of Hope. *A. S. Blackwell.* BLAC, 200.
A Sonnet to Cervantes. *M. González.* CARA, 305.
A Symphony in Gray. *G. D. Craig.* CRAI, 49.
An Autumn Song in Spring. *G. D. Craig.* CRAI, 55.
An Autumn Song in Spring. *G. D. Craig.* RES, 52.
Anthem for the Death of Paul Verlaine. *J. M. Cohen.* COH-2, 335.
Autumn Verses. *J. M. Cohen.* COH-2, 340.
Autumn Verses. *K. Flores.* FLOR-1, 226.
Autumnal. *A. Volland.* FLOR-1, 210.
Autumnal Sonnet to the Marquis of Bradomín. *R. Anderson.* TRAN, 240.
Blazon. *G. D. Craig.* CRAI, 47.
Canción Of Autumn In Springtime. *T. Walsh.* WALS, 602.
Doom. *K. Flores.* FLOR-1, 225.
Eheu! *A. Volland.* FLOR-1, 226.
Far Away. *M. González.* CARA, 306.
Far Away and Long Ago. *D. Levertov.* FLOR-1, 225.
Fatalism. *M. E. Johnson.* JOHN, 89.
Fatality. *J. M. Cohen.* COH-2, 339.
For a Cuban Lady. *G. D. Craig.* CRAI, 61.
Frieze. *G. D. Craig.* CRAI, 51.
I am the man. *G. D. Craig.* CRAI, 39.
I pursue a form.... *D. Bell.* FLOR-1, 216.
I Seek a Form. *M. González.* CARA, 304.
Leda. *D. Bell.* FLOR-1, 221.
Leda. *A. J. McVan.* TRAN, 244.
Litany for Our Lord Don Quijote. *M. Lee.* JONE-3, 26.
Litany for our Lord Don Quixote. *M. Lee.* LIT-1, 75.
Litany for Our Lord Don Quixote. *M. Lee.* LIT-2, 56.
Litany Of Our Sire, Don Quixote. *D. J. Flakoll & C. Alegría.* BENE, 19.
Margarita. *G. D. Craig.* CRAI, 63.

(DARÍO, RUBÉN)
Marguerite. *A. Volland.* FLOR-1, 214.
Melancholy. *A. Volland.* FLOR-1, 222.
Men Of Genius. *E. W. Underwood.* UND, 38.
Mine. *G. D. Craig.* CRAI, 61.
Nightfall In The Tropics. *T. Walsh.* WALS, 601.
Nocturne. *J. M. Cohen.* COH-2, 338.
Nocturne. *K. Flores.* FLOR-1, 224.
On an Open Page. *M. González.* CARA, 307.
Philosophy. *M. González.* CARA, 305.
Philosophy. *M. Lee.* FLOR-1, 221.
Portico. *T. Walsh.* JONE-3, 23.
Portico. *T. Walsh.* WALS, 606.
Race. *M. González.* CARA, 309.
Salutation to the Eagle. *G. D. Craig.* CRAI, 73.
Seashell. *A. Volland.* FLOR-1, 223.
Slings. *A. S. Blackwell.* BLAC, 188.
Sonatina. *J. Crow.* FLOR-1, 212.
Sonatina. *M. E. Johnson.* JOHN, 85.
Sonatina. *J. P. Rice.* JONE-3, 21.
Sonatina. *A. B. Poor.* POOR, 64.
Sonatina. *S. Resnick.* RES, 50.
Sonatina. *J. P. Rice.* WALS, 598.
Song of the Pines. *A. S. Blackwell.* BLAC, 184.
Sonnet to Cervantes. *A. S. Blackwell.* BLAC, 188.
Spring [A Fragment]. *A. Volland.* FLOR-1, 209.
Stories of the Cid. *A. S. Blackwell.* BLAC, 182.
Symphony in Gray Major. *D. Levertov.* FLOR-1, 215.
Symphony in Gray Major. *A. J. McVan.* JONE-3, 25.
Symphony in Gray Major. *A. J. McVan.* TRAN, 245.
Symphony in Grey Major. *J. M. Cohen.* COH-2, 333.
The Angelus. *G. D. Craig.* CRAI, 65.
The Cock. *M. González.* CARA, 310.
The Fount. *W. M. Davis.* FLOR-1, 216.
The Grandmother's Clavichord. *A. J. McVan.* TRAN, 241.
The Kings of the East. *G. D. Craig.* CRAI, 63.
The Murmur from the Stable. *A. B. Poor.* POOR, 61.
The Optimist's Salutation. *G. D. Craig.* CRAI, 65.
The Princess and the Star. *A. S. Blackwell.* BLAC, 192.
The Swan. *G. D. Craig.* CRAI, 45.
The Swan. *M. E. Johnson.* JOHN, 85.
The Swans. *D. Bell.* FLOR-1, 219.
The White Page. *A. S. Blackwell.* BLAC, 198.
To Roosevelt. *L. Kemp.* BOLD, 102.
To Roosevelt. *G. D. Craig.* CRAI, 69.
To Roosevelt. *E. C. Hills.* WALS, 595.
To the Joyful Poets. *M. González.* CARA, 303.
To Theodore Roosevelt, 1904. *R. Bly.* TRI-15, 238.
"Towers of God! Poets!" *J. M. Cohen.* COH-2, 337.
Triumphal March. *C. Guenther.* FLOR-1, 217.
Unhappy he.... *M. Lee.* FLOR-1, 222.

Verses of Autumn. *M. E. Johnson*. JOHN, 89.
Vesperal. *M. González*. CARA, 308.
Fiction
The Bourgeois King. *B. Belitt*. HOW-1, 44.
The Case of Señorita Amelia. *G. Woodruff*. MANC, 33.
The Death of the Empress of China. *W. E. Colford*. COLF, 129.
The Ruby. no tr. JONE-3, 28.
Other
My Visit to Nicaragua. no tr. LIT-1, 73.
My Visit to Nicaragua. no tr. LIT-2, 33.

297 DARTHÉS, JUAN FERNANDO CAMILO (1889-?) Argentina
(Joint author. See also DAMEL, CARLOS SANTIAGO.)
Drama
The Quack Doctor. *W. K. Jones*. JONE-1, 3.
The Quack Doctor (Excerpt). *M. L. H. Delgado*. JONE-3, 400.

298 DÁVALOS, BALBINO (1866-1951) Mexico
Poetry
My Glory. *T. Walsh*. GOLD-2, 54.
My Glory. *T. Walsh*. WALS, 635.
The Poet. *A. S. Blackwell*. BLAC, 168.

299 DÁVALOS, JUAN CARLOS (1898-1959) Argentina
Fiction
The White Wind. *A. Flores*. FLOR-2, 421.
The White Wind. *A. Flores*. FLOR-3, 208.
The White Wind. *A. Flores*. MILL, 183.

300 DÁVALOS, RENÉ ( ) Paraguay
Poetry
All on meeting you. *J. Upton*. TRI-13, 282.

301 DÁVILA, ÁNGELA MARÍA (1944-) Puerto Rico
Poetry
i have just died.... *M. Arrillaga*. MATI, 155.
I Want for My Name.... *M. Arrillaga*. MATI, 155.

302 DÁVILA, JOSÉ ANTONIO (1898-1941) Puerto Rico
Poetry
Letter of Recommendation (To The Proprietor Of The Universe).
B. Luby. BABI, 272.

303 DÁVILA, VIRGILIO (1869-1943) Puerto Rico
Poetry
Holy Week. *T. Walsh*. WALS, 704.
Nostalgia. *B. Luby*. BABI, 270.
The Town. *B. Luby*. BABI, 269.

304   DE LA TORRE, ANTONIO   (1904–   )   Argentina
     Poetry
     My Peasant Father. *W. Shand*. SHA, 66.

305   DÉBOLE, CARLOS ALBERTO   (1915–   )   Argentina
     Poetry
     Bow And Arrow. *W. Shand*. SHA, 119.
     Frog. *W. Shand*. SHA, 118.
     The Pigeon. *W. Shand*. SHA, 117.

306   DEBRAVO, JORGE   (1938–   )   Costa Rica
     Poetry
     I Affirm. *A. Edwards*. YOU, 41.

307   DEL PICCHIA, MENOTTI   (1892–   )   Brazil
     Poetry
     Bay Of Guanabara. *D. Poore*. FITT, 153.
     The Narrow Street. *D. Poore*. FITT, 153.

308   DÉLANO, POLI   (1936–   )   Chile
     Fiction
     The Boarding House. *C. Baraona*. WILL-2, 118.

309   DELGADO, JUAN B.   (1868–1929)   Mexico
     Poetry
     La Cañada. *E. W. Underwood*. UND, 137.
     Old Sea Wolf. *A. S. Blackwell*. BLAC, 172.

310   DELGADO, RAFAEL   (1853–1914)   Mexico
     Poetry
     In the Mountains. *E. W. Underwood*. UND, 138.
     Fiction
     Calandria (Excerpts). *F. Starr*. STAR, 396.

311   DELGADO, WASHINGTON   (1927–   )   Peru
     Poetry
     Exile for Life. *R. Greenwell*. HAR67-2, 21.
     Good Manners. *D. Tipton*. AHER, 29.
     History of Peru. *D. Tipton*. AHER, 27.
     Human Wisdom. *D. Tipton*. AHER, 28.
     Imperfect Times. *M. Ahern & D. Tipton*. AHER, 27.
     Life Explains & Death Spies Out. *M. Ahern & D. Tipton*.
       AHER, 30.
     Life explains & death spies out. *M. A. Maurer & D. Tipton*.
       TRI-13, 201.
     Plurality of Worlds. *M. Ahern & D. Tipton*. AHER, 31.
     Plurality of worlds. *M. A. Maurer & D. Tipton*. TRI-13,
       202.
     Serpent. *R. Greenwell*. HAR67-2, 23.
     The Foreigner. *R. Greenwell*. HAR67-2, 19.
     Other
     On the Death of Javier Heraud. *D. Tipton*. AHER, 120.

312 DELIGNE, GASTÓN F. (1861-1913) Dominican Republic
       Poetry
       To Sister Mary of the Snows. *F. E. Townsend.* TOWN, 47.

313 DENEVI, MARCO (1922-   ) Argentina
       Fiction
       Secret Ceremony. *H. de Onís.* MILL, 198.
       Secret Ceremony. *H. de Onís.* PRIZE, 1.
       Drama
       Romeo Before the Corpse of Juliet (Written by Georges Cahoon,
         adapted by M. Denevi). *G. Luzuriaga & R. Rudder.* LUZU,
         72.
       You Don't Have to Complicate Happiness (Written by Ramón
         Civedé, adapted by M. Denevi). *G. Luzuriaga & R. Rudder.*
         LUZU, 77.

314 DI BENEDETTO, ANTONIO (1922-   ) Argentina
       Fiction
       But One Could -. *H. E. Francis.* MU-73, 119.
       Koch's Butterflies. *H. E. Francis.* MU-73, 118.
       Nest In My Bones. *H. E. Francis.* MU-73, 121.

315 DIAS GOMES, ALFREDO (1922-   ) Brazil
       Drama
       Payment As Pledged. *O. Fernández.* WOOD, 46.

316 DÍAZ, JESÚS (1942-   ) Cuba
       Fiction
       Who the hell can stand this? no tr. CARZ, 115.

317 DÍAZ, VIGIL (   ) Dominican Republic
       Poetry
       Lady of the Moon. *F. E. Townsend.* TOWN, 26.

318 DÍAZ ALFARO, ABELARDO (1920-   ) Puerto Rico
       Fiction
       Josco. *N. Vandemoer.* HOW-2, 257.
       Peyo Mercé Teaches English (from: Terrazo). *B. Luby.*
         BABI, 362.
       "Santa Clo" Comes to La Cuchilla. *W. E. Colford.* COLF, 206.
       The Dogs. *H. St. Martin.* ·HOW-1, 313.

   DÍAZ GARCÉS, JOAQUÍN. See [PINO, ÁNGEL pseud.].

319 DÍAZ GUTIÉRREZ, JORGE (1930-   ) Chile
       Drama
       Love Yourselves Above All Others. *F. Colecchia & J. Matas.*
         COLE, 177.
       Man Does Not Die By Bread Alone: Notes on Torture and Other
         Forms of Dialogue (Scene from: "Introducción al elefante
         y otras zoologías"). *J. Pottlitzer.* DR, 87.

(DÍAZ GUTIÉRREZ, JORGE)
The Eve of the Execution or Genesis Was Tomorrow.
  G. Luzuriaga & R. Rudder. LUZU, 160.
The Place Where The Mammals Die. *N. Nelson.* WOOD, 184.
Other
Reflections on the Chilean Theatre (Essay). *J. Pottlitzer.*
  DR, 84.

DÍAZ LOYOLA, CARLOS. See [ROKHA, PABLO DE pseud.].

320   DÍAZ MARTÍNEZ, MANUEL (1936-   ) Cuba
      Poetry
      Ancient History. *D. Gardner.* TARN, 89.
      Bread. *A. Boyer.* BECK, 641.
      In Amsterdam. *A. Boyer.* BECK, 635.
      Love Is Like Her. *A. Boyer.* BECK, 643.
      Ode in Budapest. *A. Boyer.* BECK, 637.
      Ophelia In The Rain. *D. Gardner.* TARN, 87.

321   DÍAZ MIRÓN, SALVADOR (1853-1928) Mexico
      See also MIRÓN, SALVADOR DÍAZ
      Poetry
      Cleopatra. *M. González.* CARA, 245.
      Green Eyes. *E. W. Underwood.* UND, 35.
      Grief. *S. Beckett.* PAZ-1, 118.
      In Hoc Signo (for my daughter Rosa). *W. K. Jones.* JONE-3,
        33.
      Nox. *S. Beckett.* PAZ-1, 122.
      Snow-Flake. *A. S. Blackwell.* GOLD-2, 19.
      Snow-Flake. *A. S. Blackwell.* WALS, 536.
      The Apparition. *M. González.* CARA, 247.
      The Cloud. *A. S. Blackwell.* GOLD-2, 19.
      The Corpse. *S. Beckett.* PAZ-1, 120.
      The Deserter. *E. W. Underwood.* UND, 37.
      The Example. *J. M. Cohen.* COH-2, 327.
      The Example. *S. Beckett.* PAZ-1, 120.
      The Phantom. *S. Beckett.* PAZ-1, 121.
      The Vision. *A. J. McVan.* TRAN, 222.
      To an Araucaria. *S. Beckett.* PAZ-1, 125.
      To Gloria (Fragments). *W. K. Jones.* JONE-3, 32.
      To Pity. *A. S. Blackwell.* GOLD-2, 18.
      To Pity. *A. S. Blackwell.* JONE-3, 32.
      To Pity. *A. S. Blackwell.* WALS, 535.
      Within an Emerald. *S. Beckett.* PAZ-1, 126.

322   DÍAZ ORDÓÑEZ, VIRGILIO (1895-   ) Dominican Republic
      Poetry
      Intimacy. *F. E. Townsend.* TOWN, 68.
      The Act. *F. E. Townsend.* TOWN, 31.
      Other
      Columbus in Hispaniola. no tr. LIT-1, 40.

323 DÍAZ RODRÍGUEZ, JESÚS (1941-   ) Cuba
    Fiction
    The Cripple. *J. M. Cohen.* COH-3, 159.

324 DÍAZ VALCÁRCEL, EMILIO (1929-   ) Puerto Rico
    Fiction
    Black Sun (Excerpt). *C. V. Matters.* KAI, n.p.

325 DIEGO, ELISEO (1920-   ) Cuba
    Poetry
    Calm. *E. Randall.* TRI-13, 137.
    Difficulties Of An Equilibrist. *T. Reynolds.* TARN, 31.
    Fragment. *C. Beck.* BECK, 225.
    Fragment. *N. Tarn.* TARN, 27.
    Litany for Rubén Darío. *C. Beck.* BECK, 211.
    Man's Tools. *C. Beck.* BECK, 219.
    On This Single, This One And Only Afternoon. *N. Tarn.*
        TARN, 29.
    Only This. *C. Beck.* BECK, 227.
    Risks of Balancing. *C. Beck.* BECK, 215.
    Song of lost paradise. *E. Randall.* TRI-13, 137.
    The Child in his Bedroom. *C. Beck.* BECK, 229.
    The Face Never Seen. *C. Beck.* BECK, 231.
    The Splendor of the Depths. *C. Beck.* BECK, 223.
    The Whole Ingenuous Disguise, The Whole Of Happiness.
        N. Tarn. TARN, 27.
    Who Sees the Night. *C. Beck.* BECK, 233.
    Fiction
    Concerning Señor de la Peña. *E. Randall.* HOW-1, 310.
    How His Excellency Spent The Time. *J. MacLean.* HOW-2, 242.
    Something To Everyone. *J. MacLean.* HOW-2, 240.

326 DIEGO, JOSÉ DE (1868-1918) Puerto Rico
    Poetry
    In The Breach. *B. Luby.* BABI, 233.
    The Setting Sun. *A. B. Poor.* POOR, 73
    Ultima Actio. *B. Luby.* BABI, 233.
    Fiction
    Out In The Open. no tr. KAI, n.p.
    Other
    No (Essay). *B. Luby.* BABI, 232.

327 DIEGO PADRÓ, JOSÉ I. DE (1899-   ) Puerto Rico
    Fiction
    The Fish Sing (from: A Cowbell with Two Clappers). *B. Luby.*
        BABI, 318.

328 DIEZ CANSECO, JOSÉ (1905-1949) Peru
    Fiction
    Gaviota. *H. de Onís.* FLOR-2, 229.

329 DINIZ, FRANCISA SENHORINHA DA MOTTA (   ) Brazil
Other
What Do We Want? (Newspaper article). *J. E. Hahner.* HAH, 44.

330 DOBLEZ YZAGUIRRE, JULIETA (1943-   ) Costa Rica
Poetry
Song In Vain For A Resurrection. *L. Bradford.* MU-74, 109.
Unfinished Prayer. *A. Edwards.* YOU, 45.

331 D'OLIVEIRA, FELIPE (1891-   ) Brazil
Poetry
The Epitaph Which Was Not Graven. *L. S. Downes.* DOWN, 24.

332 DOLORES, CARMEN (1852-1910) Brazil
Fiction
Aunt Zeze's Tears. *I. Goldberg.* GOLD-1, 139.

333 [DOMECQ, BUSTOS pseud.]
BIOY CASARES, ADOLFO with BORGES, JORGE LUIS
Fiction
The Twelve Figures of the World. *D. Yates.* YATE, 65.

334 DOMÍNGUEZ, RAMIRO (1929-   ) Paraguay
Poetry
"Flour from lifeless roots." *J. Upton.* TRI-13, 281.
Fragment. *J. Upton.* TRI-13, 281.

DOMÍNGUEZ ALBA, BERNARDO. See [SINÁN, ROGELIO pseud.].

335 DOMÍNGUEZ CHARRO, FRANCISCO (1912-   ) Dominican Republic
Poetry
Chant of the Fisher. *F. E. Townsend.* TOWN, 71.

336 DONOSO, JOSÉ (1925-   ) Chile
Fiction
Ana María. *J. M. Cohen.* COH-1, 152.
Denmarker. *D. Flakoll & C. Alegría.* FLAK, 200.
Hell Has No Limits. *H. D. Taylor & S. J. Levine.* FUEN,
145.
Paseo. *L. O. Freeman.* TRI-13, 307.
Paseo. *L. O. Freeman.* HOW-1, 335.
Paseo. *L. O. Freeman.* MANC, 293.

337 DRAGÚN, OSVALDO (1929-   ) Argentina
Drama
And They Told Us We Were Immortal. *A. J. Green.* WOOD, 122.
The Man Who Turned Into a Dog. *F. Colecchia & J. Matas.*
COLE, 21.
The Story of Panchito González. *G. Luzuriaga & R. Rudder.*
LUZU, 43.
The Story of the Man Who Turned into a Dog. *G. Luzuriaga &
R. Rudder.* LUZU, 33.

338 DRUMMOND DE ANDRADE, CARLOS (1902-   ) Brazil
Poetry
Aspiration. *J. Nist & Y. Leite.* NIST, 93.
Childhood. *D. Poore.* FITT, 185.
Childhood. *H. Ruiz del Vizo.* RUIZ, 133.
Confession Of The Man From Itabira. *M. Cardozo.* NEI, 79.
Consolation at the Beach. *J. Nist & Y. Leite.* NIST, 88.
Dawn. *P. Standish.* CARA 81.
Dawn. *J. Nist & Y. Leite.* NIST, 92.
Don't Kill Yourself. *E. Bishop.* BISH, 65.
Don't Kill Yourself. *E. Bishop.* COH-1, 70.
Eternal. *M. Cardozo.* NEI, 85.
Family Portrait. *E. Bishop.* BISH, 91.
Fantasia. *D. Poore.* FITT, 187.
Garden In Liberty Square. *D. Poore.* FITT, 189.
In Search Of Poetry. *M. Cardozo.* NEI, 75.
In Search of Poetry. *P. Standish.* CARA, 82.
In the Middle of the Road. *E. Bishop.* BISH, 89.
In The Middle Of The Road. *M. Cardozo.* NEI, 77.
Infancy. *E. Bishop.* BISH, 87.
José. *J. R. Longland.* CHI, 67.
Pathetic Poem. *J. Nist & Y. Leite.* NIST, 83.
Sadness in Heaven. *J. Nist & Y. Leite.* NIST, 86.
Search for Poetry. *J. Nist & Y. Leite.* NIST, 89.
Secret. *J. Nist & Y. Leite.* NIST, 84.
Seven-Sided Poem. *E. Bishop.* BISH, 63.
The Dead in Frock Coats. *J. Nist & Y. Leite.* NIST, 87.
The Death Of Neco Andrade. *M. Cardozo.* NEI, 81.
The Dirty Hand. *J. Nist & Y. Leite.* NIST, 84.
The Itabiran's Confession. *J. R. Longland.* CHI, 65.
The Ox. *J. Nist & Y. Leite.* NIST, 87.
The Table. *E. Bishop.* BISH, 67.
They Died In Frock-Coats. *L. S. Downes.* DOWN, 48.
Travelling in the Family. *E. Bishop.* BISH, 57.
Travelling In The Family. *E. Bishop.* COH-1, 67.
Travelling In The Family. *E. Bishop.* GARR, 23.
Your Shoulders Hold Up The World. *L. S. Downes.* DOWN, 47.
Fiction
Miguel's Theft. *R. Stock.* DEL-70, 170.

339 D'SOLA, OTTO (1912-   ) Venezuela
Poetry
Before The Coming Of The Planes That Burn The Cities.
    A. Flores. FITT, 307.
Last Song To A Girl Of The Waterfront. *A. Flores.* FITT,
    307.
Plenitude. *A. Flores.* FITT, 305.

340 DUEÑAS, GUADALUPE (1920-   ) Mexico
Fiction
A Clinical Case. no tr. CRAN, 78.
The Moribund. *Z. Nelken.* TORR, 131.

341   DUQUE, MANUEL   (   ) Bolivia
      Poetry
      Dew. *A. S. Blackwell*. BLAC, 462.

342   DURÁN, ARMANDO (1938-   ) Venezuela
      Fiction
      José Barcalayo, Killer Of Pests. *N. T. di Giovanni*. MU-70,
      77.

343   DURÁN, MANUEL (1925-   ) Mexico
      Poetry
      Still Life. *P. Blackburn*. EVER, 86.
      The Garden Well. *P. Blackburn*. CRAN, 100.
      The Possessed. *P. Blackburn*. EVER, 85.
      The Power And The Glory. *P. Blackburn*. EVER, 86.

344   EANDI, HÉCTOR I. (1895-1964) Argentina
      Fiction
      Dangerous Men. *A. De Sola*. FLOR-2, 368.

345   ECHAGÜE, JUAN PABLO (1877-?   ) Argentina
      Fiction
      Doña Paula's Rooster. no tr. LIT-1, 1.
      Doña Paula's Rooster. no tr. LIT-2, 3.

346   ECHEVERRÍA, ALFONSO (1922-   ) Chile
      Fiction
      Nausicaa. *A. Echeverría*. PRIZE, 106.

347   EDELBERG, BETINA (1930-   ) Argentina
      Poetry
      Family Album. *W. Shand*. SHA, 235.
      More Than Slow. *W. Shand*. SHA, 236.

348   EDWARDS, ALBERTO (1874-1932) Chile
      Fiction
      The Case of the Travelling Corpse. *D. Yates*. YATE, 5.

349   EDWARDS, JORGE (1931-   ) Chile
      Fiction
      After the Procession. *H. St. Martin*. LAWA, 23.
      Family orders. *J. C. Murchison*. TRI-13, 413.
      Weight-Reducing Diet. *S. Hertelendy & L. Paniagua*. HOW-1,
      374.

350   EGUREN, JOSÉ MARÍA (1882-1942) Peru
      Fiction
      La Tarda. *T. Raworth*. CARA, 319.
      Lied V. *D. D. Walsh*. FITT, 471.
      Marginal. *D. D. Walsh*. FITT, 467.
      The Girl With The Blue Lamp. *D. D. Walsh*. FITT, 467.
      The Horse. *T. Raworth*. CARA, 320.

351 EHRMAN, HANS (   ) Chile
     Other
     Theatre in Chile: A Middle-Class Conundrum (Essay). no tr.
        DR, 77.

352 EICHELBAUM, SAMUEL (1894-   ) Argentina
     Drama
     A Twentieth Century Bully (Excerpt). *D. A. Flory.* JONE-3,
        406.

353 [EISEN, W. I. pseud.]
     AISEMBERG, ISAAC
     Fiction
     Checkmate in Two Moves. *D. Yates.* YATE, 203.

354 ELIZONDO, SALVADOR (1932-   ) Mexico
     Fiction
     Bridge of Stone. *H. Carpentier.* CARP, 318.

355 ELOY BLANCO, ANDRÉS (   ) Venezuela
     Poetry
     Paint Me Little Black Angels. *H. Ruiz del Vizo.* RUIZ, 121.

356 ENRIQUETA, MARÍA (1875-?   ) Mexico
     Poetry
     Landscape. *J. R. Longland.* TRAN, 235.
     Sad Song. *A. S. Blackwell.* BLAC, 162.
     Sad Song. *I. Goldberg.* GOLD-2, 61.

357 ESCARDÓ, ROLANDO (1925-1960) Cuba
     Poetry
     Caves. *C. Beck.* BECK, 293.
     Challenge. *C. Beck.* BECK, 287.
     Death. *C. Beck.* BECK, 295.
     Feats of Balance. *C. Beck.* BECK, 297.
     Getting Out. *C. Beck.* BECK, 289.
     Island. *C. Beck.* BECK, 301.
     Meeting with the Hours. *C. Beck.* BECK, 291.
     The Valley of Giants. *C. Beck.* BECK, 285.
     Vigil. *C. Beck.* BECK, 299.

358 ESCOBAR, EDUARDO (1942-   ) Colombia
     Poetry
     Goodbye to Neruda Without Raising My Hand. *W. Barnstone.*
        LOW, 210.
     Like waterdrops that skid along the wall. *P. Blackburn.*
        CARP, 387.
     To say that I'm on the eighth floor. *P. Blackburn.* CARP,
        385.

359 ESCOBAR, FROILÁN (1944-   ) Cuba
Poetry
Worries. *T. Raworth*. TARN, 121.

360 ESCOBAR URIBE, JORGE (1886-1918) Colombia
Poetry
Fiat Lux. *W. K. Jones*. JONE-3, 100.
In the Presence of a Skull. *W. K. Jones*. JONE-3, 98.
When I Hear the Francia Waltz. *W. K. Jones*. JONE-3, 99.

361 ESCUDERO, GONZALO (1903-   ) Ecuador
Poetry
God. *D. Fitts*. FITT, 385.
The Dolmens. *D. Fitts*. FITT, 385.
Zoo. *R. O'Connell*. FITT, 387.

362 ESCUTI ORREGO, SANTIAGO (   ) Chile
Poetry
After the Duel. *A. B. Poor*. POOR, 45.

363 ESPÍN, VILMA (   ) Cuba
Other
Women in Revolutionary Cuba (Interview). *J. E. Hahner*.
HAH, 164.

364 ESPINAL, JAIME (1940-   ) Colombia
Fiction
Migraines and Phantoms. *M. Espinal*. CARP, 388.

365 ESTENGER, RAFAEL (1899-   ) Cuba
Poetry
Colloquium. *H. Ruiz del Vizo*. RUIZ, 52.

366 ESTEVES, JOSÉ DE JESÚS (   ) Puerto Rico
Poetry
To The Castilian Language. *G. Pando*. KAI, n.p.

367 ESTORINO, ABELARDO (1925-   ) Cuba
Drama
Cain's Mangoes. *J. M. Cohen*. COH-3, 115.

368 ESTRADA, GENARO (1887-1937) Mexico
Poetry
Back to the Sea. *E. W. Underwood*. UND, 141.
Lament For Lost Love. *D. D. Walsh*. FITT, 449.
Little Song In The Air. *D. D. Walsh*. FITT, 447.
Paraphrase Of Horace. *D. D. Walsh*. FITT, 451.
Other
The Colonial City (Essay from: Visionario de la Nueva Espa-
ña). *H. de Onís*. ARC, 401.
The House (Essay). *E. W. Underwood*. UND, 140.
The Colonial City: Mexico (Essay). no tr. LIT-2, 31.

56

369   ESTRADA, RAFAEL (1901–1934) Costa Rica
      Poetry
      Mexican Soldiers. *D. D. Walsh.* FITT, 171.
      Traces. *D. D. Walsh.* FITT, 171.
      Twilight. *D. D. Walsh.* FITT, 173.

370   ESTRELLA GUTIÉRREZ, FERMÍN (1900–   ) Argentina
      Poetry
      Days Of Adventure. *W. Shand.* SHA, 43.
      Solitude. *W. Shand.* SHA, 42.
      The Statue. *W. Shand.* SHA, 43.
      Time Asleep. *W. Shand.* SHA, 43.

371   ESTUPIÑAN BASS, NELSON (   ) Ecuador
      Poetry
      A Candle for Pablo. *L. Veltfort.* LOW, 69.

372   FABBRI, TECLA (   ) Brazil
      (Joint author. See also CARI, TERESA and LOPES, MARIA.)
      Other
      To the Young Seamstresses of São Paulo (Newspaper article).
        J. E. Hahner. HAH, 114.

373   FÁBREGA, DEMETRIO (1881–1932) Panama
      Poetry
      The Idyl of the Mountain. *A. S. Blackwell.* BLAC, 524.

374   FÁBREGA, DEMETRIO J. (1932–   ) Panama
      Poetry
      Book of the Reluctant Lady (Excerpt). no tr. YOU, 103.

375   FABREGAS, ELBA (1922–   ) Argentina
      Poetry
      Demented Stone. *D. Flakoll & C. Alegría.* FLAK, 171.

376   FARIA, JOSÉ ESCOBAR (1914–   ) Brazil
      Poetry
      The Street. *L. S. Downes.* DOWN, 60.

377   FARIAS DE ISSASI, TERESA (   ) Mexico
      Drama
      The Sentence of Death. *L. Saunders.* SHAY, 275.

378   FARIÑA NÚÑEZ, ELOY (1885–1925) Paraguay
      Poetry
      The Serpent. *W. K. Jones.* JONE-3, 137.

379   FAUSTINO, MÁRIO (1930–   ) Brazil
      Poetry
      A Life All Of Words. *M. Cardozo.* NEI, 165.
      Fragment. *M. Cardozo.* NEI, 169.

(FAUSTINO, MÁRIO)
The World I Vanquished Gave Me A Love. *F. P. Hepplethwaite.*
YOU, 26.
This Month I Feel Will See Me Dead. *M. Cardozo.* NEI, 167.

380 FEIJÓO, SAMUEL (1914–   ) Cuba
Poetry
At the Bedside of a Sick Comrade. *C. Beck.* BECK, 151.
Dinner at the State Farm. *C. Beck.* BECK, 153.
On The Death By Fire Of Gladys, The Girl Of The Canaries.
A. Kerrigan. TARN, 23.
Simple. *A. Boyer.* BECK, 147.
Since We Are Many. *C. Beck.* BECK, 155.
The Song of Man Facing Death. *A. Boyer.* BECK, 149.
The Song Of The Man At Death. *T. Raworth.* TARN, 25.
Trip to the Trenches I. *A. Boyer.* BECK, 143.
Trip to the Trenches II. *A. Boyer.* BECK, 145.
Visit to the Trenches. *C. Beck.* BECK, 157.
Fiction
Soldier Eloy. no tr. CARZ, 33.

381 FERIA, LINA DE (1945–   ) Cuba
Poetry
'When My Old Age.' *T. Raworth.* TARN, 131.
'When My Papers.' *A. Kerrigan.* TARN, 133.

382 FERNÁNDEZ, PABLO ARMANDO (1930–   ) Cuba
Poetry
A Peasant Girl Calls Her Yeye Cari (from: The Book of
Heroes). *J. M. Cohen.* COH-3, 87.
Abel Reflects. *J. Gibson & C. Middleton.* BECK, 407.
Abel Reflects. *J. Gibson, A. Boyars & C. Middleton.* COH-1,
234.
'Barracks and nets' (Excerpt). *M. Randall.* BOLD, 458.
Barracks and nets (Excerpt). *M. Randall.* TRI-13, 115.
Birth Of Eggo. *N. Tarn.* TARN, 45.
Denunciation. *J. Gibson & C. Middleton.* BECK, 409.
Denunciation. *J. Gibson, A. Boyars & C. Middleton.* COH-1,
234.
Epiphany. *A. Boyars & C. Middleton.* BECK, 393.
From Man to Death. *J. Gibson.* BECK, 411.
From Man To Death. *T. Reynolds.* TARN, 51.
Goodness Does Not Abide in Me. *R. Llopis.* BECK, 399.
Islands. *T. Reynolds.* TARN, 49.
July 26, 1959. *J. M. Cohen.* BOLD, 459.
July 26, 1959 (from: The Book of Heroes). *J. M. Cohen.*
COH-3, 86.
Meditation and Elegy of the Poet Raoul. *J. Gibson &
C. Middleton.* BECK, 403.
Modulor. *C. Beck.* BECK, 401.
Origin of Eggo. *C. Middleton.* BECK, 395.

Origin of Eggo. *J. Gibson, A. Boyars & C. Middleton.*
COH-1, 233.
Surrender of Eshu. *N. Tarn.* TARN, 47.
The Heroes. *J. Hill.* CARA, 221.
The Surrender of Eshu. *C. Beck.* BECK, 397.
Trajan. *J. Hill.* CARA, 220.
Twelve. *J. Gibson & C. Middleton.* BECK, 405.
Twelve (from: The Book of Heroes). *J. M. Cohen.* COH-3, 86.

383 FERNÁNDEZ CHERICIÁN, DAVID (1940-   ) Cuba
Poetry
A Song of Peace. *C. Beck.* BECK, 727.
A Song of Peace. no tr. MARQ, 195.
Camagüey, 30 November 1966. *D. Gardner.* TARN, 101.
Classified Section. *R. Márquez.* MARQ, 191.
Inventory. *D. Gardner.* TARN, 99.
On The Third World. *R. Márquez.* MARQ, 193.
Tree and Then Forest. *R. Llopis.* BECK, 733.

384 FERNÁNDEZ GRANADOS, ENRIQUE (1862-1920) Mexico
Poetry
Remembrance. *A. S. Blackwell.* BLAC, 128.
To Some Violets. *A. S. Blackwell.* BLAC, 126.
To Some Violets. *A. S. Blackwell.* GOLD-2, 32.
Wine Of Lesbos. *E. W. Underwood.* UND, 43.

385 FERNÁNDEZ MORENO, BALDOMERO (1886-1950) Argentina
Poetry
Dalmira. *T. Raworth.* CARA, 18.
Return. *P. Gannon.* GAN, 31.
Seventy Balconies and Not A Single Flower. *D. J. Flakoll &*
C. Alegría. BENE, 27.
Sonnet. *T. Raworth.* CARA, 18.

386 FERNÁNDEZ MORENO, CÉSAR (1919-   ) Argentina
Poetry
Life. *W. Shand.* SHA, 144.
The Island. *W. Shand.* SHA, 143.

387 FERNÁNDEZ RETAMAR, ROBERTO (1930-   ) Cuba
Poetry
A Man And A Woman. *T. Reynolds.* TARN, 59.
Adoration Of The Kings. *J. M. Cohen.* COH-3, 35.
Being Asked About The Persians. *N. Tarn.* TARN, 61.
Epitaph for an Invader. *R. Márquez.* MARQ, 179.
For an Instant. *A. Boyer.* BECK, 375.
From the Vedado, a Cuban writes to a decidedly European
friend. *T. Reynolds.* TRI-13, 141.
Girls and Boys, Young Ladies and Gentlemen. *D. J. Flakoll &*
C. Alegría. BENE, 119.
Homeland. *A. Boyer.* BECK, 377.

(FERNÁNDEZ RETAMAR, ROBERTO)
Homeland. *J. Hill.* CARA, 218.
How Lucky They Are, The Normal Ones. *T. Reynolds.* TARN, 59.
It Would Be Nice To Deserve This Epitaph. *R. Márquez.* MARQ, 185.
It's Better to Light a Candle than to Curse the Darkness. *R. Márquez & M. Randall.* MARQ, 183.
Last Station of the Ruins. *A. Boyer.* BECK, 365.
Night Stroll. *A. Boyer.* BECK, 369.
No Word Does You Justice. *A. Boyer.* BECK, 373.
Of Reality. *J. M. Cohen.* COH-3, 35.
Sonata for Surviving Those Days & Piano. *T. Reynolds.* CARP, 359.
The Other. *A. Boyer.* BECK, 363.
The other. *T. Reynolds.* TRI-13, 140.
The Uglies. *T. Reynolds.* CARP, 363.
To Whom It May Concern. *A. Boyer.* BECK, 385.
Today's Poem. *J. Hill.* CARA, 218.
We Do Well to Remember. *R. Márquez.* MARQ, 181.
With the Same Hands. *A. Boyer.* BECK, 371.
You Were Right, Tallet: We Are Men of Transition. *A. Boyer.* BECK, 379.
You Were Right, Tallet: We Are Transitional People. *T. Reynolds.* CARP, 365.
Other
Caliban: Notes Toward A Discussion Of Culture In Our America (Essay). *L. Garafola, D. A. McMurray & R. Márquez.* MR, 7.

388   FERNÁNDEZ SIMÓ, ALFREDO (1915-   ) Dominican Republic
Poetry
Poem I. *F. E. Townsend.* TOWN, 75.
Poem 6. *F. E. Townsend.* TOWN, 74.

389   FERRARI AMORES, ALFONSO (   ) Argentina
Fiction
A Scrap of Tinfoil. *D. Yates.* YATE, 123.

390   FERRARO, ARIEL (1925-   ) Argentina
Poetry
Birth Of Art. *W. Shand.* SHA, 193.
Tree By The Side Of Men. *W. Shand.* SHA, 194.

391   FERREIRA, BUARQUE DE HOLLANDA AURÉLIO (1910-   ) Brazil
Fiction
My Father's Hat. *W. L. Grossman.* GRO, 107.

392   FERREIRA LÓPEZ, RAMÓN (1921-   ) Cuba
Fiction
Dream With No Name. *P. Blackburn.* PRIZE, 360.

393 FERREIRO, ADOLFO (   ) Paraguay
　　　Poetry
　　　Early morning memory. *J. Upton*. TRI-13, 289.
　　　Masquerade. *J. Upton*. TRI-13, 290.

394 FERRER, JOSÉ MIGUEL (1903-   ) Venezuela
　　　Poetry
　　　Nocturne Of Sin And Its Accusation. *R. O'Connell*. FITT,
　　　　391.

395 FERRETIS, JORGE (1902-   ) Mexico
　　　Fiction
　　　The Failure. *H. Kurz*. HAYDN, 898.

396 FERREYRA BASSO, JUAN G. (1910-   ) Argentina
　　　Poetry
　　　Epistle. *W. Shand*. SHA, 97.
　　　The Fallen Horseman. *W. Shand*. SHA, 95.

397 FIALLO, FABIO S. (1866-1942) Dominican Republic
　　　Poetry
　　　Broken Wings. *A. S. Blackwell*. BLAC, 508.
　　　Broken Wings. *A. S. Blackwell*. RES, 68.
　　　Forever. *F. E. Townsend*. TOWN, 28.
　　　Her Name Was Belkis. *F. E. Townsend*. TOWN, 54.
　　　In the Churchyard. *F. E. Townsend*. TOWN, 29.
　　　Nostalgia. *M. Lee*. JONE-3, 67.
　　　Nostalgia. *M. Lee*. WALS, 591.
　　　The Bells Ring "Gloria." *A. S. Blackwell*. BLAC, 506.
　　　The Roses of My Rose Tree. *A. S. Blackwell*. BLAC, 502.
　　　Would I Were Thy Mirror. *A. S. Blackwell*. BLAC, 502.
　　　Fiction
　　　The Marble Bust (from: Fragile Tales). no tr. LIEB, 948.

398 FIGUEIRA, GASTÓN (1905-   ) Uruguay
　　　Poetry
　　　Ballad of Life. *W. K. Jones*. JONE-3, 180.
　　　Ballad Of Life. *W. K. Jones*. MILL, 263.
　　　I Believe in You, Pan America. *D. M. Tercero*. LIT-1, 34.
　　　I Believe In You, Pan America. *D. M. Tercero*. LIT-2, 5.
　　　Maracatu (an Afro-Brazilian street dance). *W. K. Jones*.
　　　　JONE-3, 181.
　　　Prayer to the Moon of the Tropics. *W. K. Jones*. JONE-3,
　　　　181.
　　　The Pineapple. *W. K. Jones*. JONE-3, 184.
　　　The Pineapple (from: "For the Children of America").
　　　　W. K. Jones. MILL, 264.
　　　The Southern Cross. *A. S. Blackwell*. JONE-3, 183.

399 FIGUEROA, EDWIN (1925-   ) Puerto Rico
　　　Fiction
　　　Salón Boricua (Excerpt). *P. Vallés*. KAI, n.p.

400 FINOT, ENRIQUE (1891-   ) Bolivia
Other
Gabriel René-Moreno, A Great Bolivian Writer (1834-1908).
    no tr. LIT-1, 10.

401 FISCHER, ALMEIDA (1916-   ) Brazil
Fiction
The Island. *R. W. Horton.* COEL, 23.

402 FLORES, MARCO ANTONIO (1937-   ) Guatemala
Poetry
Goodbye To The Man I Was. *E. Dorn & G. Brotherston.* DORN,
    n.p.
Havanna 59. *R. Márquez.* MARQ, 287.
Havanna 1959. *E. Dorn & G. Brotherston.* DORN, n.p.
Mother. *R. Márquez.* MARQ, 283.
On Jail. *R. Márquez.* MARQ, 275.
Otto René The Poet. *E. Dorn & G. Brotherston.* DORN, n.p.
Requiem For Luis Augusto. *E. Dorn & G. Brotherston.* DORN,
    n.p.

403 FLORES, R. (   ) Puerto Rico
Poetry
Cocktail. Originally Engl. MR, 279.

404 FLÓREZ, JULIO (1867-1923) Colombia
Poetry
Danger. *A. S. Blackwell.* BLAC, 418.
Hymn To Aurora. *T. Walsh.* WALS, 687.
Love's Messages. *A. S. Blackwell.* BLAC, 416.

405 FLORIT, EUGENIO (1903-   ) Cuba
Poetry
Acquarium. *H. R. Hays.* HAYS, 109.
Atlantic. *H. R. Hays.* HAYS, 105.
Death In The Sun. *H. R. Hays.* HAYS, 115.
Elegy For Your Absence. *H. R. Hays.* HAYS, 99.
Nocturne. *H. R. Hays.* HAYS, 97.
On Someone's Death. *M. Lee.* FITT, 31.
Stanzas to a Statue. *J. Hill.* CARA, 203.
Strophes To A Statue. *D. D. Walsh.* FITT, 35.
The Baby Girl. *D. D. Walsh.* FITT, 29.
The Dead Nereid. *H. R. Hays.* HAYS, 101.
The Martyrdom Of Saint Sebastian. *D. D. Walsh.* FITT, 33.
The Present Evening. *H. R. Hays.* HAYS, 111.
The Signal. *H. R. Hays.* HAYS, 111.
To the Dead Butterfly. *J. Hill.* CARA, 204.
To The Dead Butterfly. *R. O'Connell.* FITT, 31.

406 FOMBONA PACHANO, JACINTO (1901-1951) Venezuela
       Poetry
       A Warning For Abraham Lincoln. *A. Flores.* FITT, 281.
       America, My Sweet. *H. R. Hays.* HAYS, 313.
       Dance Of The Lost Key. *H. R. Hays.* HAYS, 321.
       Death Over The Air. *A. Flores.* FITT, 283.
       I Announce The Kingdom Of The Star. *H. R. Hays.* HAYS, 325.
       I Announce the Kingdom of the Star. *H. R. Hays.* JONE-3,
         101.
       Since Tomorrow Is Sunday. *H. R. Hays.* HAYS, 307.
       The Clouds Have Already Told Me. *H. R. Hays.* HAYS, 317.
       The Coca Tree. *H. R. Hays.* HAYS, 303.
       The Complaint. *H. R. Hays.* HAYS, 311.
       The Puddle. *H. R. Hays.* HAYS, 305.
       While I Sang My Song. *A. Flores.* FITT, 287.

407 FRAIRE, ISABEL (1936-   ) Mexico
       Poetry
       A Re-encounter With What Was Believed Lost. *A. Edkins.*
         MU-69, 123.
       The dunes. *T. Reynolds.* TRI-13, 332.
       "This was in the time...." *T. Reynolds.* TRI-13, 333.
       8 1/2. *T. Reynolds.* MU-69, 123.

408 FRANCO, JOSÉ (1931-   ) Panama
       Poetry
       "Elegía a Griselda Almar" (Excerpt). no tr. YOU, 101.
       Land of Pain and Weeping (Excerpt). no tr. YOU, 102.

409 FRANCO, LUIS L. (1898-   ) Argentina
       Poetry
       Goat-Pen. *A. Fife.* FIFE, 65.
       Goat-Pen. *M. Lee.* FITT, 203.
       Song Of The Hungry Children. *W. Shand.* SHA, 20.

410 FRANK, MIGUEL (1920-   ) Chile
       Drama
       The Man of the Century. *W. K. Jones.* JONE-1, 113.

411 FRAU, ANTONIO OLIVER (1902-1945)   Puerto Rico
       Fiction
       The Red Seed. *B. Luby.* BABI, 355.

412 FRÍAS, JOSÉ D. (1891-1936) Mexico
       Poetry
       Sonata of Beethoven. *E. W. Underwood.* UND, 143.

413 FROTA, LÉLIA COELHO (1937-   ) Brazil
       Poetry
       Little Barcarole. *F. P. Hebblethwaite.* YOU, 22.

414   FRUGONI, EMILIO   (1880-1969)   Uruguay
      Poetry
      Adventure. *M. González*. CARA, 363.
      The Circle. *M. González*. CARA, 362.

   FUENTE BENAVIDES, RAFAEL DE LA. See [ADÁN, MARTÍN pseud.].

415   FUENTES, CARLOS   (1929-   )   Mexico
      Fiction
      Aura. *L. Kemp*. COH-1, 107.
      Deed. *G. McWhirter*. MU-70, 26.
      Holy Place. *S. J. Levine*. FUEN, 5.
      The Cost Of Living. *A. Austin*. LAWA, 121.
      The Life Line (from: La región más transparente). *L. Kemp*.
         EVER, 75.
      The Doll Queen. *M. S. Peden*. MANC, 259.
      The doll queen. *A. Moncy*. TRI-15, 264.
      The Life Line. *L. Kemp*. MILL, 265.
      The Two Elenas. *L. Mades*. HOW-1, 364.

416   FUENTES, JOSÉ LORENZO   (1928-   )   Cuba
      Fiction
      Señor García. no tr. CARZ, 105.

417   FUENTES, NORBERTO   (1943-   )   Cuba
      Fiction
      Captain Descalzo. *T. Reynolds*. CARP, 400.
      Capitán Descalzo. *V. Ortiz*. LAWA, 145.
      For The Night. *T. Reynolds*. CARP, 404.
      Honor Cleaned. *V. Ortiz*. MANC, 405.
      Order #13. *T. Reynolds*. CARP, 406.
      Share and Share Alike. *V. Ortiz*. LAWA, 155.

418   FULLEDA LEÓN, GERARDO   (1942-   )   Cuba
      Poetry
      A Man. *E. Randall*. TARN, 109.

419   FUTORANSKY, LUISA   (1939-   )   Argentina
      Poetry
      The Roles Of Orpheus And Eurydice. *W. Shand*. SHA, 272.
      Twenty Years Since Auschwitz, Bergen-Belsen And The Others.
         W. Shand. SHA, 273.

420   GALLEGOS, RÓMULO   (1884-1969)   Venezuela
      Fiction
      A Man of Character. *J. C. MacLean*. ONIS-2, 226.
      Doña Bárbara (Excerpt). *R. Malloy*. JONE-3, 218.
      Peace on High. *H. St. Martin*. MANC, 61.
      Poor Nigger (Excerpt). *H. de Onís*. ARC, 467.
      Poor Nigger (Excerpt). *H. de Onís*. ONIS-1, 280.
      The Devil's Twilight. *G. M. Molinari*. HOW-1, 67.

421 GALTIER, LYSANDRO Z. D. (1902-   ) Argentina
    Poetry
    The Part Of The Darkness. *W. Shand.* SHA, 52.
    Through The Labyrinth. *W. Shand.* SHA, 51.

422 GÁLVEZ, JOSÉ (1885-?) Peru
    Other
    Arequipa and Lake Titicaca (Essay). no tr. LIT-2, 40.

423 GÁMBARO, GRISELDA (1928-   ) Argentina
    Drama
    The Camp. *W. I. Oliver.* OLIV, 47.

424 GAMBOA, FEDERICO (1864-?) Mexico
    Fiction
    Suprema Ley (Excerpts). *F. Starr.* STAR, 408.

425 GAMBOA, JOSÉ JOAQUÍN (1878-1931) Mexico
    Drama
    An Old Yarn. *W. K. Jones.* JONE-3, 430.
    An Old Yarn. *W. K. Jones.* JONE-4, 70.

426 GANDÍA, ZENO (1855-1930) Puerto Rico
    Fiction
    The Redeemers (Excerpt). *B. Luby.* BABI, 103.

427 GARCÍA, FATHER DAVID (   ) Puerto Rico
    Other
    Mass Of The People, Church Of Saint Mark's In The Bowery
       (Mass). *M. C. López Kelly.* BABI, 469.
    Order For Holy Matrimony, Church Of Saint Mark's In The
       Bowery (Church ritual). *M. C. López Kelly.* BABI, 475.
    Psalm 5, Listen To My Protest. *M. C. López Kelly.* BABI,
       477.
    Psalm 21, Why Have You Forgotten Me? *M. C. López Kelly.*
       BABI, 478.

428 GARCÍA CALDERÓN, VENTURA (1887-1960) Peru
    Fiction
    The Lottery Ticket. *R. Phibbs.* HAYDN, 912.
    The Pin. *H. de Onís.* ONIS-1, 249.

429 GARCÍA MÁRQUEZ, GABRIEL (1928-   ) Colombia
    Fiction
    Balthazar's Marvellous Afternoon. *J. S. Bernstein.* LAWA,
       163.
    Balthazar's Marvelous Afternoon. *J. S. Bernstein.* CARP,
       258.
    Balthazar's Marvelous Afternoon. *J. S. Bernstein.* MANC,
       281.
    Isabel's Soliloquy: Watching the Rain in Macondo.
       R. Southern. FRA-J, 67.

(GARCÍA MÁRQUEZ, GABRIEL)
  The Day After Saturday. *J. Franco*. COH-1, 182.
  The Handsomest Drowned Man in the World. *G. Rabassa*.
    HOW-1, 351.
  Tuesday Siesta. *J. S. Bernstein*. MILL, 290.
  Tuesday siesta. *J. S. Bernstein*. TRI-13, 209.

430 GARCÍA MARRUZ, FINA (1923-   ) Cuba
     Poetry
     Noon. *T. Raworth*. TARN, 39.

431 GARCÍA MORALES, LUIS (1930-   ) Venezuela
     Poetry
     Always. *T. Hoeksema*. MU-73, 59.
     Now. *T. Hoeksema*. MU-73, 57.
     Return. *R. Schulte*. MU-73, 53.
     This Melody. *T. Hoeksema*. MU-73, 57.
     Trial By Fire. *T. Hoeksema*. MU-73, 61.

432 GARCÍA ROBLES, VÍCTOR (1933-   ) Argentina
     Poetry
     Know Ye What Happens Amidst Copious Tears and with Four-
       Letter Words. *L. E. Yglesias*. MARQ, 63.

433 GARCÍA SARAVÍ, GUSTAVO (1920-   ) Argentina
     Poetry
     Gratefulness. *W. Shand*. SHA, 152.
     This Morning I Discovered.... *W. Shand*. SHA, 151.

434 GARCÍA TERRÉS, JAIME (1924-   ) Mexico
     Poetry
     Debate. *P. Blackburn*. EVER, 89.
     Ipanema. *W. S. Merwin*. PAZ-2, 91.
     The Park At Montsouris: A Savage Elegy. *P. Blackburn*.
       EVER, 87.

435 GARIBAY, RICARDO (   ) Chile
     Other
     Pablo Neruda's Funeral (Eyewitness account). *M. Schoijet*.
       LOW, 93.

436 GARRIDO, VÍCTOR (1919-   ) Dominican Republic
     Poetry
     Pax. *F. E. Townsend*. TOWN, 40.

437 GARRO, ELENA (1920-   ) Mexico
     Drama
     A Solid Home. *F. Colecchia & J. Matas*. COLE, 35.
     A Solid House. *K. Kemp*. EVER, 62.

   GARVAJAL, MARÍA ISABEL. See [LYRA, CARMEN pseud.].

438 GAUTIER-BENÍTEZ, JOSÉ (1850–1880) Puerto Rico
       Poetry
       Poem Of Puerto Rico. *B. Luby*. BABI, 89.
       Porto Rico. *A. S. Blackwell*. BLAC, 516.
       Puerto Rico. *W. K. Jones*. JONE-2, 243.
       Return. *B. Luby*. BABI, 92.

439 GELMÁN, JUAN (1930–   ) Argentina
       Poetry
       Algiers. *E. Randall & R. Márquez*. MARQ, 57.
       Better. no tr. YOU, 13.
       Customs. *H. St. Martin*. CARP, 397.
       Dawn. *W. Shand*. SHA, 239.
       Deeds. *J. Brof*. CARP, 399.
       Epochs. *E. Randall & R. Márquez*. MARQ, 55.
       Eyes. *E. Randall & R. Márquez*. MARQ, 53.
       History. *R. Márquez*. MARQ, 59.
       In The Letter File. *W. Shand*. SHA, 239.
       Poem V. *W. Shand*. SHA, 237.
       Poetic Art. *W. Shand*. SHA, 238.
       The Game We Play. *J. Brof*. CARP, 397.
       The Guest. *W. Shand*. SHA, 238.
       The Heartache And Thousand Natural Shocks. *R. Márquez*.
         MR, 120.
       The Victory. *D. J. Flakoll & C. Alegría*. BENE, 123.
       theory re daniela rocca. *P. Morgan*. TRI-13, 251.
       Victory. *J. Brof*. CARP, 399.

440 GERCHUNOFF, ALBERTO (1883–1950) Argentina
       Fiction
       The Owl. *W. E. Colford*. COLF, 92.
       The Owl. *H. de Onís*. ONIS-1, 210.

441 GHIRALDO, ALBERTO (1874–1946) Argentina
       Poetry
       For Thee. *A. S. Blackwell*. BLAC, 338.

442 GIANNUZZI, JOAQUÍN O. (1924–   ) Argentina
       Poetry
       All This Ends. *W. Shand*. SHA, 186.
       Epitaph. *W. Shand*. SHA, 185.

443 GIMINEZ PASTOR, ARTHUR (   ) Argentina
       Poetry
       Homage to Darío. *A. B. Poor*. POOR, 67.

444 GIRÓ, VALENTÍN (1883–1949) Dominican Republic
       Poetry
       The Timorous Nymph. *F. E. Townsend*. TOWN, 86.
       To a Farmer. *F. E. Townsend*. TOWN, 83.

445 GIRONDO, OLIVERIO (1891-1965) Argentina
Poetry
Café-Concert. *T. Raworth*. CARA, 22.
Las Sierpes Street. *M. B. Davis*. FITT, 443.
Scarecrow (Excerpt). *T. Raworth*. CARA, 23.

446 GIRRI, ALBERTO (1918-) Argentina
Poetry
A Metaphor. *C. Maurer*. CHI, 161.
Alternatives, Complements. *W. Shand*. SHA, 148.
Epistle To Hieronymus Bosch. *J. M. Cohen*. COH-1, 141.
Everyone Is Job. *W. Shand*. SHA, 147.
Mutation. *T. Raworth*. CARA, 41.
Rhetoric Variations. *W. Shand*. SHA, 149.
Sperlonga. *T. Raworth*. CARA, 42.
The Necessary Condition. *W. Shand*. SHA, 145.
To A City, Suddenly Considered From A Certain Angle.
    C. Maurer. CHI, 155.
To The Brotherhood Of Wise Men. *C. Maurer*. CHI, 157.
Until The Dawn. *C. Maurer*. CHI, 159.

447 GÓMEZ DE READ, ERNESTINA (   ) Dominican Republic
Poetry
Communion. *F. E. Townsend*. TOWN, 80.
To My Beloved. *F. E. Townsend*. TOWN, 82.

448 GÓMEZ JAIME, ALFREDO (1878-?) Colombia
Poetry
A Sketch. *A. S. Blackwell*. BLAC, 420.
Problem. *M. Lee*. LIT-2, 28.

449 GÓMEZ KEMP, VICENTE (   ) Cuba
Poetry
Sharp Song. *H. Ruiz del Vizo*. RUIZ, 33.

450 GÓMEZ P., CLEMENCIA DAMIRON (   ) Dominican Republic
Poetry
Son of Mine. *F. E. Townsend*. TOWN, 64.

451 GÓMEZ RESTREPO, ANTONIO (1869-?) Colombia
Poetry
Eyes. *T. Walsh*. WALS, 619.
The Generalife. *T. Walsh*. WALS, 621.
Toledo. *T. Walsh*. WALS, 620.
Other
Gonzalo Jiménez de Quesada, Founder of Bogotá. no tr.
    LIT-1, 31.

452 GÓMEZ SANJURJO, JOSÉ MARÍA (1930-) Paraguay
Poetry
"I cannot find...." *J. Upton*. TRI-13, 288.
"If the breeze today." *J. Upton*. TRI-13, 289.

453 GONÇALVES DIAS, ANTONIO (1823-1864) Brazil
Poetry
Bed of Green Leaves. *P. Standish.* CARA, 53.
For a Birthday. *P. Standish.* CARA, 55.

454 GÓNGORA, HELCÍAS MARTÁN (1922-   ) Colombia
Poetry
Negro. *H. Ruiz del Vizo.* RUIZ, 101.
Negro Rhythm. *H. Ruiz del Vizo.* RUIZ, 100.

455 GONZÁLEZ ALLER, FAUSTINO (   ) Cuba
Fiction
The Yoke. *I. A. Langnas.* PRIZE, 201.

456 GONZALES OBREGÓN, LUIS (1865-?) Mexico
Other
Changes in Mexico. *F. Starr.* STAR, 120.
Luisa Martínez. *F. Starr.* STAR, 123.
Sor Juana Inés de la Cruz. *F. Starr.* STAR, 124.
The Inquisition. *F. Starr.* STAR, 128.

457 GONZÁLEZ, ANA H. (   ) Cuba
Poetry
Black Ballad Of The Negro. *H. Ruiz del Vizo.* RUIZ, 83.

458 GONZÁLEZ, ANISIA MERUELO (   ) Cuba
Poetry
Portrait From Havana. *H. Ruiz del Vizo.* RUIZ, 78.

459 GONZÁLEZ, JOSÉ LUIS (1926-   ) Puerto Rico
Fiction
The Letter. *B. Luby.* BABI, 368.
There's a Little Colored Boy in the Bottom of the Water.
   L. Kemp. KAI, n.p.

460 GONZÁLEZ, OTTO RAÚL (1921-   ) Guatemala
Poetry
To the Scavenger. *D. Flakoll & C. Alegría.* FLAK, 80.

461 GONZÁLEZ, REINALDO (1940-   ) Cuba
Fiction
Four in a Jeep. *J. Franco.* COH-3, 175.
Honey for New Year's. no tr. CARZ, 215.

462 GONZÁLEZ B., JORGE (1879-?) Chile
Poetry
To the Old Guitar. *A. S. Blackwell.* BLAC, 306.

463 GONZÁLEZ DE CASCORRO, RAÚL (1922-   ) Cuba
Fiction
The return of the pimp. no tr. CARZ, 157.

464   GONZÁLEZ GUERRERO, FRANCISCO (   ) Mexico
       Poetry
       Apparition. *E. W. Underwood.* UND, 145.
       Fountain. *E. Roach.* CRAN, 97.
       Fountain. *E. W. Underwood.* UND, 146.

465   GONZÁLEZ LANUZA, EDUARDO (1900-   ) Argentina
       Poetry
       Poem for a gramophone record. *H. Manning.* GAN, 63.
       Voices. *W. Shand.* SHA, 44.
       Why? *W. Shand.* SHA, 45.

466   GONZÁLEZ LEÓN, ADRIANO (1931-   ) Venezuela
       Fiction
       The Rainbow. *H. R. Hays.* CARP, 272.
       Drama
       Imagen de Caracas (Fragment of Text). *C. Rennert.* DR, 136.

467   GONZÁLEZ LEÓN, FRANCISCO (1868?-1945) Mexico
       Poetry
       Hours. *S. Beckett.* PAZ-1, 146.

468   GONZÁLEZ MARTÍNEZ, ENRIQUE (1871-1952) Mexico
       Poetry
       A Hidden Spring. *A. S. Blackwell.* BLAC, 104.
       A Hidden Spring. *A. S. Blackwell.* GOLD-2, 59.
       A Spectre. *M. González.* CARA, 255.
       Afternoon in the Country. *G. D. Craig.* CRAI, 151.
       As Sister And Brother. *M. E. Johnson.* JOHN, 119.
       Change. *E. W. Underwood.* UND, 54.
       Do You Recall? *M. E. Johnson.* JOHN, 115.
       Do You Remember? *A. S. Blackwell.* BLAC, 114.
       Homesick Memory. *E. W. Underwood.* UND, 51.
       House With Two Doors. *S. Beckett.* PAZ-1, 162.
       House With Two Doors. *E. W. Underwood.* UND, 48.
       In a Stately Garden. *E. du Gué Trapier.* TRAN, 233.
       Last Journey. *S. Beckett.* PAZ-1, 168.
       Life Escapes Me. *G. D. Craig.* CRAI, 147.
       Like Brother and Sister. *A. S. Blackwell.* BLAC, 106.
       Like Brother and Sister. *A. S. Blackwell.* GOLD-2, 55.
       My Grief Is A Rosebush Always In Flower.... *E. W. Under-
         wood.* UND, 52.
       Noli Me Tangere. *E. W. Underwood.* UND. 56.
       Pain. *S. Beckett.* PAZ-1, 163.
       Pity That Passes. *G. D. Craig.* CRAI, 149.
       Plus Ultra. *M. González.* CARA, 256.
       Romance of the Living Corpse. *S. Beckett.* PAZ-1, 166.
       Sower Of Stars. *A. S. Blackwell.* GOLD-2, 57.
       The Ballad of Mad Fortune. *E. W. Underwood.* RES, 72.
       The Ballad Of Mad Fortune. *E. W. Underwood.* UND, 55.
       The Captive. *E. W. Underwood.* UND, 47.
       The Castle. *A. S. Blackwell.* GOLD-2, 58.

The Condemned. *S. Beckett.* PAZ-1, 163.
The Dead Rebel. *A. S. Blackwell.* BLAC, 116.
The Dead Rebel. *A. S. Blackwell.* LIT-1, 71.
The Enclosed Garden. *J. M. Cohen.* COH-2, 341.
The Fountain. *E. W. Underwood.* UND, 54.
The Grief Of Autumn. *E. W. Underwood.* UND, 46.
The Impossible Return. *M. E. Johnson.* JOHN, 123.
The Prayer of the Barren Rock. *A. S. Blackwell.* BLAC, 102.
The Prayer of the Barren Rock. *J. P. Rice.* JONE-3, 41.
The Prayer Of The Barren Rock. *J. P. Rice.* WALS, 641.
The Sower of Stars. *A. S. Blackwell.* BLAC, 100.
The Sower of Stars. *A. S. Blackwell.* LIT-1, 72.
The Sower of Stars. *A. S. Blackwell.* LIT-2, 53.
The Swan. *R. Bly & P. Blackburn.* SIX60-4, 3.
The Useless Voyage. *E. W. Underwood.* UND, 54.
The Voice Of Long Ago. *E. W. Underwood.* UND, 53.
Then Twist The Neck Of This Delusive Swan. *J. P. Bishop.* FITT, ix.
Three Birds. *A. S. Blackwell.* BLAC, 110.
Throttle The Swan. *M. Lee.* WALS, 640.
To a Stone by the Wayside. *A. S. Blackwell.* BLAC, 108.
To the Spirit of the Tree. *A. S. Blackwell.* BLAC, 112.
To the Traveller. *A. S. Blackwell.* BLAC, 116.
Tomorrow. *C. M. Hutchings.* JONE-3, 42.
Tomorrow poets will sing. *G. D. Craig.* CRAI, 149.
Twist the Neck of the Swan. *R. Bain.* JONE-3, 41.
Useless Days. *E. W. Underwood.* UND, 50.
When It Is Given You To Find A Smile. *S. Beckett.* PAZ-1, 161.
When You Know How To Find A Smile. *M. E. Johnson.* JOHN, 117.
Wring the neck of the swan. *G. D. Craig.* CRAI, 147.
Wring The Neck Of The Swan. *M. E. Johnson.* JOHN, 115.
Wring the Neck of the Swan. *G. D. Craig.* RES, 70.
Wring the Swan's Neck. *S. Beckett.* PAZ-1, 160.

469   GONZÁLEZ ROJO, ENRIQUE (1899-1939) Mexico
      Poetry
      Naked Woman. *E. W. Underwood.* UND, 99.
      Stones. *E. W. Underwood.* UND, 100.
      The Midday Sea. *E. W. Underwood.* UND, 98.

470   GONZÁLEZ SANTANA, JOAQUÍN (1938-   ) Cuba
      Poetry
      Cerro, My Neighborhood. *A. Romeo.* BECK, 703.
      Grandfather Rufino. *A. Romeo.* BECK, 699.
      So That Kisses Do Not Die, As Always. *A. Romeo.* BECK, 701.
      This Divine Will of the People. *A. Romeo.* BECK, 697.

471 GONZÁLEZ TUÑÓN, RAÚL (1905-   ) Argentina
Poetry
Red Light District Of Barcelona. *W. Shand.* SHA, 75.
The Old Cathedrals. *W. Shand.* SHA, 73.
The Poet Died At Dawn. *W. Shand.* SHA, 72.

472 GONZÁLEZ Y CONTRERAS, GILBERTO (1904-   ) El Salvador
Poetry
Church. *D. Fitts.* FITT, 197.
Heat. *D. Fitts.* FITT, 197.

473 GONZÁLEZ ZELEDÓN, MANUEL (1864-1936) Costa Rica
Fiction
The Two Musicians. no tr. LIT-1, 33.
The Two Musicians (from: La Propia). no tr. LIT-2, 16.

474 GORDILLO CERVANTES, FERNANDO (1940-1967) Nicaragua
Poetry
A dead youth. *E. Dorn & G. Brotherston.* BOLD, 502.
A Dead Youth. *E. Dorn & G. Brotherston.* DORN, n.p.
Andrés. *E. Dorn & G. Brotherston.* DORN, n.p.
Now you know he died. *E. Dorn & G. Brotherston.* BOLD, 503.
Now You Know He Died. *E. Dorn & G. Brotherston.* DORN, n.p.
The dead. *E. Dorn & G. Brotherston.* BOLD, 503.
The Dead. *E. Dorn & G. Brotherston.* DORN, n.p.
The price of a country. *E. Dorn & G. Brotherston.* BOLD,
502.
The Price of a Country. *E. Dorn & G. Brotherston.* DORN,
n.p.

475 GOROSTIZA, JOSÉ (1901-   ) Mexico
Poetry
A Poor Little Conscience. *D. D. Walsh.* FITT, 25.
Aquarium. *R. Benson.* BENS, 27.
Aquarium. *D. D. Walsh.* FITT, 23.
Autumn. *H. R. Hays.* HAYS, 177.
Autumn. *E. W. Underwood.* UND, 170.
Death Without End (Excerpt). *R. Benson.* BENS, 41.
Death Without End (Excerpt). *R. Benson.* PAZ-2, 161.
Elegy. *R. Benson.* BENS, 25.
Fireflies. *R. Benson.* BENS, 31.
Fisherman Of The Moon. *H. R. Hays.* HAYS, 175.
Moon Fisher. *R. Benson.* BENS, 17.
Nocturne. *R. Benson.* BENS, 19.
Pauses II. *H. R. Hays.* HAYS, 177.
Prelude. *R. Benson.* BENS, 35.
Prelude. *H. R. Hays.* HAYS, 187.
Presence and Flight. *M. González.* CARA, 268.
Seashore. *E. W. Underwood.* UND, 168.
The Aquarium. *E. W. Underwood.* UND, 167.
The Bloom Hoists Its Banner. *H. R. Hays.* HAYS, 179.
The Sea Rejoices. *R. Benson.* BENS, 15.

Twilight. *E. W. Underwood*. UND, 171.
Who Is It? *H. R. Hays*. HAYS, 183.
Who Will Buy Me an Orange? *R. Benson*. BENS, 13.
Who Will Buy Me an Orange? *H. R. Hays*. HAYS, 173.
Women. *R. Benson*. BENS, 21.
Women. *D. D. Walsh*. FITT, 25.

476 GRAÇA ARANHA, JOSÉ PEREIRA DA (1868-1931) Argentina
Fiction
Canaán (Excerpt). *M. J. Llorente*. ARC, 54.

477 GRAMCKO, IDA (1925-) Venezuela
Poetry
Dream. *D. Flakoll & C. Alegría*. FLAK, 197.
To Neruda Incommunicado. *M. Brand*. LOW, 40.

478 GRANATA, MARÍA (1923-) Argentina
Poetry
Song With Your Semblance. *W. Shand*. SHA, 174.
The Visitor. *W. Shand*. SHA, 175.

479 GRANDA, EULER (1939?-) Ecuador
Poetry
A Date And The Sea. *R. Connally*. YOU, 56.

480 GREIFF, LEÓN DE (1895-) Colombia
Poetry
The Story of Sergio Stepansky. *J. Hill*. CARA, 184.

481 GRIEBEN, CARLOS F. (1921-) Argentina
Poetry
Man. *W. Shand*. SHA, 160.
The Immobile Heart. *W. Shand*. SHA, 161.

482 GRINBERG, MIGUEL (   ) Argentina
Poetry
Americania. *P. Morgan*. TRI-13, 240.

483 GRÜNEWALD, JOSÉ LINO (1931-) Brazil
Poetry
a dice/facet/hazard/sunset (fig. death). no tr. BANN, 117.
ageravaged. *E. Morgan*. WILL-1, n.p.
forma. no tr. WILL-1, n.p.
go and come. no tr. WILL-1, n.p.
pastime. no tr. BANN, 118.
petroleum. *H. de Campos*. WILL-1, n.p.
river/ray. no tr. BANN, 116.
stone. *H. de Campos*. WILL-1, n.p.
that/soil/callus/lime/solitary/here/ceases (subjunctive).
  no tr. BANN, 115.
to see. *H. de Campos*. WILL-1, n.p.
"two oxen." *H. de Campos*. WILL-1, n.p.

484 GUANES, ALEJANDRO (1872-1925) Paraguay
Poetry
The Hour of Tears. *W. K. Jones*. JONE-3, 138.
Your Soul. *A. S. Blackwell*. BLAC, 468.

485 GUARNIERI, ROSSINI CAMARGO (1914-   ) Brazil
Poetry
When, Brothers? *L. S. Downes*. DOWN, 58.

486 GUERRA, DORA (1925-   ) El Salvador
Poetry
Adventure. no tr. YOU, 61.
Tidings of Your Death. *D. Flakoll & C. Alegría*. FLAK, 130.

487 GUERRA, FÉLIX (1939-   ) Cuba
Poetry
This Is The Century I Love. *A. Mitchell*. TARN, 95.

488 GUERRERO, JULIO (1862-?   ) Mexico
Other
Atavisms. *F. Starr*. STAR, 158.
Governmental Difficulties. *F. Starr*. STAR, 155.
Mexico's Lowest Class. *F. Starr*. STAR, 165.
The Mexican Atmosphere. *F. Starr*. STAR, 152.
Uncertainty and Gaming. *F. Starr*. STAR, 162.

489 GUERRERO, PABLO HERNANDO (   ) Cuba
Poetry
Don't Hide. *E. Dorn & G. Brotherston*. DORN, n.p.

490 GUEVARA, ERNESTO CHE (1928-1967) Argentina
Poetry
Song to Fidel. *E. Dorn & G. Brotherston*. BOLD, 445.
Song to Fidel. *E. Dorn & G. Brotherston*. DORN, n.p.

491 GUEVARA, LUIS CAMILO (1937-   ) Venezuela
Poetry
Looking Up. *L. Getsi & M. A. Serna-Maytorena*. MU-73, 81.
Sudden Encounter And Eternity. *L. Getsi & M. A. Serna-Maytorena*. MU-73, 83.
The Sun. *L. Getsi & M. A. Serna-Maytorena*. MU-73, 79.

492 GUEVARA, PABLO (1930-   ) Peru
Poetry
An Attack, 1940. *M. Ahern & D. Tipton*. AHER, 44.
Babylon, O Babylon. *D. Tipton*. AHER, 46.
'Civil Marriage' (Excerpt). *M. Ahern & D. Tipton*. AHER, 49.
Guita Brüner. *M. Ahern & D. Tipton*. AHER, 43.
Heaven Hell. *M. Ahern & D. Tipton*. AHER, 47.

My Father. *D. Tipton.* AHER, 42.
The Bourgeois are Beasts. *E. Hollis & D. Tipton.* AHER, 48.

493 GUIBERT, FERNANDO (1912-   ) Argentina
Poetry
The Poet At The Foot Of Buenos Aires (Excerpts). *W. Shand.*
SHA, 109.

494 GUILLÉN, NICOLÁS (1902-   ) Cuba
Poetry
A Song For Antillan Children. *H. Ruiz del Vizo.* RUIZ, 58.
Angela Davis. *R. Márquez.* MARQ, 169.
Arrival. *S. Schwartz.* MU-69, 41.
Ballad Of My Two Grandfathers. *G. R. Coulthard.* COUL, 111.
Ballad Of The Güije. *H. R. Hays.* HAYS, 231.
Ballad of the Little Black Dwarf. *J. M. Cohen.* COH-2, 413.
Ballad Of The River Sprites. *G. R. Coulthard.* COUL, 114.
Ballad of the Two Grandfathers. *D. J. Flakoll & C. Alegría.*
BENE, 53.
Ballad Of The Two grandfathers. *H. R. Hays.* HAYS, 225.
Barren Stone. *L. Hughes.* HUGH, 380.
Big-Lipped Negro. *H. R. Hays.* HAYS, 223.
Blade. *L. Hughes.* JONE-3, 75.
Can You. *A. Romeo.* BECK, 53.
Cane. *L. Hughes.* HUGH, 374.
Cane. *L. Hughes.* JONE-3, 74.
Cantaliso In A Bar. *L. Hughes.* FITT, 267.
Dead Soldier. *L. Hughes.* FITT, 265.
Dead Soldier. *L. Hughes.* HUGH, 376.
Elegy. *G. R. Coulthard.* COUL, 113.
Execution. *J. L. Grucci.* JONE-3, 77.
Federico. *B. F. Carruthers.* HUGH, 381.
Guadalupe, W. I. *N. Braymer & L. Lowenfels.* BRAY, 38.
Guitar. *A. Romeo.* BECK, 49.
How To Become a Southern Governor. *L. Raphael & M. Raphael.*
BECK, 57.
I Came in a Slave-Boat. *A. Romeo.* BECK, 61.
I Don't Know Why You Think. *J. Hill.* CARA, 201.
I Have. *R. Márquez.* MARQ, 165.
I, Juan, Negro. *L. Raphael & M. Raphael.* BECK, 33.
It's All Right. *A. Romeo.* BECK, 43.
Kilnstone. *S. Schwartz.* MU-69, 39.
Land in the Sierra and Below. *A. Romeo.* BECK, 65.
Little Rock. *N. Braymer & L. Lowenfels.* BRAY, 39.
Little Rock. *P. Blackburn.* GARR, 31.
Madrigal. *N. Braymer & L. Lowenfels.* BRAY, 37.
Marching. *J. Hill.* CARA, 200.
Proposition. *L. Hughes.* HUGH, 380.
Reveille At Daybreak. *H. R. Hays.* HAYS, 235.
Sensemaya. *H. R. Hays.* HAYS, 229.
Sensemaya: A Chant For Killing A Snake. *G. R. Coulthard.*
COUL, 109.

(GUILLÉN, NICOLÁS)
    Sensemaya (Chant to Kill a Snake). *W. K. Jones*. JONE-3, 75.
    Sightseers In A Courtyard. *L. Hughes*. HUGH, 374.
    'Soldier, I Can't Figure Why.' *H. R. Hays*. FITT, 263.
    Song About An Eviction. *H. Ruiz del Vizo*. RUIZ, 56.
    Students. *L. Raphael & M. Raphael*. BECK, 59.
    Sunday Reading. *R. Márquez*. MARQ, 173.
    Sweat And Whip. *H. Ruiz del Vizo*. RUIZ, 55.
    The Bourgeoisie. *R. Márquez*. MR, 278.
    The Caribe. *A. Romeo*. BECK, 47.
    The Flowers That Grow High. *D. A. McMurray*. MARQ, 157.
    The Mocking-Bird Sings in Turquino. *A. Romeo*. BECK, 29.
    The Name   Family Elegy. *St. Martin*. CARP, 147.
    The Rivers. *A. Romeo*. BECK, 51.
    To Chile. *N. Suarez, J. Rodeiro & D. Rosenblatt*. LOW, 106.
    Two Children. *H. R. Hays*. FITT, 265.
    Two Weeks. *L. Hughes*. HUGH, 379.
    Visit To A Tenement. *D. Fitts*. FITT, 271.
    Wake For Papa Montero. *L. Hughes*. FITT, 275.
    Wake For Papa Montero. *L. Hughes*. HOW-2, 229.
    Wake For Papa Montero. *L. Hughes*. HUGH, 377.
    Way Back When. *A. Romeo*. BECK, 37.
    Yellow Girl. *H. R. Hays*. HAYS, 221.

495   GUILLÉN ZELAYA, ALFONSO (1888-1947) Honduras
    Poetry
    Lord, I Ask A Garden. *W. G. Williams*. WALS, 751.

496   GUIMARAENS, ALPHONSUS DE (1870-1921) Brazil
    Poetry
    Serenade. *P. Standish*. CARA, 61.
    Sonnet. *P. Standish*. CARA, 60.

497   GUIMARAENS FILHO, ALPHONSUS DE (1918-   ) Brazil
    Poetry
    Green Moon. *L. S. Downes*. DOWN, 67.

498   GUIMARÃES ROSA, JOÃO (1908-1967) Brazil
    Fiction
    The Third Bank Of The River. *R. P. Joscelyne*. COH-1, 97.
    The Third Bank of the River. *W. L. Grossman*. GRO, 125.
    The Third Bank of the River. *W. L. Grossman*. HOW-1, 177.
    The Third Bank of the River. *B. Shelby*. MANC, 189.

499   GÜIRALDES, RICARDO (1886-1927) Argentina
    Fiction
    Don Segundo Sombra (Excerpt). *H. de Onís*. JONE-3, 243.
    Misery and the Devil (from: Don Segundo Sombra, Shadows on
      the Pampa). *H. de Onís*. ONIS-1, 214.
    Rosaura. *A. Brenner*. FRAN, 181.
    The Gauchos' Hearth. *P. Emigh*. HOW-1, 73.
    The Old Ranch. *H. de Onís*. ONIS-2, 165.

500 GÜIRAO, RAMÓN (1908–1949) Cuba
     Poetry
     Rumba Dancer. *H. Ruiz del Vizo.* RUIZ, 26.

501 GULLAR, FERREIRA (1930–   ) Argentina
     Poetry
     Clouds' Work. *P. Blackburn.* BISH, 171.
     The House. *J. R. Longland.* CHI, 99.

502 GUTIÉRREZ, CARLOS MARÍA (1926–   ) Uruguay
     Poetry
     Objective Conditions. *R. Cohen & M. Randall.* MARQ, 473.
     3:15 AM/–4°. *R. Cohen & M. Randall.* MARQ, 475.
     Voting Instructions. *R. Cohen & M. Randall.* MARQ, 479.
     White Stone on White Stone. *R. Cohen & M. Randall.* MARQ,
        485.
     Fiction
     The Irregular Armies. *M. Randall.* MR, 126.

503 GUTIÉRREZ, EDUARDO (1853–1890) Argentina
     (Joint author. See also PODESTA, JOSÉ J.)
     Drama
     Juan Moreira. *C. Escudero & W. K. Jones.* JONE-3, 371.

504 GUTIÉRREZ HERMOSILLO, ALFONSO (1905–1935) Mexico
     Poetry
     Earth. *D. Fitts.* FITT, 61.
     Fugue. *D. Fitts.* FITT, 59.

505 GUTIÉRREZ NÁJERA, MANUEL (1859–1895) Mexico
     See also NÁJERA, MANUEL GUTIÉRREZ
     Poetry
     Butterflies. *E. W. Underwood.* UND, 22.
     Calicot. *E. W. Underwood.* UND, 16.
     Dead Waters. *S. Beckett.* PAZ-1, 133.
     Dead Waves. *A. S. Blackwell.* GOLD-2, 30.
     For A Menu. *E. W. Underwood.* UND, 19.
     In the Depths of Night. *T. Walsh.* WALS, 557.
     Non Omnis Moriar. *S. Beckett.* PAZ-1, 138.
     Non Omnis Moriar. *E. W. Underwood.* UND, 14.
     Out of Doors. *T. Walsh.* WALS, 551.
     Para El Corpiño. *E. W. Underwood.* UND, 20.
     Pax Anima (Excerpt). *S. Beckett.* PAZ-1, 137.
     Rip-Rip (from: Smoke-Coloured Tales). no tr. LIEB, 943.
     Sad Night. *E. W. Underwood.* UND, 24.
     Schubert's Serenade. *J. Wendell.* TRAN, 224.
     Shubert's Serenade. *E. W. Underwood.* UND, 9.
     Sometime. *E. W. Underwood.* UND, 13.
     The Duchess Job. *W. K. Jones.* JONE-3, 35.
     The Duchess Job. *E. W. Underwood.* UND, 5.
     To Be. *S. Beckett.* PAZ-1, 135.
     To Salvador Díaz Mirón. *E. W. Underwood.* UND, 12.

(GUTIÉRREZ NÁJERA, MANUEL)
To the Wife of the Corregidor. *A. S. Blackwell*. JONE-3, 37.
When I Die. *M. E. Johnson*. JOHN, 45.
When I Die. *A. J. McVan*. JONE-3, 34.
When I Die. *M. E. Johnson*. RES, 38.
When I Die. *A. J. McVan*. TRAN, 223.
When That Time Comes. *M. González*. CARA, 251.
When The Day Comes. *S. Beckett*. PAZ-1, 139.
White. *A. S. Blackwell*. GOLD-2, 27.
White. *A. S. Blackwell*. WALS, 552.
Whiteness. *M. E. Johnson*. JOHN, 45.
Other
Lenten Sermons of "El Duque Job." no tr. JONE-3, 30.

506 GUZMÁN, MARTÍN LUIS (1887-?) Mexico
Fiction
A Perilous Sleep (from: The Eagle and the Serpent). *H. de Onís*. ARC, 517.
Pancho Villa On The Cross (from: The Eagle and the Serpent). *H. de Onís*. ARC, 510.
The Carnival of the Bullets (from: The Eagle and the Serpent). *H. de Onís*. ONIS-1, 325.
The Eagle and the Serpent (Excerpt). *R. A. Goldberg*. JONE-3, 270.

507 GUZMÁN CRUCHAGA, JUAN (1895-) Chile
Poetry
Distant. *G. D. Craig*. CRAI, 183.
Song. *W. K. Jones*. JONE-3, 118.
The Four Roads. *G. D. Craig*. CRAI, 183.
The Song of Smoke. *C. M. Hutchings*. JONE-3, 119.

508 HADDAD, JAMIL ALMANSUR (1914-) Brazil
Poetry
The Second Poem Of The Violin. *L. S. Downes*. DOWN, 59.

509 HAHN, OSCAR (1938-) Chile
Poetry
The living man. *J. Upton*. TRI-13, 385.
Vision of Hiroshima. *J. Upton*. TRI-13, 384.

510 HARRIAGUE, MAGDALENA (1930-) Argentina
Poetry
Information Window. *W. Shand*. SHA, 240.
Space. *W. Shand*. SHA, 240.

511 HEITOR, LYRA (1893-) Brazil
Other
History Of The Reign Of Dom Pedro II (from: History of Dom Pedro II). *H. de Onís*. ARC, 287.

78

512 HELIODORO VALLE, RAFAEL (1891-   ) Honduras
    <u>Other</u>
    Corn. no tr. LIT-1, 59.

513 HELÚ, ANTONIO (   ) Mexico
    <u>Fiction</u>
    Piropos at Midnight. *D. Yates*. YATE, 83.

514 HENDERSON, CARLOS (1947?-   ) Peru
    <u>Poetry</u>
    We Learned From the Surrealist Poets. no tr. HAR68-5, 23.

515 HENESTROSA, ANDRÉS (1906-   ) Mexico
    <u>Fiction</u>
    Biguu. *Z. Nelken*. TORR, 75.
    The Bat. *Z. Nelken*. TORR, 73.
    The Zapotec Prometheus. *Z. Nelken*. TORR, 77.

516 HENRÍQUEZ, ENRIQUE (1859-1940) Dominican Republic
    <u>Poetry</u>
    In the Café Martin. *F. E. Townsend*. TOWN, 20.
    The Song of the Miser. *F. E. Townsend*. TOWN, 19.

517 HENRÍQUEZ, GUSTAVO JULIO (   ) Dominican Republic
    <u>Poetry</u>
    Anxiety. *F. E. Townsend*. TOWN, 57.
    Solitude. *F. E. Townsend*. TOWN, 56.

518 HENRÍQUEZ, RAFAEL A. (1899-   ) Dominican Republic
    <u>Poetry</u>
    Singing, she goes her way. *F. E. Townsend*. TOWN, 33.

519 HENRÍQUEZ UREÑA, PEDRO (1884-?   ) Dominican Republic
    <u>Other</u>
    Discontent And Promise (from: <u>Seis Ensayos en Busca de</u>
    <u>nuestra Expresión</u>). no tr. LIT-2, 20.

520 HERAUD, JAVIER (1942-1963) Peru
    <u>Poetry</u>
    A Guerrilla's Goodbye. *M. Ahern*. AHER, 82.
    A Guerrilla's Word. *M. Ahern*. AHER, 81.
    A Guerrilla's Word. *M. A. Maurer*. HAR67-3, 56.
    A Guerrilla's Word. *R. Márquez*. MARQ, 399.
    A New Journey. *M. Ahern*. AHER, 87.
    A New Journey. *M. A. Maurer*. HAR67-3, 51.
    A new journey. *M. A. Maurer*. TRI-15, 242.
    Ars Poetica. *E. Dorn & G. Brotherston*. DORN, n.p.
    Ars Poetica. *E. Randall*. MARQ, 401.
    At home. *P. Blackburn*. TRI-13, 111.
    Earth Poems (Excerpt). *M. Ahern*. AHER, 84.
    Earth Poems. *M. A. Maurer*. HAR67-3, 54.

(HERAUD, JAVIER)
Epilogue. *P. Blackburn.* TRI-13, 115.
Flies. *E. Dorn & G. Brotherston.* DORN, n.p.
I Give You My Word. *E. Dorn & G. Brotherston.* DORN, n.p.
In Praise of Days Destruction and Eulogy to Darkness.
  R. Márquez. MARQ, 397.
Only. *P. Blackburn.* TRI-13, 112.
Poem. *E. Dorn & G. Brotherston.* DORN, n.p.
Some Things. *P. Blackburn.* TRI-13, 112.
Summer. *M. Ahern.* AHER, 82.
Summer. *M. A. Maurer.* HAR67-3, 50.
Summer. *M. A. Maurer.* TRI-15, 244.
The Art of Poesy. *M. A. Maurer.* HAR67-3, 57.
The Art of Poetry. *P. Blackburn.* CARP, 427.
The Art of Poetry. *E. Randall.* MARQ, 401.
The Keys Of Death. *M. A. Maurer.* HAR67-3, 49.
The keys of death. *M. A. Maurer.* TRI-15, 241.
The new journey. *E. Dorn & G. Brotherston.* BOLD, 504.
The New Journey. *E. Dorn & G. Brotherston.* DORN, n.p.
The poem. *P. Blackburn.* TRI-13, 106.
The river. *P. Blackburn.* TRI-13, 113.
Waiting For Autumn. *M. A. Maurer.* HAR67-3, 52.
Word of the Guerrilla Fighter. *P. Blackburn.* CARP, 429.

521 HEREDIA, JOSÉ RAMÓN (1900-   ) Venezuela
  Poetry
  My Poem To The Children Killed In The War In Spain.
    D. Fitts. FITT, 523.

522 HERMES VILLORDO, OSCAR (1928-   ) Argentina
  Poetry
  If You Had To Look For Me. *W. Shand.* SHA, 222.
  In The North, Towards The East. *W. Shand.* SHA, 220.

523 HERNÁNDEZ, FELISBERTO (1902-1963) Uruguay
  Fiction
  The Crocodile. *A. Beringer.* CARP, 32.

524 HERNÁNDEZ, JOSÉ P. H. (1892-1922) Puerto Rico
  Poetry
  Madrigal. *B. Luby.* BABI, 294.
  Starry Eyes. no tr. KAI, n.p.

525 HERNÁNDEZ, JUAN JOSÉ (1930-   ) Argentina
  Poetry
  One Morning. *W. Shand.* SHA, 250.
  Poem. *W. Shand.* SHA, 249.
  Fiction
  Danaë. *H. E. Francis.* MU-70, 71.
  The favorite. *J. C. Murchison.* TRI-13, 356.

526 HERNÁNDEZ, LUIS (1943-   ) Peru
   Poetry
   For Arnold. *C. A. de Lomellini & O. Bingham-Powell.*
      HAR67-4, 75.

527 HERNÁNDEZ, LUISA JOSEFINE (1928-   ) Mexico
   Drama
   Dialogues. *F. Colecchia & J. Matas.* COLE, 125.
   The Mulatto's Orgy. *W. I. Oliver.* OLIV, 219.

528 HERNÁNDEZ AQUINO, LUIS (1907-   ) Puerto Rico
   Poetry
   Elegy Before The Ruins Of Caparra. *B. Luby.* BABI, 281.
   Fiction
   Death Roamed the Guasio River (Excerpt). no tr. KAI, n.p.

529 HERNÁNDEZ CATÁ, ALFONSO (1885-1940) Cuba
   Fiction
   The Servant Girl. *H. Kurz.* HAYDN, 927.

530 HERNÁNDEZ CRUZ, VÍCTOR (1949-   ) Puerto Rico
   Poetry
   Back to/Back to. Originally Engl. MATI, 208.
   Cocaine Galore 1. Originally Engl. MATI, 210.
   The Cha Cha Cha at Salt Lake City Bus Terminal. Originally
      Engl. MATI, 216.
   The Fiction Magazine/Volume One. Originally Engl. MATI,
      212.
   Other
   #1 exploration [from: 19 Necromancers from Now (Poetic Es-
      say)]. Originally Engl. BABI, 441.
   #2 trans-atlantic flight [from: 19 Necromancers from Now
      (Poetic essay)]. Originally Engl. BABI, 442.
   #6 bodega [from: 19 Necromancers from Now (Poetic essay)].
      Originally Engl. BABI, 443.
   #8 night writers (riding) [from: 19 Necromancers from Now
      (Poetic essay)]. Originally Engl. BABI, 444.
   #9 song & dance [from: 19 Necromancers from Now (Poetic es-
      say)]. Originally Engl. BABI, 446.

531 HERNÁNDEZ FRANCO, TOMÁS (1904-   ) Dominican Republic
   Poetry
   Salutation to Frankie Alegria. *F. E. Townsend.* TOWN, 97.

532 HERNÁNDEZ MÍYARES, ENRIQUE (1854-1914) Cuba
   Poetry
   The Fairest One. *A. Coester.* WALS, 538.
   The Most Beautiful. *A. S. Blackwell.* BLAC, 498.
   The Most Beautiful. *A. S. Blackwell.* JONE-3, 68.

533 HERRERA, FLAVIO (1895-   ) Guatemala
      Fiction
      Coffee: Its Life Story (from: The Tempest). *H. de Onís*.
        ARC, 86.

534 HERRERA, PORFIRIO (   ) Dominican Republic
      Poetry
      The Fountain. *F. E. Townsend*. TOWN, 43.

535 HERRERA SEVILLANO, DEMETRIO (1902-   ) Panama
      Poetry
      Training. *D. Fitts*. FITT, 123.

536 HERRERA & REISSIG, JULIO (1875-1910) Uruguay
      Poetry
      A Mournful Dawn. *G. D. Craig*. CRAI, 127.
      Anguish and Love. *G. D. Craig*. CRAI, 129.
      Heraldic Declaration. *M. González*. CARA, 361.
      July. *M. E. Johnson*. JOHN, 113.
      Meditative Absence. *D. Hall*. GARR, 135.
      Night. *D. Hall*. GARR, 137.
      Supper. *G. D. Craig*. CRAI, 129.
      The Carts. *T. Walsh*. JONE-3, 168.
      The Carts. *T. Walsh*. WALS, 685.
      The Cura. *T. Walsh*. WALS, 683.
      The Doleful Shadow. *G. D. Craig*. CRAI, 127.
      The Evening Meal. *M. González*. CARA, 360.
      The House on the Mountain. *A. S. Blackwell*. BLAC, 444.
      The House on the Mountain. *D. Hall*. GARR, 135.
      The House on the Mountain. *A. S. Blackwell*. LIT-1, 71.
      The Parish Church. *T. Walsh*. JONE-3, 169.
      The Parish Church. *T. Walsh*. WALS, 684.
      The Priest. *T. Walsh*. JONE-3, 169.
      The Quarrel. *M. Lee*. JONE-3, 170.
      The Return. *M. E. Johnson*. JOHN, 113.
      The Return from the Fields. *J. M. Cohen*. COH-2, 342.
      The Soirée. *M. González*. CARA, 359.
      The Theatre of the Humble. *J. M. Cohen*. COH-2, 343.

537 HINE, DAVID (1858-?   ) Costa Rica
      Poetry
      The Bright Star. *A. S. Blackwell*. BLAC, 480.

538 HINOSTROZA, RODOLFO (1941-   ) Peru
      Poetry
      Cronica II, III (Excerpt). *M. Shipman*. HAR67-2, 33.
      Othello's Report. *M. Ahern & D. Tipton*. AHER, 56.
      The Night. *M. Ahern & D. Tipton*. AHER, 57.
      To a Dead Childhood. *M. Ahern & D. Tipton*. AHER, 53.
      Other
      On the Situation of the Writer in Peru (Essay). *D. Tipton*.
        AHER, 116.

539 HÜBNER BEZANILLA, JORGE (1892-1964) Chile
     Poetry
     The River. *A. S. Blackwell.* BLAC, 294.
     The Wind. *A. S. Blackwell.* BLAC, 296.

540 HUERTA, EFRAÍN (1914-   ) Mexico
     Poetry
     Recollection Of Love. *D. Fitts.* FITT, 341.
     The Drunken Girl. *P. Levine.* PAZ-2, 113.
     The Men of the Dawn. *P. Levine.* PAZ-2, 107.
     The Sounds Of Dawn. *D. Fitts.* FITT, 339.

541 HUIDOBRO, MATÍAS MONTES (1931-   ) Cuba
     Drama
     The Guillotine. *F. Colecchia & J. Matas.* COLE, 93.

542 HUIDOBRO, VICENTE (1893-1948) Chile
     Poetry
     Adam. *D. Pettinella.* SIX64-7, 77.
     Adieu. *G. D. Craig.* CRAI, 237.
     Altazor   Preface. *J. Hill.* CARA, 110.
     Altazor: Canto III. *E. Weinberger.* CHI, 37.
     Altazor, Fragment of Canto I. *J. Rothenberg.* CARP, 15.
     Altazor, or Journey By Parachute (Fragments). *R. Lebovitz.*
       MU-69, 29.
     Ars Poetica. *E. Weinberger.* CHI, 27.
     Ballad of That Which Does Not Return. *T. Raworth.* CARA,
       106.
     Bell Tower. *G. D. Craig.* CRAI, 243.
     'Bewitching Drowned.' *J. Staples.* FITT, 375.
     'Bring Games.' *J. Staples.* FITT, 371.
     Drama. *G. O'Brien.* CHI, 29.
     Emigrant to America. *T. Raworth.* CARA, 104.
     Emigrant To America. *H. R. Hays.* HAYS, 69.
     Equatorial. *R. Benson.* BENS, 51.
     Horizon. *G. D. Craig.* CRAI, 239.
     'I Am Partly Moon....' *J. Staples.* FITT, 371.
     In. *H. R. Hays.* HAYS, 79.
     Landscape. *A. Torres-Ríoseco.* JONE-3, 125.
     Looks And Memories. *D. Pettinella.* SIX64-7, 79.
     Monument to the Sea. *E. Arenal.* CARP, 25.
     Nature Vive. *D. Fitts.* FITT, 379.
     Nature Vive. *H. R. Hays.* HAYS, 77.
     Nature Vive. *H. R. Hays.* JONE-3, 125.
     Nipponese. *T. Raworth.* CARA, 102.
     On the Tomb of a Poet. *T. Raworth.* CARA, 101.
     Poem To Make Trees Grow. *E. Weinberger.* CHI, 33.
     Poetry is a Heavenly Crime. *W. S. Merwin.* CARP, 23.
     Poster. *T. Raworth.* CARA, 105.
     Prelude To Hope. *H. R. Hays.* HAYS, 71.
     Put Out Your Pipe. *T. Raworth.* CARA, 103.

(HUIDOBRO, VICENTE)
  Romance. *G. O'Brien.* CHI, 31.
  Round. *D. D. Walsh.* FITT, 377.
  Serenade Of Laughing Life. *H. R. Hays.* HAYS, 81.
  She. *D. Fitts.* FITT, 381.
  Spring Morning. *G. D. Craig.* CRAI, 241.
  The Alert. *T. Raworth.* CARA, 103.
  The Art Of Poetry. *M. B. Davis.* FITT, 377.
  The Path Was So Long. *G. D. Craig.* CRAI, 241.
  There is a Cataclysm Inside Us. *J. Rothenberg.* CARP, 19.
  Time Of Waiting. *H. R. Hays.* HAYS, 75.
  Unstill Life. *D. J. Flakoll & C. Alegría.* BENE, 45.
  'You Have Never Known The Tree of Tenderness....'
    J. Staples. FITT, 373.

543 HURTADO, OSCAR (1919-) Cuba
    Poetry
    Hamlet on the Staircase. *C. Beck.* BECK, 189.
    The Return. *A. Boyer.* BECK, 181.
    Fiction
    Letter from a judge. no tr. CARZ, 79.

544 IBÁÑEZ, JORGE (1940-) Costa Rica
    Poetry
    What No One Knows. *A. Edwards.* YOU, 43.

545 IBÁÑEZ, ROBERTO (1907-) Uruguay
    Poetry
    Elegy For The Drowned Men Who Return. *L. Mallan &*
    D. D. Walsh. FITT, 549.

546 IBARBOUROU, JUANA DE (1895-) Uruguay
    Poetry
    Clinging To Life. *M. E. Johnson.* JOHN, 157.
    Compass Rose. *J. Bardin.* LIT-1, 92.
    Crystal Brook. *J. Bardin.* LIT-1, 92.
    Dejection. *M. E. Johnson.* JOHN, 161.
    Fleeting Restlessness. *M. E. Johnson.* JOHN, 157.
    Fleeting Restlessness. *E. du Gué Trapier.* JONE-3, 173.
    Fleeting Restlessness. *E. du Gué Trapier.* TRAN, 263.
    In Praise of the Spanish Language. *R. Bain & W. K. Jones.*
     JONE-3, 174.
    Like the Springtime. no tr. JONE-3, 175.
    Lullabies. *P. T. Manchester.* JONE-3, 173.
    March Twilight. *W. K. Jones.* JONE-3, 171.
    Rainy Night. *R. Humphries.* FITT, 491.
    The Hour. *S. Resnick.* RES, 90.
    The Nest. *D. J. Flakoll & C. Alegría.* BENE, 49.
    The Shepherdess. *B. Proske.* TRAN, 262.
    The Smith. *B. Proske.* TRAN, 261.
    The Strong Bond. *S. Resnick.* RES, 92.

The Sweet Miracle. *A. S. Blackwell.* BLAC, 448.
The Sweet Miracle. *A. S. Blackwell.* LIT-2, 59.
Woman. *M. E. Johnson.* JOHN, 161.

547 ICAZA, FRANCISCO ASÍS DE (1863-1925) Mexico
Poetry
A Village of Andalusia. *E. W. Underwood.* UND, 88.
Autumn. *E. W. Underwood.* UND, 91.
Eastern Music. *E. W. Underwood.* UND, 90.
For the Poor Blind Man. *S. Beckett.* PAZ-1, 141.
Golden. *S. Beckett.* PAZ-1, 141.
Landscape Colours. *A. J. McVan.* TRAN, 228.
Landscape of the Sun. *E. W. Underwood.* UND, 89.
Poor Blind Man. *E. W. Underwood.* UND, 90.
Responding Voice. *S. Beckett.* PAZ-1, 140.
The Song by the Way. *A. S. Blackwell.* BLAC, 128.
The Song by the Way. *A. S. Blackwell.* RES, 60.
Wayfaring. *S. Beckett.* PAZ-1, 141.

548 ICAZA, JORGE (1906-   ) Ecuador
Fiction
Big Precipice. *H. St. Martin.* MANC, 79.
Huasipungo (Excerpt). *W. K. Jones.* JONE-3, 190.

549 ICAZA SÁNCHEZ, HOMERO (1925-   ) Panama
Poetry
"Necessary Poem." no tr. YOU, 95.

550 IGLESIAS, CÉSAR ANDRÉU (1910-   ) Puerto Rico
Fiction
The Collapse (from: The Vanquished). *B. Luby.* BABI, 316.

551 IGNAZA, ALCIDES (1914-   ) Cuba
Poetry
Day's Story (Variation). *R. Llopis.* BECK, 207.
Loneliness. *R. Llopis.* BECK, 199.
Objective. *S. Carranza.* BECK, 205.
Presence. *R. Llopis.* BECK, 195.
Sister. *R. Llopis.* BECK, 197.
Wife and Comrade. no tr. BECK, 201.
Within. *S. Carranza.* BECK, 203.

552 INCHÁUSTEGUI CABRAL, HÉCTOR (1912-   ) Dominican Republic
Poetry
Return to Man. *F. E. Townsend.* TOWN, 61.

553 ISAACSON, JOSÉ (1922-   ) Argentina
Poetry
Aroma Of An Unknown Flower. *D. Tipton.* HAR67-4, 85.
How To Create You. *D. Tipton.* HAR67-4, 82.
Longed For Perfume. *W. Shand.* SHA, 169.

(ISAACSON, JOSÉ)
   Ode To Joy (I want to name you). *W. Shand.* SHA, 170.
   Recognition. *D. Tipton.* HAR67-4, 83.
   Retreat. *D. Tipton.* HAR67-4, 87.
   Silence Of The River. *D. Tipton.* HAR67-4, 86.
   Song. *D. Tipton.* HAR67-4, 88.

554 ISLA, L. A. (   ) Chile
    Fiction
    The Case of the "Southern Arrow." *D. Yates.* YATE, 131.

555 [IVANOVITCH, DMITRI pseud.] (1888-?) Colombia
    BETANCOURT, JOSÉ
    Poetry
    The Child Asleep. *T. Walsh.* WALS, 749.

556 IVO, LÉDO (1924-) Brazil
    Poetry
    Vain Enchantment. *L. S. Downes.* DOWN, 80.

557 IZA, ANA MARÍA (1947?-) Ecuador
    Poetry
    Formula. *R. Connally.* YOU, 52.

558 [JACOB, PORFIRIO BARBA pseud.] (1883-1942) Colombia
    OSORIO, MIGUEL ÁNGEL
    Poetry
    The Queen. *J. Hill.* CARA, 182.

559 JAIMES FREYRE, RICARDO (1868-1933) Bolivia
    Poetry
    Dawn. *G. D. Craig.* CRAI, 91.
    Eternal Farewell. *G. D. Craig.* CRAI, 89.
    Fleetingness. *M. E. Johnson.* JOHN, 93.
    Inner Landscapes. *A. S. Blackwell.* BLAC, 454.
    Sonnet. *T. Raworth.* CARA, 49.
    The Ancestors. *A. S. Blackwell.* BLAC, 456.
    The Ancestors. *A. S. Blackwell.* JONE-3, 115.
    The Idol. *A. S. Blackwell.* BLAC, 460.
    The Mournful Voices. *G. D. Craig.* CRAI, 95.
    The Portal. *G. D. Craig.* CRAI, 91.
    The Sad Voices. *M. E. Johnson.* JOHN, 91.
    The Song of Evil. *T. Raworth.* CARA, 50.
    Fiction
    Indian Justice. *W. E. Colford.* COLF, 45.

560 JAMÍS, FAYAD (1930-) Cuba
    Poetry
    Auschwitz was not the garden of my childhood. *T. Reynolds.*
     TRI-13, 142.
    For this Liberty. *R. F. Hardy.* BECK, 423.

I hear my name. *T. Reynolds.* TRI-13, 141.
Life. *R. F. Hardy.* BECK, 429.
Life. *J. M. Cohen.* BOLD, 460.
Life. *J. M. Cohen.* COH-3, 58.
On The River Bank. *J. M. Cohen.* COH-3, 58.
Poem in Minas del Frío. *R. F. Hardy.* BECK, 425.
Poem In Nanking. *D. Ossman & C. Hagen.* TARN, 55.
Shut Up You Shit. *A. Mitchell.* TARN, 57.
Sometimes. *D. Flakoll & C. Alegría.* FLAK, 128.
The Hanging in the Cafe Bonaparte. *R. F. Hardy.* BECK, 433.
The Lost Scarf. *R. F. Hardy.* BECK, 431.
The Milky Way. *D. Ossman & C. Hagen.* TARN, 55.
The Victory of Playa Girón. *R. F. Hardy.* BECK, 437.
To an Illiterate. *R. F. Hardy.* BECK, 439.

561 JARA, VICTOR (   ) Chile
     Poetry
     Chile Stadium. *J. Jara.* LOW, 89.

562 JARDIM, LUÍS (1901-   ) Brazil
     Fiction
     The Enchanted Ox. *W. L. Grossman.* GRO, 53.

563 JESÚS, CAROLINA MARIA DE (   ) Brazil
     Other
     Child of the Dark: The Diary of Carolina Maria de Jesús
        (Excerpt). *D. St. Clair.* HAH, 138.

564 JESÚS, SALVADOR M. DE (   ) Puerto Rico
     Fiction
     "When he stood up...." *S. M. de Jesús.* KAI, n.p.

565 JIMÉNEZ, RAMÓN EMILIO (1886-?) Dominican Republic
     Poetry
     A Lesson from the Tree. *F. E. Townsend.* TOWN, 92.
     Before Class. *F. E. Townsend.* TOWN, 89.
     Hymn to Truth. *F. E. Townsend.* TOWN, 90.
     My Dolly. *F. E. Townsend.* TOWN, 91.

566 JODOROWSKY, ALEJANDRO (   ) Chile
     Drama
     The Mole (Excerpts from a film script). *C. Rennert.* DR, 57.
     Other
     A Mass Changes Me More (Interview by Sergio Guzik).
        J. Pottlitzer. DR, 70.

567 JODOROWSKY, RAQUEL (1935-   ) Chile
     Poetry
     "Like wild beasts held by the mane." *C. A. de Lomellini &*
        R. Jodorowsky. HAR67-4, 69.

(JODOROWSKY, RAQUEL)
Still Alone Under The Satellites. *C. Cotton*. MU-74, 91.
The Mask Of The Oracle In The Temple. *S. Mondragón &
R. Schulte*. MU-69, 119.

568 JOGLAR CACHO, MANUEL (1898-   ) Puerto Rico
Poetry
To Saint John Of The Cross. *B. Luby*. BABI, 294.

569 JOHNSON, LUISA (   ) Chile
Poetry
Devotional. *M. Williams*. WILL-2, 33.
Notice. *M. Williams*. WILL-2, 31.

570 JONQUIÉRES, EDUARDO (1918-   ) Argentina
Poetry
A High Price. *W. Shand*. SHA, 133.
Birthday. *W. Shand*. SHA, 134.
Not Even Worth While. *W. Shand*. SHA, 135.

571 JOUBLANC RIVAS, LUCIANO (1896-   ) Mexico
Poetry
Sadness. *E. W. Underwood*. UND, 147.

572 JUARROZ, ROBERTO (1925-   ) Argentina
Poetry
A fly is walking head downward on the ceiling. *W. S. Merwin*.
CARP, 313.
Death no longer faces mirrors. *S. Mondragón & R. Schulte*.
MU-69, 71.
I think that in this moment. *S. Mondragón & R. Schulte*.
MU-69, 71.
It's raining onto thought. *W. S. Merwin*. CARP, 317.
Man. *S. Mondragón & R. Schulte*. MU-69, 69.
One day I will find a word. *S. Mondragón & R. Schulte*.
MU-69, 69.
Poems Of Otherness No. 15. *W. Shand*. SHA, 195.
Poems Of Otherness No. 28. *W. Shand*. SHA, 196.
Poems Of Unity No. 4. *W. Shand*. SHA, 197.
Somewhere there's a man. *W. S. Merwin*. CARP, 315.

573 KOCIANCICH, VLADY (1942-   ) Argentina
Fiction
False Limits. *N. T. di Giovanni & V. Kociancich*. MU-70,
54.

574 KORSI, DEMETRIO (1898-   ) Panama
Poetry
Incident Of Dance. *H. Ruiz del Vizo*. RUIZ, 117.

575   KRUPKIN, ILKA   (1902-   ) Argentina
       Poetry
       Cantata To The Time Of The Fatherland 1816-1966. *W. Shand*.
         SHA, 53.

576   LAGUADO, ARTURO   (1919-   ) Colombia
       Fiction
       The Return. *M. A. Serna-Maytorena & T. Hoeksema*. MU-70,
         110.

577   LAGUERRE, ENRIQUE A.   (1906-   ) Puerto Rico
       Fiction
       The Cockfight (from: The Flare-up). *B. Luby*. BABI, 333.
       The Strike (from: The Flare-up). *B. Luby*. BABI, 339.

578   [LAIR, CLARA pseud.]   (1895-   ) Puerto Rico
       NEGRÓN MUÑOZ, MERCEDES
       Poetry
       Lullaby (Excerpt). no tr. KAI, n.p.

579   LALEAU, LÉON   (   ) Chile
       Poetry
       Delicate Silence. *N. R. Shapiro*. MR, 125.

580   LAMARCHE, MARTHA   (   ) Dominican Republic
       Poetry
       In Your Snare. *F. E. Townsend*. TOWN, 66.

581   LAMBERG, FERNANDO   (1928-   ) Chile
       Poetry
       LXXI. *D. A. McMurray*. MR, 280.

582   LARRANAGA PORTUGAL, MANUEL   (1868-?   ) Mexico
       Poetry
       Sonnet. *E. W. Underwood*. UND, 104.

583   LARRETA, ENRIQUE   (1875-?   ) Argentina
       Poetry
       The Pillow. *P. Gannon*. GAN, 29.

584   [LARS, CLAUDIA pseud.]   (1899-   ) El Salvador
       BRANNON BEERS, CARMEN
       Poetry
       Heads And Tails. *D. D. Walsh*. FITT, 199.
       Part One (from: On Angel and Man). no tr. YOU, 62.
       Sketch Of The Frontier Woman. *D. D. Walsh*. FITT, 199.
       Sketch of the Frontier Woman. *D. D. Walsh*. JONE-3, 63.

585 LASTRA, PEDRO (1932-   ) Chile
     Poetry
     Don Quixote Contradicts The Cervantes Scholars For Purely
          Personal Reasons. *R. de Costa.* CHI, 169.
     Recovery Of The Astrolabe. *R. de Costa.* CHI, 165.
     Reflections Of Achilles. *R. de Costa.* CHI, 167.

586 LATORRE, CARLOS (1916-   ) Argentina
     Poetry
     Always Reason. *W. Shand.* SHA, 124.
     Till We Meet Again. *W. Shand.* SHA, 125.

587 LATORRE, MARIANO (1886-1955) Chile
     Fiction
     A Woman of Mystery. *H. Kurz.* HAYDN, 864.
     Captain Oyarzo (from: The Oceans of Chile). *H. de Onís.*
          ARC, 124.
     The Old Woman of Peralillo. *H. de Onís.* ONIS-1, 259.

588 LAUER, MIRKO (1947-   ) Peru
     Poetry
     Cruel Photograph without Light at Daybreak. *D. Tipton.*
          AHER, 110.
     Tanks. *D. Tipton.* AHER, 113.
     The Angels. *D. Tipton.* AHER, 109.
     The Classics Revisited. *D. Tipton.* AHER, 111.
     The Roses of the Map. *M. Lauer.* HAR67-4, 77.

589 LEBRÓN SAVIÑÓN, MARIANO (1922-   ) Dominican Republic
     Poetry
     Second Chant to the Sea. *F. E. Townsend.* TOWN, 99.

590 LEDESMA, ROBERTO (1901-   ) Argentina
     Poetry
     Ransom. *P. Gannon.* GAN, 73.

591 LEGUIZAMON, MARTINIANO (1858-1935) Argentina
     Poetry
     Triste. *A. J. McVan.* TRAN, 185.

592 LEÑERO, VICENTE (1933-   ) Mexico
     Fiction
     The perfect adventure. *M. S. Peden.* TRI-13, 367.

593 LEÓN DEL VALLE, JOSÉ (1866-1924) Mexico
     Poetry
     The Last of the Aztecs. *A. S. Blackwell.* BLAC, 156.

594 LEÓN-PORTILLA, MIGUEL (1920-   ) Mexico
     Other
     A Náhuatl Concept of Art. *A. Bové & L. Kemp.* EVER, 157.

595 LEZAMA LIMA, JOSÉ (1912-   ) Cuba
     Poetry
     An Obscure Meadow Lures Me. *N. Tarn*. MU-69, 49.
     An Obscure Meadow Lures Me. *N. Tarn*. TARN, 19.
     Boredom of the second day. *E. Randall*. TRI-13, 138.
     Cry of the Wishful Man. *J. Hill*. CARA, 210.
     Fragments (Excerpt). *J. Hill*. CARA, 214.
     Nocturnal Fish. *J. Hill*. CARA, 209.
     Now has no weight. *E. Randall*. TRI-13, 139.
     Ode to Julián del Casal. *C. Beck*. BECK, 129.
     Rhapsody for the Mule. *D. D. Walsh, J. Rodríguez Feo &*
        D. Fitts. BECK, 121.
     Rhapsody For The Mule. *D. D. Walsh, J. Rodríguez Feo &*
        D. Fitts. FITT, 229.
     Summons Of The Desirer. *N. Tarn*. MU-69, 47.
     Summons Of The Desirer. *N. Tarn*. TARN, 21.
     'Tell Me, Ask Me.' *N. Tarn*. TARN, 17.
     The cords. *E. Randall*. TRI-13, 140.
     The First Bower of Friendship (Excerpt). *J. Hill*. CARA,
        212.
     Fiction
     Paradiso (Excerpt). *T. Reynolds*. CARP, 350.

596 LIACHO, LÁZARO (1906-   ) Argentina
     Poetry
     Encounter. *W. Shand*. SHA, 84.
     Firm Ground. *W. Shand*. SHA, 83.
     Submission. *W. Shand*. SHA, 84.

597 LIHN, ENRIQUE (1929-   ) Chile
     Poetry
     Bel Epoch. *D. Oliphant*. CHI, 147.
     Coliseum. *M. Williams*. TRI-13, 353.
     Europeans. *R. Márquez*. MARQ, 107.
     Graveyard at Punta Arenas. *M. Williams*. CARP, 347.
     Graveyard At Punta Arenas. *M. Williams*. WILL-2, 43.
     Jonah. *J. M. Cohen*. COH-1, 249.
     Jonah. *M. Williams*. TRI-13, 352.
     Market place. *W. Witherup & S. Echeverría*. TRI-13, 355.
     Memories of A Marriage. *R. Connally*. YOU, 37.
     Memories of Marriage. *T. Raworth*. CARA, 159.
     Monologue Of An Old Man With Death. *M. Williams*. WILL-2,
        37.
     Mud. *W. Witherup & S. Echeverría*. TRI-13, 349.
     Newly Born. *D. Flakoll & C. Alegría*. FLAK, 225.
     Rooster. *M. Williams*. CARP, 349.
     Rooster. *M. Williams*. WILL-2, 41.
     The Dark Room. *W. Witherup & S. Echeverría*. TRI-13, 350.
     The Friends Of The House. *J. M. Cohen*. COH-1, 248.
     The Invasion. *J. M. Cohen*. COH-1, 247.
     The Tree-Clump In The Garden. *J. M. Cohen*. COH-1, 247.
     You are perfectly monstrous in your silence. *W. Witherup &*
        S. Echeverría. TRI-13, 354.

(LIHN, ENRIQUE)
Fiction
Rice Water. *M. Williams*. CARP, 332.

598 LILLO, BALDOMERO (1867-1923) Chile
Fiction
The Abyss. *W. E. Colford*. COLF, 36.

599 LILLO, SAMUEL A. (1870-1958) Chile.
Poetry
To Vasco Núñez de Balboa. *L. Elliott*. WALS, 699.

600 LIMA, JORGE MATEUS DE (1893-1953) Brazil
Poetry
Christian's Poem. *D. Poore*. FITT, 89.
Christmas Poem. *J. Nist & Y. Leite*. NIST, 54.
Daddy John. *D. Poore*. FITT, 75.
Distribution of Poetry. *J. Nist & Y. Leite*. NIST, 48.
Distribution of Poetry. *P. Standish*. CARA, 72.
First Canto   The Foundation of the Island (Excerpt).
   P. Standish. CARA, 73.
Fulo's Ballad. *H. Ruiz del Vizo*. RUIZ, 129.
Goodbye to Poetry. *J. Nist & Y. Leite*. NIST, 55.
I Announce Consolation to You. *J. Nist & Y. Leite*. NIST,
   52.
Invention Of Orpheus Canto VII. *M. Cardozo*. NEI, 101.
Invention Of Orpheus Canto VIII Biography. *M. Cardozo*.
   NEI, 103.
Papa John. *J. Nist & Y. Leite*. NIST, 49.
Paraclete. *D. Poore*. FITT, 85.
Poem Of Any Virgin. *D. Poore*. FITT, 79.
Rag Doll. *J. Nist & Y. Leite*. NIST, 53.
Songs. *R. M. Anderson*. TRAN, 197.
Stranger, Stranger. *M. Cardozo*. NEI, 107.
That Black Girl, Fulô. no tr. TRE, 10.
That Nigger Fulô. *L. S. Downes*. DOWN, 38.
That Nigger Fulow. *M. Cardozo*. NEI, 97.
The Big Mystical Circus. *D. Poore*. FITT, 81.
The Bird. *D. Poore*. FITT, 77.
The Enormous Hand. *J. Jordan*. BISH, 19.
The Great Mystical Circus. *M. Cardozo*. NEI, 109.
The Multiplication of the Creature. *J. Nist & Y. Leite*.
   NIST, 51.
The River and the Serpent. *J. Nist & Y. Leite*. NIST, 50.
The Sleep Before. *J. Nist & Y. Leite*. NIST, 52.
The Trumpets. *M. Cardozo*. NEI, 95.
The Words Will Resurrect. *J. Nist & Y. Leite*. NIST, 47.
Words Of Farewell. *M. Cardozo*. NEI, 95.

601 LIMA, JOSÉ MARÍA (1934-   ) Puerto Rico
     Poetry
     deaths lurk also in navels.... *M. Arrillaga.* MATI, 101.
     The Heroes. *M. Arrillaga.* MATI, 103.

602 LINDO, HUGO (1917-   ) El Salvador
     Poetry
     A Station That Travels (from: Navegante Río). no tr. YOU,
        64.
     Sleeping in the Salt. *D. Flakoll & C. Alegría.* FLAK, 194.

603 LINS DO REGO, JOSÉ (1901-   ) Brazil
     Fiction
     Old Totonha (from: Menino de Engenho). *H. de Onís.*
        ONIS-1, 387.
     The Masters and the Slaves (from: Menino de Engenho).
        H. de Onís. ONIS-1, 384.

604 LIRA, CARMEN (1888-1949) Costa Rica
     Fiction
     Ulvieta. *A. S. Hasbrouck.* JONE-3, 310.

605 LISBOA, HENRIQUETA (   ) Brazil
     Poetry
     Minor Elegy. *J. R. Longland.* MU-74, 125.
     Palm Tree On The Beach. *J. R. Longland.* CHI, 87.
     Problem. *L. S. Downes.* DOWN, 52.
     The Veil. *J. R. Longland.* CHI, 89.

606 LISPECTOR, CLARICE (1924-   ) Brazil
     Fiction
     Marmosets. *E. Bishop.* HOW-1, 326.
     The Crime of the Mathematics Professor. *W. L. Grossman.*
        GRO, 146.
     The Imitation of the Rose. *G. Pontiero.* MANC, 317.
     The Smallest Woman in the World. *E. Bishop.* HOW-1, 320.

607 LLANA, MARÍA ELENA (1936-   ) Cuba
     Fiction
     The two of us. no tr. CARZ, 175.

608 LLINÁS, JULIO (1929-   ) Argentina
     Poetry
     City. *W. Shand.* SHA, 231.
     Omens. *W. Shand.* SHA, 231.
     Roots. *W. Shand.* SHA, 230.
     Seas. *W. Shand.* SHA, 231.
     The Dance. *W. Shand.* SHA, 231.
     The Great Tide. *W. Shand.* SHA, 232.

609 LLOPIS, ROGELIO (1926-   ) Cuba
Fiction
A Horrible Man. *J. Franco.* COH-3, 140.
Lycanthropy. no tr. CARZ, 183.

610 LLORÉNS TORRES, LUIS (1878-1944) Puerto Rico
Poetry
Bolívar. *M. González.* CARA, 349.
Bolívar. *M. Lee.* JONE-3, 79.
Maceo. *M. González.* CARA, 350.
The Güiro in A-E-I-O-U. *D. Sánchez-Méndez.* MATI, 9.
The Ugly Duckling. *D. Sánchez-Méndez.* MATI, 3.
Vida Criolla. *J. Nieto.* BABI, 35.
Vida Criolla. no tr. KAI, n.p.

611 LLUCH MORA, FRANCISCO (1925-   ) Puerto Rico
Poetry
Fatherland. *B. Luby.* BABI, 276.

612 LOANDA, FERNANDO FERREIRA DE (1924-   ) Brazil
Poetry
Ode For Jack London. *L. S. Downes.* DOWN, 81.

613 LOBATO, JOSÉ BENTO MONTEIRO (1883-1948) Brazil
Fiction
The Farm Magnate (from: Urupês). no tr. LIEB, 926.
The Farm Magnate. no tr. MILL, 276.
The Funny-Man Who Repented. *H. Kurz.* HAYDN, 941.
The Vengeance of the Redwood. *H. de Onís.* ONIS-1, 372.

614 LOLO, EDUARDO (1945-   ) Cuba
Poetry
'Anna.' *T. Reynolds.* TARN, 135.
'If You Get Up.' *S. Schwartz.* TARN, 139.

615 LOPES, MARIA (   ) Brazil
(Joint author. See also CARI, TERESA and FABBRI, TECLA.)
Other
To the Young Seamstresses of São Paulo (Newspaper article).
J. E. Hahner. HAH, 114.

616 LÓPEZ, CÉSAR (1933-   ) Cuba
Poetry
'I Can't Talk About Him.' *M. Randall.* TARN, 79.
Notes from a Trip Abroad. *C. Beck.* BECK, 565.
The City's First Book (Fragments). *C. Beck.* BECK, 573.
'What Happened to Her.' *A. Kerrigan.* TARN, 83.
'When a Man Dies.' *D. Gardner.* TARN, 81.
Who Can Be Certain. *C. Beck.* BECK, 579.

617   LÓPEZ, LUIS CARLOS   (1883-1950)   Colombia
      (Luis Carlos López de Escuariza)
      Poetry
      Country Girl, Don't Stay Away....   *D. D. Walsh.*   FITT, 219.
      From My Farm.   *A. J. McVan.*   TRAN, 212.
      Old Maids.   *H. R. Hays.*   HAYS, 55.
      River-Folk.   *T. Walsh.*   WALS, 711.
      Rubbish.   *H. R. Hays.*   JONE-3, 96.
      Rubbish IV.   *H. R. Hays.*   HAYS, 57.
      Rubbish VII.   *H. R. Hays.*   HAYS, 59.
      Summer Afternoon.   *A. Fife.*   FIFE, 65.
      The Mayor.   *H. R. Hays.*   HAYS, 53.
      The Village Barber.   *T. Walsh.*   JONE-3, 97.
      To A Dog.   *H. R. Hays.*   HAYS, 61.
      To My Native City.   *H. R. Hays.*   HAYS, 57.
      To Satan.   *H. R. Hays.*   HAYS, 61.
      Tropic Siesta.   *D. D. Walsh.*   FITT, 221.
      Tropic Siesta.   *D. D. Walsh.*   JONE-3, 97.
      Verses to the Moon.   *W. G. Williams.*   JONE-3, 97.
      Verses to the Moon.   *W. G. Williams.*   WALS, 713.
      Vespers.   *D. D. Walsh.*   FITT, 223.
      Village Night.   *D. D. Walsh.*   FITT, 221.

618   LÓPEZ, RAFAEL   (1873-1943)   Mexico
      Poetry
      Manuel de la Parra.   *E. W. Underwood.*   UND, 74.
      Venus Poised.   *S. Beckett.*   PAZ-1, 169.
      Other
      Colonial Puebla.   *E. W. Underwood.*   UND, 42.

619   LÓPEZ, RENÉ   (   )   Cuba
      Poetry
      The Sculptor.   *J. I. C. Clarke.*   WALS, 746.

620   LÓPEZ ALBÚJAR, ENRIQUE   (1872-?   )   Peru
      Fiction
      Adultery.   *H. Kurz.*   HAYDN, 915.
      Ushanan Jampi.   *H. de Onís.*   ONIS-1, 238.

621   LÓPEZ MERINO, FRANCISCO   (1904-1928)   Argentina
      Poetry
      My Cousins, On Sundays....   *R. O'Connell.*   FITT, 473.
      Song For Afterwards.   *R. O'Connell.*   FITT, 473.

622   LÓPEZ PORTILLO Y ROJAS, JOSÉ   (1850-1923)   Mexico
      Fiction
      La Parcela (Excerpt).   *F. Starr.*   STAR, 316.

623   LÓPEZ SURIA, VIOLETA   (1929-   )   Puerto Rico
      Poetry
      Ode 1962.   *B. Luby.*   BABI, 303.

624 LÓPEZ VELARDE, RAMÓN (1888-1921) Mexico
Poetry
Ants. *M. González.* CARA, 261.
Ants. *H. R. Hays.* JONE-3, 47.
Ants. *H. R. Hays.* HAYS, 31.
Ants. *S. Beckett.* PAZ-1, 181.
Ants. *D. Eichhorn.* PAZ-2, 189.
Gentle Fatherland. *H. R. Hays.* HAYS, 37.
Humbly. *D. Justice.* PAZ-2, 195.
Humbly. *S. Beckett.* PAZ-1, 184.
I Honour You in Dread. *S. Beckett.* PAZ-1, 183.
Ill-starred Return. *J. M. Cohen.* COH-2, 359.
In the Wet Shadows. *S. Beckett.* PAZ-1, 173.
My Cousin Agatha. *D. Eichhorn.* PAZ-2, 185.
My Cousin Agueda. *W. K. Jones.* JONE-3, 46.
My Cousin Águeda. *H. R. Hays.* HAYS, 27.
My Cousin Agueda. *S. Beckett.* PAZ-1, 172.
My Heart. *E. W. Underwood.* UND, 68.
My Heart Atones.... *S. Beckett.* PAZ-1, 176.
Now, as Never.... *S. Beckett.* PAZ-1, 174.
Our Lives Are Pendulums. *H. R. Hays.* HAYS, 29.
The Ascension And The Assumption. *H. R. Hays.* HAYS, 35.
The Chandelier. *D. Eichhorn.* PAZ-2, 191.
The Dream of the Black Gloves. *D. Justice.* PAZ-2, 201.
The Malefic Return. *S. Beckett.* PAZ-1, 179.
The Maleficent Return. *M. E. Johnson.* JOHN, 179.
The Sound Of The Heart. *H. R. Hays.* HAYS, 35.
The Spell of Return. *E. W. Underwood.* JONE-3, 46.
The Spell of Return. *E. W. Underwood.* UND, 67.
The Tear. *M. González.* CARA, 260.
The Tear. *S. Beckett.* PAZ-1, 182.
Wet Earth. *S. Beckett.* PAZ-1, 178.
Wet Land. *E. W. Underwood.* UND, 66.
Your Teeth. *S. Beckett.* PAZ-1, 177.

625 LÓPEZ Y FUENTES, GREGORIO (1897-   ) Mexico
Fiction
A Letter to God. *W. E. Colford.* COLF, 149.
A Letter to God. *D. A. Yates.* FLOR-3, 244.
A Letter to God. *S. L. Shelby.* JONE-3, 286.
"We Need a God." no tr. LIT-1, 69.

626 LOYÁCONO, HUGO (   ) Chile
Poetry
Victor Jara (Excerpt). *I. Langman.* LOW, 88.

627 LOZANO JR., RAFAEL (1899-   ) Mexico
Poetry
The Aztec Flutist. *E. W. Underwood.* UND, 166.

628   LUCAS, FABIO   (   )   Brazil
      Other
      Cultural aspects of Brazilian literature (Essay).
        A. Severino. TRI-13, 33.

629   LUCIANO, FELIPE   (1947-   )   Puerto Rico
      Poetry
      Message to a Dope Fiend.... Originally Engl. MATI, 202.
      The Library. Originally Engl. MATI, 204.

630   LUGONES, LEOPOLDO   (1874-1938)   Argentina
      Poetry
      A Carnival Prayer. *T. Raworth*. CARA, 12.
      A Message. *A. S. Blackwell*. BLAC, 326.
      A Message. *W. K. Jones*. JONE-3, 151.
      Adagio. *T. Raworth*. CARA, 14.
      Disdain. *G. D. Craig*. CRAI, 109.
      Drops of Gold. *A. J. McVan*. JONE-3, 152.
      Drops of Gold. *A. J. McVan*. TRAN, 187.
      How the Mountains Talk. *A. S. Blackwell*. BLAC, 332.
      How The Mountains Talk. *A. S. Blackwell*. WALS, 664.
      Journey. *M. Lee*. JONE-3, 151.
      Journey. *M. Lee*. LIT-1, 23.
      Journey. *M. Lee*. LIT-2, 7.
      Morning Song. *B. G. Proske*. TRAN, 189.
      Nocturne. *T. Raworth*. CARA, 13.
      Serenade. *A. S. Blackwell*. BLAC, 330.
      Song. *S. Resnick*. RES, 78.
      Sonnet. *P. Gannon*. GAN, 25.
      The Bachelor. *G. D. Craig*. CRAI, 97.
      The Gift of Day. *G. Strange*. JONE-3, 150.
      The Gift Of Day. *G. Strange*. WALS, 669.
      The Hailstorm. *T. Raworth*. CARA, 16.
      The Lay of the Rosy Lips. *G. D. Craig*. CRAI, 111.
      The Morning Star. *T. Raworth*. CARA, 15.
      The Palm-Tree. *A. S. Blackwell*. BLAC, 328.
      The Palm-Tree. *A. S. Blackwell*. LIT-1, 6.
      The Palm-Tree. *A. S. Blackwell*. LIT-2, 7.
      The White Solitude. *M. E. Johnson*. JOHN, 103.
      The withered rose. *P. Gannon*. GAN, 27.
      To the Cattle and Harvest Fields. *G. D. Craig*. CRAI, 107.
      To Thee. *A. S. Blackwell*. BLAC, 332.
      Twilight Elegy. *M. E. Johnson*. JOHN, 107.
      Fiction
      Death of a Gaucho. *A. Brenner*. FRAN, 81.
      The Cult of the Flower. no tr. JONE-3, 153.
      Yzur. *W. E. Colford*. COLF, 79.
      Yzur. *W. E. Colford*. HOW-1, 49.
      Yzur. *G. Woodruff*. MANC, 41.
      Other
      Sarmiento The Educator (from: History of Sarmiento).
        H. de Onís. ARC, 339.

631 LUIS, RAÚL (1934-   ) Cuba
     Poetry
     Fantasy. *R. Llopis*. BECK, 587.
     Hunger. *R. Llopis*. BECK, 593.
     Return. *S. Carranza*. BECK, 595.
     Song. *R. Llopis*. BECK, 589.
     The Soldier's Rain Knapsack. *S. Carranza*. BECK, 591.
     Time Passes. *R. Llopis*. BECK, 585.

632 LUISI, LUISA (1899-   ) Uruguay
     Poetry
     I Am a Tree. *A. S. Blackwell*. BLAC, 450.
     Other
     Two Great Uruguayan Writers (Essay). no tr. LIT-1, 88.

633 LUJÁN, FERNANDO (1912-   ) Costa Rica
     Poetry
     Song of the Long Drouth. *A. J. McVan*. TRAN, 214.

634 LYNCH, BENITO (1880-1951) Argentina
     Fiction
     The Sorrel Colt. no tr. FLOR-4, 209.
     The Sorrel Colt. *H. Kurz*. HAYDN, 922.

635 [LYRA, CARMEN pseud.] (1888-1951) Costa Rica.
     GARVAJAL, MARÍA ISABEL
     Other
     Brer Rabbit, Businessman (Folklore). *H. de Onís*. ONIS-1,
        320.
     The Tales of My Aunt Panchita (Prologue). *H. de Onís*.
        ONIS-1, 317.

636 MACHADO, ANÍBAL MONTEIRO (1895-1964) Brazil
     Fiction
     The Piano. *W. L. Grossman*. GRO, 75.
     The Piano. *W. L. Grossman*. HOW-1, 94.

637 MADARIAGA, FRANCISCO (1927-   ) Argentina
     Poetry
     A Monkey's Tears. *W. Shand*. SHA, 214.
     Love Is Continuous. *W. Shand*. SHA, 216.
     The Belle And Society. *W. Shand*. SHA, 215.
     The Journey Of The Wolf. *W. Shand*. SHA, 215.
     The Vegetable Rails. *W. Shand*. SHA, 214.

638 MAGALHÃES JÚNIOR, RAIMUNDO (1907-   ) Brazil
     Fiction
     The Immunizer. *W. L. Grossman*. GRO, 6.

639 MAGALLANES MOURE, M. (1875-1923) Chile
Poetry
Hymn to Love. *A. S. Blackwell.* BLAC, 298.
My Mother. *L. Elliott.* WALS, 689.
The Rendezvous. *G. Strange.* WALS, 691.

640 MAGGI, CARLOS (1922-   ) Uruguay
Drama
The Library. *W. I. Oliver.* OLIV, 105.

641 MAIA, CARLOS VASCONCELOS (1923-   ) Brazil
Fiction
Largo Da Palma. *R. W. Horton.* COEL, 221.

642 MAISIAS Y CALLE, DIEGO (   ) Peru
Poetry
The Three Epochs. *A. B. Poor.* POOR, 72.

643 MALDONADO DENIS, MANUEL (1933-   ) Puerto Rico
Other
The Political Situation in Puerto Rico (Essay). *S. Pollock.*
MR, 221.

644 MALÉ, BELKIS CUZA (1942-   ) Cuba
Poetry
Deadly Woman. *T. Raworth.* TARN, 111.
Thus The Poets In Their Sad Likenesses. *N. Tarn.* TARN,
113.

645 MALINOW, INÉS (1925?-   ) Argentina
Poetry
Pain Creates Life For You. *W. Shand.* SHA, 199.
You Have Chosen The Paramo. *W. Shand.* SHA, 198.
You Want To Increase The Pain. *W. Shand.* SHA, 199.

646 MALLEA, EDUARDO (1903-   ) Argentina
Fiction
Fiesta In November. *A. De Sola.* FLOR-1, 11.
The City Beside the Motionless River (Excerpt). *H. Manning.*
JONE-3, 295.
The Heart's Reason. *H. de Onís.* ONIS-2, 177.

647 MALUENDA LABARCA, RAFAEL (1885-1963) Chile
Fiction
As God Wills. *E. Schaefer.* JONE-3, 319.
Escape. *A. De Sola.* FLOR-2, 473.

648 MAÑACH, JORGE (1898-1961) Cuba
Other
Martí In Prison [from: Martí, The Apostol (Biography)].
H. de Onís. ARC, 320.

649 MANCINI, JULES (1875-1928) Colombia
     Other
     Bolívar's First Campaign (from: Bolívar And The Emancipa-
     tion of the Colonies). *H. de Onís*. ARC, 249.

650 MANCO, SILVERIO (   ) Argentina
     Drama
     Juan Moreira. *J. Fassett*. BIER, 2.

651 MANRIQUE CABRERA, FRANCISCO (1908-   ) Puerto Rico
     Poetry
     Batey. *B. Luby*. BABI, 284.

652 MANUEL, FRANCISCO (   ) Brazil
     Poetry
     To Liberty. *A. B. Poor*. POOR, 38.

653 MAPLES ARCE, MANUEL (1900-   ) Mexico
     Poetry
     City. *M. Strand*. PAZ-2, 165.
     80H.P. *E. W. Underwood*. UND, 162.
     Paroxysm. *E. W. Underwood*. UND, 159.
     Parting. *E. W. Underwood*. UND, 161.

654 MARECHAL, LEOPOLDO (1900-   ) Argentina
     Poetry
     Cortège. *D. Fitt*. FITT, 545.
     "Didactics Of Joy" (Extracts No. 4 and No. 5). *W. Shand*.
       SHA, 47.
     Madrigal in silva. *P. Gannon*. GAN, 61.
     Of The Tree. *W. Shand*. SHA, 46.
     To Elbialove unsung. *P. Morgan*. TRI-13, 242.

655 MARGENAT, HUGO (1934-1957) Puerto Rico
     Poetry
     At the Front. *D. Sánchez-Méndez*. MATI, 85.
     God is good. *D. Sánchez-Méndez*. MATI, 93.
     Hard Wood. *D. Sánchez-Méndez*. MATI, 87.
     I Am Multitude. *D. Sánchez-Méndez*. MATI, 95.
     I and God, We Have Returned. *D. Sánchez-Méndez*. MATI, 79.
     Links. *D. Sánchez-Méndez*. MATI, 89.
     Only Once. *D. Sánchez-Méndez*. MATI, 79.
     September. *D. Sánchez-Méndez*. MATI, 83.
     Silence (Excerpt). no tr. KAI, n.p.
     The Ice Hand. *D. Sánchez-Méndez*. MATI, 81.
     You Should Know. *D. Sánchez-Méndez*. MATI, 85.

656 MARÍN, JUAN (1900-1963) Chile
     Fiction
     Parallel 53 South (Excerpt). *H. de Onís*. ARC, 449.
     The Funeral. *Z. Nelken*. TORR, 169.

657 MARÍN, PACHÍN (1863-1897) Puerto Rico
Poetry
The Nightingale. *B. Luby*. BABI, 94.
The Rag. *B. Luby*. BABI, 96.

658 MARÍN, RAMÓN JULIA (1878-1917) Puerto Rico
Fiction
In the Hinterland (Excerpt). no tr. KAI, n.p.

659 MARQUÉS, RENÉ (1919-) Puerto Rico
Fiction
Death. *G. R. Coulthard*. COUL, 116.
Give Us This Day. *C. Randolph*. FLAK, 158.
Island of Manhattan. *F. Edwards & G. Ortiz*. MANC, 339.
Purification on Cristo Street (Excerpt). *C. Pilditch*.
   KAI, n.p.
There's a Body Reclining On The Stern. *H. St. Martin*.
   CARP, 236.
Three Men By The River. *R. Márquez*. MR, 87.
Drama
The Fanlights. *R. J. Wiezell*. WOOD, 4.
The House of the Setting Sun. *W. K. Jones*. JONE-3, 460.

660 MÁRQUEZ SALAS, ANTONIO (1919-) Venezuela
Fiction
Like God! *D. Flakoll & C. Alegría*. FLAK, 47.

661 MARRÉ, LUIS (1929-) Cuba
Poetry
'And There Was Also A Ranch In Hell.' *D. Gardner*. TARN, 43.
Death Head-On. *A. Boyer*. BECK, 319.
'I Had In My Hand.' *D. Gardner*. TARN, 41.
If I'm Asked.... *A. Boyer*. BECK, 321.
Poem. *A. Boyer*. BECK, 315.
Song. *S. Carranza*. BECK, 307.
Storming Paradise. *A. Boyer*. BECK, 323.
Testament. *A. Boyer*. BECK, 317.
To the Town Crier of Santiago. *C. Beck*. BECK, 311.
Written at Mr. Kennedy's Death. *A. Boyer*. BECK, 313.
Your Name. *C. Beck*. BECK, 309.
Your Name. *J. M. Cohen*. COH-3, 99.

662 MARRERO NÚÑEZ, JULIO (1910-) Puerto Rico
Fiction
The Interpreter. *B. Luby*. BABI, 321.

663 MARTÍ, JOSÉ (1853-1895) Cuba
Poetry
My Little Horseman. *W. K. Jones*. JONE-3, 69.
Poetry is Sacred. *W. K. Jones*. JONE-3, 71.
Simple Stanzas XXXIX. *B. Proske*. TRAN, 218.

(MARTÍ, JOSÉ)
    Simple Verses. *M. E. Johnson.* JOHN, 51.
    Simple Verses. *S. Resnick.* RES, 40.
    Thirst for Beauty. *J. Hill.* CARA, 193.
    Winged Goblet. *J. Hill.* CARA, 194.
    Yoke and Star. *W. K. Jones.* JONE-3, 70.
    <u>Other</u>
    Letter to Federico Henriquez Y Carvajal. no tr. LIT-1, 36.
    Sayings. no tr. LIT-1, 38.
    The Indians of America. no tr. LIT-2, 18.

664   MARTÍNEZ, DAVID (1921-   ) Argentina
    <u>Poetry</u>
    Flowering Yellow. *W. Shand.* SHA, 164.
    Passion Of A Memory. *W. Shand.* SHA, 163.

665   MARTÍNEZ, JOSÉ DE JESÚS (1929-   ) Panama
    <u>Poetry</u>
    "Lamentations." no tr. YOU, 96.
    <u>Poems to Her</u> (Excerpt). no tr. YOU, 98.

666   MARTÍNEZ CAPÓ, JUAN (1923-   ) Puerto Rico
    <u>Poetry</u>
    Peasant. *B. Luby.* BABI, 300.

667   MARTÍNEZ DE LA VEGA, PEPE (   ) Mexico
    <u>Fiction</u>
    The Dead Man Was a Lively One. *D. Yates.* YATE, 175.

668   MARTÍNEZ ESTRADA, EZEQUIEL (1895-1964) Argentina
    <u>Poetry</u>
    Infinity and Eternity. *T. Raworth.* CARA, 26.
    Last Quarter. *T. Raworth.* CARA, 25.

669   MARTÍNEZ MATOS, JOSÉ (1930-   ) Cuba
    <u>Poetry</u>
    Battle. *C. Beck.* BECK, 443.
    Defense. *C. Beck.* BECK, 455.
    Letter from the Trenches. *C. Beck.* BECK, 447.
    My Answer. *C. Beck.* BECK, 449.
    Poetry. *C. Beck.* BECK, 451.
    The Man Who Was For Autumn. *C. Beck.* BECK, 445.
    The Mighty Voice. *C. Beck.* BECK, 457.
    The Nightingale. *C. Beck.* BECK, 453.

670   MARTÍNEZ MORENO, CARLOS (1917-   ) Uruguay
    <u>Fiction</u>
    The Aborigines. *D. Rubin.* PRIZE, 65.
    The Pigeon. *G. Pontiero.* FRA-J, 137.
    The siren. *J. C. Murchison.* TRI-13, 452.

671 MARTÍNEZ QUEIROLO, JOSÉ (1951-   ) Ecuador
     Drama
     R.I.P. *G. Luzuriaga & R. Rudder.* LUZU, 57.

672 MARTOS, MARCOS (1942-   ) Peru
     Poetry
     Casa Nuestra (Excerpt). *D. Tipton.* AHER, 90.
     Our House. *D. Tipton.* AHER, 89.
     Politics. *D. Tipton.* AHER, 92.
     Quijote. *D. Tipton.* AHER, 89.

673 MASTRONARDI, CARLOS (1900-   ) Argentina
     Poetry
     A Theme Of The Night And The Man. *W. Shand.* SHA, 49.
     The Forgotten Kings. *W. Shand.* SHA, 48.

674 MATAS, JULIO (1931-   ) Cuba
     Drama
     Ladies At Play. *F. Colecchia & J. Matas.* COLE, 163.

675 MATILLA, ALFREDO (1937-   ) Puerto Rico
     Poetry
     catalogue of lunatics-kimberna. *E. G. Matilla.* MATI, 119.
     subway. *A. Matilla.* MATI, 117.

676 MATOS PAOLI, FRANCISCO (1915-   ) Puerto Rico
     Poetry
     Biography of a Poet. *D. Sánchez-Méndez.* MATI, 29.
     Democracy. *D. Sánchez-Méndez.* MATI, 31.
     Invocation To The Fatherland. *B. Luby.* BABI, 275.
     The Death of God. *D. Sánchez-Méndez.* MATI, 33.
     The Leader's Name is Pedro. *D. Sánchez-Méndez.* MATI, 27.

677 MATTO DE TURNER, CLORINDA (1854-1909) Peru
     Fiction
     Birds Without Nests (Excerpt).*G. Karnezis.* JONE-2, 169.

678 MAYA, RAFAEL (1898-   ) Colombia
     Poetry
     Far Over Yonder. *R. Humphries.* FITT, 457.

679 MAZAS GARBAYO, GONZALO (1904-   ) Cuba
     Fiction
     The Valley. *W. E. Colford.* COLF, 172.

680 MEDEIROS E ALBUQUERQUE, JOSÉ DE (1867-?   ) Brazil
     Fiction
     The Vengeance of Felix. *I. Goldberg.* GOLD-1, 107.

681 MEDINA VIDAL, JORGE (1930-   ) Uruguay
     Poetry
     No One Weeps. *R. Connally.* YOU, 114.

682 MÉDIZ BOLIO, ANTONIO (1884-1957) Mexico
     Poetry
     Theatrical Sword. *E. W. Underwood.* UND, 132.

683 MEIRELES, CECÍLIA (1901-1964) Brazil
     Poetry
     A Sketch. *M. Cardozo.* NEI, 115.
     Aria. *P. Standish.* CARA, 78.
     Ballad Of The Ten Ballerinas Of The Casino. *M. Cardozo.*
       NEI, 125.
     Ballad of the Ten Casino Dancers. *J. Merrill.* BISH, 39.
     Destiny. *L. S. Downes.* DOWN, 44.
     Guitar. *M. Cardozo.* NEI, 123.
     Guitar. *J. Nist & Y. Leite.* NIST, 73.
     Introduction. *J. Nist & Y. Leite.* NIST, 71.
     Laughter. no tr. TRE, 16.
     Medieval Sandal. *J. Nist & Y. Leite.* NIST, 75.
     Motive. *J. Nist & Y. Leite.* NIST, 72.
     Museum. *J. Nist & Y. Leite.* NIST, 76.
     Pastoral. *J. Nist & Y. Leite.* NIST, 76.
     Portrait. *A. Levitin.* CHI, 83.
     Portrait. *M. Cardozo.* NEI, 113.
     Portrait. *J. Nist & Y. Leite.* NIST, 71.
     Presence. *P. Standish.* CARA, 79.
     Pyrargyrite Metal, 9. *J. Merrill.* BISH, 47.
     Romance LXXXIV or The Horses Of The Inconfidência.
       M. Cardozo. NEI, 127.
     Second Rose Motif. *J. Merrill.* BISH, 35.
     Still Life. no tr. TRE, 14.
     The Androgynous One. *M. Cardozo.* NEI, 121.
     The Archangel. *J. Nist & Y. Leite.* NIST, 77.
     The Bath Of The Buffalos. *A. Levitin.* CHI, 81.
     The Cycle Of The Sabía Songbird. *M. Cardozo.* NEI, 117.
     The Dead Horse. *J. Merrill.* BISH, 43.
     The Gates of Midnight. *J. Nist & Y. Leite.* NIST, 78.
     The Roosters Will Crow. *J. Nist & Y. Leite.* NIST, 74.
     Tree-Cricket. no tr. TRE, 18.
     Vigil. *J. Merrill.* BISH, 37.

684 MEJÍA SÁNCHEZ, ERNESTO (1923-   ) Nicaragua
     Poetry
     The Recluse. *D. Flakoll & C. Alegría.* FLAK, 156.

685 MELÉNDEZ, CONCHA (1904-   ) Puerto Rico
     Poetry
     The Mountains Know. *B. Luby.* BABI, 146.

686 MELÉNDEZ MUÑOZ, MIGUEL (1884-1966) Puerto Rico
     Fiction
     Two Letters. *B. Luby.* BABI, 111.

687   MELLO, THIAGO DE   (1926–   )   Brazil
      Poetry
      Song of Armed Love. *R. Márquez & D. A. McMurray*. MARQ, 99.
      The Statues of Man (A Permanent Act of Law). *R. Márquez &*
         T. Pax. MARQ, 91.

688   MELO FRANCO, AFFONSO ARINHOS DE   (1868–1916)   Brazil
      Other
      The Yara (Legend). *H. de Onís*. ONIS-1, 363.

689   MENDES, MURILO   (1902–   )   Brazil
      Poetry
      Anonymity. *J. Nist & Y. Leite*. NIST, 102.
      Baroque Poem. *P. Standish*. CARA, 86.
      Destruction. *J. Nist & Y. Leite*. NIST, 102.
      Final Judgment of the Eyes. *J. Nist & Y. Leite*. NIST, 98.
      Gambling. *J. Nist & Y. Leite*. NIST, 103.
      Half Bird. *J. Nist & Y. Leite*. NIST, 99.
      Horses. *W. S. Merwin*. BISH, 55.
      I Give Alms. *L. S. Downes*. DOWN, 49.
      Look, Timeless. *J. Nist & Y. Leite*. NIST, 99.
      Map. *W. S. Merwin*. BISH, 49.
      Newest Prometheus. *J. Nist & Y. Leite*. NIST, 104.
      Poem Seen from the Outside. *J. Nist & Y. Leite*. NIST, 101.
      Rose Ideas. *P. Standish*. CARA, 88.
      Something. *P. Standish*. CARA, 87.
      Spiritual Poem. *J. Nist & Y. Leite*. NIST, 101.
      The Culprit. *J. Nist & Y. Leite*. NIST, 100.
      The Three Circles. *J. Nist & Y. Leite*. NIST, 100.
      Two-edged Sword. *J. Nist & Y. Leite*. NIST, 103.
      USSR. *J. Nist & Y. Leite*. NIST, 97.

690   MÉNDEZ, ÁNGEL LUIS   (1944–   )   Puerto Rico
      Poetry
      áurea petra maría. *E. G. Matilla*. MATI, 197.
      initials. *E. G. Matilla*. MATI, 199.
      pronouns of passage. *E. G. Matilla*. MATI, 195.

691   MÉNDEZ, FRANCISCO   (1908–   )   Guatemala
      Poetry
      Blood On A Stone. *D. D. Walsh*. FITT, 193.

692   MÉNDEZ BALLESTER, MANUEL   (1909–   )   Puerto Rico
      Drama
      Crossroad. *B. Luby*. BABI, 377.

693   MÉNDEZ CALZADA, ENRIQUE   (1898–   )   Argentina
      Fiction
      Christ in Buenos Aires. *E. C. García*. JONE-3, 363.

694 MÉNDEZ DORICH, RAFAEL (1903-   ) Peru
    Poetry
    Porcelain Of The North. *D. D. Walsh*. FITT, 421.
    She Was Carrying The Lamp. *D. D. Walsh*. FITT, 421.
    The Duchess's White Cats. *D. D. Walsh*. FITT, 423.

695 MENDOZA, RAFAEL (   )
    Poetry
    This Pablo. *C. Hayes*. LOW, 19.

696 MENÉN DESLEAL, ALVARO (   ) El Salvador
    Drama
    Black Light. *G. Luzuriaga & R. Rudder*. LUZU, 83.

697 MENÉNDEZ, ALDO (1918-   ) Cuba
    Poetry
    Fishing Port. *R. Llopis*. BECK, 173.
    Mara. *R. Llopis*. BECK, 171.
    Raimundo. *C. Beck*. BECK, 169.
    Revolution. *C. Beck*. BECK, 167.
    Ship. *S. Carranza*. BECK, 165.
    We Always Sang. *S. Carranza*. BECK, 161.

698 MENÉNDEZ ALBERDI, ADOLFO (1912-   ) Cuba
    Poetry
    Fable of the Family Table. *R. Llopis*. BECK, 107.
    In the Afternoon at Six. *S. Carranza*. BECK, 109.
    Song of the Militiaman Recently Married. *S. Carranza*.
      BECK, 111.
    The Deserter. *R. Llopis*. BECK, 117.

699 MENESES, GUILLERMO (1911-   ) Venezuela
    Fiction
    The Sloop Isabel Arrived This Evening.... *A. Flores*.
      FLOR-2, 283.

700 MENESES, PORFIRIO (1915-   ) Peru
    Fiction
    The Little Dark Man. *D. Flakoll & C. Alegría*. FLAK, 11.

701 MERCADO, JOSÉ (1863-1911) Puerto Rico
    Poetry
    The Castillian Language. *B. Luby*. BABI, 96.

702 MEYER, AUGUSTO (1902-   ) Brazil
    Poetry
    Mirror. *L. S. Downes*. DOWN, 46.
    Picture. *M. Cardozo*. NEI, 89.
    Prodigality: To A Cicada. *M. Cardozo*. NEI, 87.
    The Looking Glass. *M. Cardozo*. NEI, 93.
    The Speech, By A Fly. *M. Cardozo*. NEI, 91.

703 MIESES BURGOS, FRANKLIN (1907-   ) Dominican Republic
      Poetry
      Song of the Lassie Who Walked Alone. *F. E. Townsend.*
        TOWN, 59.

704 MILANO, DANTE (1899-   ) Brazil
      Poetry
      Nocturne. *L. S. Downes.* DOWN, 43.

705 MILLÁN, GONZALO (   ) Chile
      Poetry
      And I keep singing you like a bad Popular Song. *J. Upton.*
        TRI-13, 383.
      Clinical bulletin. *J. Upton.* TRI-13, 383.

706 MILLIET, SÉRGIO (1898-1966) Brazil
      (Sérgio Milliet Da Costa E Silva)
      Poetry
      Birthday. *M. Cardozo.* NEI, 39.
      Poem. *L. S. Downes.* DOWN, 42.
      Run away flying low. *M. Cardozo.* NEI, 41.
      Saudade. *M. Cardozo.* NEI, 41.

707 MIR, PEDRO (1913-   ) Dominican Republic
      Poetry
      Amen to Butterflies. *R. Márquez.* MARQ, 211.

708 MIRANDA, JOSÉ TAVORES DE (1919-   ) Brazil
      Poetry
      Poem At Thirty. *L. S. Downes.* DOWN, 70.

709 MIRÓN, SALVADOR DÍAZ (1853-1928) Mexico
      See also DÍAZ MIRÓN, SALVADOR
      Poetry
      Envy. *A. S. Blackwell.* BLAC, 120.
      Snow-flake. *A. S. Blackwell.* BLAC, 118.
      The Cloud. *A. S. Blackwell.* BLAC, 122.
      To Pity. *A. S. Blackwell.* BLAC, 120.

710 MISTRAL, GABRIELA (1889-1957) Chile
      Poetry
      A Sonnet of Death. *R. Gill.* JONE-3, 121.
      Absence. *K. Flores.* FLOR-1, 298.
      Autumn. *M. Kittel.* FLOR-1, 294.
      Ballad. *D. J. Flakoll & C. Alegría.* BENE, 31.
      Ballad. *M. Kittel.* FLOR-1, 292.
      Ballad of the Star. *S. Resnick.* RES, 84.
      Ballad of the Star. *A. J. McVan.* TRAN, 199.
      Deep Sleep. *K. G. C.* FITT, 43.
      Earth And The Woman. *L. Hughes.* MILL, 301.
      Ecstasy. *M. Lee.* LIT-1, 24.
      Ecstasy. *M. Lee.* LIT-2, 58.

(MISTRAL, GABRIELA)
Fear. *L. Hughes*. MILL, 303.
Foreigner. *T. Raworth*. CARA, 121.
God Wills It. *K. G. C*. FITT, 47.
Hymn to the Tree. *A. S. Blackwell*. BLAC, 236.
If You'll Just Go To Sleep. *L. Hughes*. MILL, 300.
In Memoriam. *I. K. Macdermott*. LIT-1, 12.
Intimate. *G. D. Craig*. CRAI, 197.
Intimate. *K. Flores*. FLOR-1, 291.
Intimate. *D. Conzelman*. JONE-3, 121.
Little Feet. *A. S. Blackwell*. BLAC, 264.
Little Feet. *A. Fife*. FIFE, 67.
Little Hands. *A. S. Blackwell*. BLAC, 266.
Little Hands. no tr. LIT-2, 13.
Midnight. *T. Raworth*. CARA, 122.
Night. *S. Resnick*. RES, 82.
Night. *A. J. McVan*. TRAN, 200.
Paradise. *L. Hughes*. MILL, 302.
Poem of the Boy. *A. Fife*. FIFE, 69.
Poems of the Home. *A. S. Blackwell*. BLAC, 256.
Prayer for the Nest. *A. S. Blackwell*. BLAC, 252.
Rocking. *M. Kittel*. FLOR-1, 296.
Rocking. *S. Resnick*. RES, 80.
Serene Woods. *M. Kittel*. FLOR-1, 294.
Song. *G. D. Craig*. CRAI, 201.
Sonnets Of Death (Excerpt). *R. Gill*. WALS, 735.
The Children Dance. *A. S. Blackwell*. BLAC, 266.
The Enemy. *A. S. Blackwell*. BLAC, 240.
The Enemy. *A. S. Blackwell*. LIT-2, 12.
The Jars. *A. S. Blackwell*. BLAC, 244.
The Liana. *D. Dana*. COH-1, 15.
The Little Girl That Lost A Finger. *M. Lee*. FITT, 39.
The Prayer. *G. D. Craig*. CRAI, 203.
The Prayer. *D. D. Walsh*. FITT, 39.
The Rose. *K. Flores*. FLOR-1, 297.
The Rural Teacher. *G. D. Craig*. CRAI, 195.
The Rural Teacher. *I. K. Macdermott*. JONE-3, 123.
The Sad Mother. *A. S. Blackwell*. BLAC, 254.
The Stable. *L. Hughes*. MILL, 298.
The Stranger. *K. Flores*. FLOR-1, 297.
The Thistle. *A. S. Blackwell*. BLAC, 248.
The Thorn-Tree. *A. S. Blackwell*. BLAC, 252.
Thirst. *A. S. Blackwell*. BLAC, 246.
Vessels. *A. S. Blackwell*. BLAC, 246.
White Clouds. *A. S. Blackwell*. BLAC, 262.
Fiction
Earthen Jugs. *K. Flores*. FLOR-1, 296.
Why Reeds Are Hollow. *W. J. Smith*. HOW-1, 79.

Other
Silhouette Of The Mexican Indian Woman. *H. de Onís.* ARC,
76.
The Human Geography of Chile. no tr. LIT-1, 19.
To the Children (Essay). *K. Flores.* FLOR-1, 293.
To the Children (Essay). *A. S. Blackwell.* BLAC, 240.

711 MOJARRO, TOMÁS (1932-   ) Mexico
Fiction
The Harp. *L. Kemp.* PRIZE, 134.

712 MOLINA, ENRIQUE (1910-   ) Argentina
Poetry
A Natural Chair. *W. Shand.* SHA, 100.
Descent Into Oblivion. *T. Hoeksema.* MU-69, 45.
Hue. *R. Márquez.* MARQ, 39.
Information. *R. Márquez.* MARQ, 47.
Life Before Birth. *T. Raworth.* CARA, 36.
Market. *W. Shand.* SHA, 98.
Memory. *T. Hoeksema.* MU-69, 43.
Night Watch. *R. Márquez.* MARQ, 49.
Nocturnal Hollow. *W. Shand.* SHA, 98.
Old ferret. *J. Upton.* TRI-13, 443.
Renegade. *J. Upton.* TRI-13, 443.
To Settle Down. *W. Shand.* SHA, 99.
"What trade can suit me?" *J. Upton.* TRI-13, 444.

713 MOLINA SOLIS, JUAN F. (1850-?   ) Mexico
Other
The Horrors of 1648 in Yucatan. *F. Starr.* STAR, 108.

714 MOLINARI, RICARDO E. (1898-   ) Argentina
Poetry
A Rose for Stefan George. *T. Raworth.* CARA, 27.
Elegy. *W. Shand.* SHA, 23.
Elegy. *W. Shand.* SHA, 28.
"No, it will not come back, neither the light nor the
morning...." *J. M. Cohen.* COH-2, 379.
Ode. *J. M. Cohen.* COH-1, 28.
Ode. *J. M. Cohen.* COH-2, 377.
Poem. *W. Shand.* SHA, 24.
Poem. *W. Shand.* SHA, 27.
Short Ode To Melancholy. *W. Shand.* SHA, 26.
Sonnet III. *H. Manning.* GAN, 49.
"Yes, nothing comes back except pure dream...." *J. M. Cohen.*
COH-2, 380.

715 MOLINAS ROLÓN, GUILLERMO (1892-1947) Paraguay
Poetry
Spring. *W. K. Jones.* JONE-3, 139.

716   MONDRAGÓN, SERGIO (1936-   ) Mexico
       Poetry
       Coatlicue. *M. A. de Maurer*. HAR67-4, 61.
       Guru. *W. S. Merwin*. PAZ-2, 51.
       In July and in Hebrew. *E. Randall*. TRI-13, 337.
       Risk. *M. A. de Maurer*. HAR67-4, 65.
       Urns, flies and locusts. *E. Randall*. TRI-13, 336.

717   MONETA, CARLOS J. (   ) Argentina
       Poetry
       picture girl. *P. Morgan*. TRI-13, 235.
       the emperor of rain. *P. Morgan*. TRI-13, 236.
       the struggle of poets. *P. Morgan*. TRI-13, 236.

718   MONTENEGRO, CARLOS (1900-   ) Cuba
       Fiction
       Twelve Corals. *N. Vandemoer*. HOW-2, 267.

719   MONTENEGRO, ERNESTO (1885-?   ) Chile
       Poetry
       To Modern Poets. *R. Gill*. WALS, 740.

720   MONTERDE, FRANCISCO (1894-   ) Mexico
       Other
       The Road to Taxco (Essay). *E. W. Underwood*. UND, 131.

721   MONTERROSO, AUGUSTO (1922-   ) Guatemala
       Fiction
       First Lady. *D. Flakoll & C. Alegría*. FLAK, 66.

722   MONTES DE OCA, MARCO ANTONIO (1931-   ) Mexico
       Poetry
       A Little Set of Morals. *M. González*. CARA, 296.
       Assumption of the triple image. *J. Upton*. TRI-13, 446.
       Behind Memory. *D. J. Flakoll & C. Alegría*. BENE, 127.
       Nameless. *J. Upton*. TRI-13, 448.
       On The Threshold Of A Plea. *L. Kemp*. EVER, 105.
       Song For Celebrating What Won't Die. *W. Stafford*. GARR,
       325.
       The Fool's Farewell. *J. M. Cohen*. COH-1, 216.
       The Garden Which the Gods Frequented. *W. S. Merwin*. PAZ-2,
       63.
       The Light in Its Stand. *W. S. Merwin*. PAZ-2, 61.
       The Lip Cracks. *J. M. Cohen*. COH-1, 217.
       With fixed bayonet. *J. Upton*. TRI-13, 445.
       9. *W. Stafford*. GARR, 321.

723   MONTOYA ROJAS, RODRIGO (   ) Peru
       Other
       The Cholo From Pacaraos (Recorded interview). *C. A. de Lo-
       mellini*. HAR67-3, 9.

724   MOOCK, ARMANDO   (1894-1942) · Chile
      Drama
      The Youngster (Excerpt). *W. K. Jones.*   JONE-3, 417.

725   MORA, OCTÁVIO   (1933-   )   Brazil
      Poetry
      The Table. *F. P. Hebblethwaite.*   YOU, 28.

726   MORAES, VINÍCIUS DE   (1913-   )   Brazil
      Poetry
      Ballad of the Red Light District. *J. Nist & Y. Leite.*
        NIST, 120.
      Christmas Poem. *A. Brown.* BISH, 101.
      Christmas Poem. *A. Brown.* COH-1, 150.
      Christmas Poem. *J. Nist & Y. Leite.* NIST, 126.
      Death. *J. Nist & Y. Leite.* NIST, 120.
      Death-bed. *L. S. Downes.* DOWN, 55.
      Epitaph. *J. Nist & Y. Leite.* NIST, 122.
      Final Elegy (Excerpt). *P. Standish.* CARA, 92.
      Imitation of Rilke. *J. Nist & Y. Leite.* NIST, 117.
      Longing for Manuel Bandeira. *J. Nist & Y. Leite.* NIST,
        117.
      Natural History of Pablo Neruda (Excerpt). *N. Braymer &*
        C. Dobzynski. LOW, 206.
      Piece. *J. Nist & Y. Leite.* NIST, 123.
      Recipe For A Woman. *M. Cardozo.* NEI, 137.
      Rocking the Dead Son. *J. Nist & Y. Leite.* NIST, 124.
      Song. *R. Wilbur.* BISH, 95.
      Sonnet Of Farewell. *M. Cardozo.* NEI, 135.
      Sonnet of Intimacy. *E. Bishop.* BISH, 103.
      Sonnet of Separation. *M. Cardozo.* NEI, 135.
      Sonnet on Fidelity. *A. Brown.* BISH, 97.
      Sonnet on Separation. *A. Brown.* BISH, 111.
      Sonnet On Separation. *A. Brown.* COH-1, 151.
      The Acrobats. *J. Nist & Y. Leite.* NIST, 118.
      The Diver. *M. Cardozo.* NEI, 131.
      The Pear. *A. Brown.* BISH, 99.
      The Verb in the Infinite. *P. Standish.* CARA, 94.
      Woman Recipe. *P. Blackburn.* BISH, 105.

727   MORALES, JORGE LUIS   (1930-   )   Puerto Rico
      Poetry
      Hymn To The Sun. *B. Luby.* BABI, 301.

728   MOREIRA DA FONSECA, JOSÉ PAULO   (1922-   )   Brazil
      Poetry
      Night Wind. *L. S. Downes.* DOWN, 78.
      Poem. *L. S. Downes.* DOWN, 78.

729   MOREJÓN, NANCY   (1944-   ) Cuba
       Poetry
       A Disillusionment for Rubén Darío. *S. Carranza.* BECK, 781.
       Central Park Some People (3 P.M.). *S. Carranza.* BECK, 783.
       Freedom Now. *R. Márquez.* MARQ, 207.
       'Love Slides Down the Sides.' *T. Reynolds.* TARN, 123.
       Present, Angela Domínguez. *S. Carranza.* BECK, 779.
       Some People/Central Park/3:00 P.M. *N. Tarn.* TARN, 125.
       The Achaens. *R. Márquez.* MARQ, 203.

730   MOREL, TOMÁS   (   ) Dominican Republic
       Poetry
       Accordian. *F. E. Townsend.* TOWN, 41.
       Flamboyant Tree. *F. E. Townsend.* TOWN, 42.

731   MORENO JIMENES, DOMINGO   (1894-   ) Dominican Republic
       Poetry
       Schoolmistress. *F. E. Townsend.* TOWN, 38.

732   MORENO JIMENO, MANUEL   (1913-   ) Peru
       Poetry
       The Damned. *H. R. Hays.* FITT, 299.

    [MORLEY, HELENA pseud.]. See BRANT, ALICE.

733   [MORO, CÉSAR pseud.]   (1904-1956) Peru
       QUÍSPEZ ASÍN, CÉSAR
       Poetry
       The Illustrated World. *M. Lee.* FITT, 413.
       Vision Of Moth-Eaten Pianos Falling To Pieces. *M. Lee.*
         FITT, 411.
       You Come In The Night With The Fabulous Smoke Of Your Hair.
         H. R. Hays. FITT, 409.

734   MOSQUERA, RICARDO   (1918-   ) Argentina
       Poetry
       The Tireless Peddler. *W. Shand.* SHA, 138.
       To Leopoldo Lugones. *W. Shand.* SHA, 136.
       What Bitter Solitude. *W. Shand.* SHA, 136.

735   MOTA, MAURO   (1912-   ) Brazil
       (Mauro Ramos Da Mota E Albuquerque)
       Poetry
       Memory. *L. S. Downes.* DOWN, 53.
       The Cock. *M. Strand.* BISH, 113.

736   MOURA, EMILIO   (1902-   ) Brazil
       Poetry
       In The Depths Of Night. *L. S. Downes.* DOWN, 50.

737   MOYANO, DANIEL (1930-   ) Argentina
      Fiction
      Vaudeville Artists. *N. T. di Giovanni.* CARP, 306.

738   MUÑOZ, RAFAEL JOSÉ (1928-   ) Venezuela
      Poetry
      Death On The Road. *B. Belitt.* MU-73, 31.
      Winter Pastoral. *B. Belitt.* MU-73, 29.

739   MUÑOZ MARÍN, LUIS (1898-   ) Puerto Rico
      Poetry
      Pamphlet. *M. Lee.* FITT, 225.
      Proletarians. *M. Lee.* FITT, 225.
      Symphony In White. *T. Walsh.* WALS, 769.
      The Pamphlet. *B. Luby.* BABI, 199.
      Other
      A Good Civilization (Speech). *B. Luby.* BABI, 200.

740   MUÑOZ RIVERA, LUIS (1859-1916) Puerto Rico
      Poetry
      Parenthesis (Excerpt). no tr. KAI, n.p.
      To Her. *R. Gill.* WALS, 589.
      Other
      Give Us Our Independence (Speech). *B. Luby.* BABI, 185.
      What I Have Been, What I Am, What I Shall Be (Speech).
         B. Luby. BABI, 183.

741   MURENA, HÉCTOR A. (1923-   ) Argentina
      Poetry
      Arpeggios Of A Winter Evening. *W. Shand.* SHA, 176.
      Death of Edgar Allan Poe. *D. Flakoll & C. Alegría.* FLAK,
         96.
      I Know. *W. Shand.* SHA, 178.
      The Lost Poem. *W. Shand.* SHA, 177.
      Fiction
      The Cavalry Colonel. *G. Brotherston.* FRA-J, 45.

742   MUTIS, ALVARO (1923-   ) Colombia
      Poetry
      A Word. *J. Hill.* CARA, 188.
      Every Poem. *W. S. Merwin.* CARP, 267.
      The Death of Matías Aldecoa. *W. S. Merwin.* CARP, 269.

 [NABORÍ, INDIO pseud.]. See ORTA RUIZ, JESÚS.

743   NÁJERA, MANUEL GUTIÉRREZ (1859-1895) Mexico
      See also GUTIÉRREZ NÁJERA, MANUEL
      Poetry
      Dead Waves. *A. S. Blackwell.* BLAC, 2.
      Ephemera. *A. S. Blackwell.* BLAC, 6.
      In the Country. *A. S. Blackwell.* BLAC, 22.
      Longing. *A. S. Blackwell.* BLAC, 22.

(NÁJERA, MANUEL GUTIÉRREZ)
Pax Animae. *A. S. Blackwell*. BLAC, 24.
Souls and Birds. *A. S. Blackwell*. BLAC, 10.
To an Unknown Goddess. *A. S. Blackwell*. BLAC, 16.
To The Wife of the Corregidor. *A. S. Blackwell*. BLAC, 30.
Whiteness. *A. S. Blackwell*. BLAC, 12.

744 NAJLIS, MICHELE (   ) Nicaragua
Poetry
To Fernando (1). *E. Dorn & G. Brotherston*. DORN, n.p.
To Fernando (2). *E. Dorn & G. Brotherston*. DORN, n.p.

745 NALÉ ROXLO, CONRADO (1898-   ) Argentina
Poetry
A Guiding Song. *W. Shand*. SHA, 30.
Conformity. *W. Shand*. SHA, 29.
From Another Sky. *W. Shand*. SHA, 30.
Mystery Of The Bell-Ringer's Daughters. *W. Shand*. SHA, 31.
Nocturne. *M. B. Davis*. FITT, 507.
The Game. *M. B. Davis*. FITT, 507.
The Unforeseen. *M. B. Davis*. FITT, 509.
Today. *H. Manning*. GAN, 47.

746 NAVARRO, FRANCISCO (1902-   ) Mexico
Drama
The City (Excerpt). *W. K. Jones*. JONE-3, 435.

747 NAVARRO, JOSÉ GABRIEL (1881-?) Ecuador
Other
Quito (Essay). no tr. LIT-1, 45.

748 NAVARRO LUNA, MANUEL (1894-   ) Cuba
Poetry
A Father's Poem. *A. Boyer*. BECK, 19.
Comrade. *A. Boyer*. BECK, 25.
Playa Girón. *A. Romeo*. BECK, 15.
Stepparents. *A. Boyer*. BECK, 23.
The Captain. *A. Romeo*. BECK, 13.
The Deep Heart. *A. Boyer*. BECK, 21.
The Song of the Star. *A. Romeo*. BECK, 9.

NEGRÓN MUÑOZ, MERCEDES. See [LAIR, CLARA pseud.].

749 NERUDA, MATILDE URRUTIA (   ) Chile
Other
Pablo's Death. *A. Zitron*. LOW, 23.

750 NERUDA, PABLO (1904-1973) Chile
(Neftalí Ricardo Reyes Basualto)
Poetry
A Certain Weariness. *M. Williams*. WILL-2, 63.
Alberto Rojas Jiménez Comes Flying. *H. R. Hays*. HAYS, 255.

Alturas De Macchu Picchu, III (from: Canto General).
   J. *Wright*. SIX64-7, 3.
America, I Do Not Call Your Name Without Hope (from: Canto
   General). R. *Bly*. BLY, 95.
Anguish Of Death (from: Canto General). J. *Wright*. BLY,
   77.
2. Apogee Of Celery [from: "Tres Cantos Materiales" (Three
   Material Songs)]. J. L. *Grucci*. PELL, 35.
Arsenal By Night. G. D. *Craig*. CRAI, 227.
Atacama [from: "Canto General De Chile" (General Song Of
   Chile)]. J. L. *Grucci*. PELL, 45.
Autumn Returns. J. L. *Grucci*. PELL, 32.
Barcarolle. R. *Benson*. BENS, 87.
Barcarolle. M. E. *Johnson*. JOHN, 197.
Bestiary. M. *Williams*. WILL-2, 53.
"Body of a woman, white hills, white thighs" (from: Twenty
   Poems of Love and One Ode of Desperation). R. *Bly*. BLY,
   19.
Botany [from: "Canto General De Chile" (General Song of
   Chile)]. J. L. *Grucci*. PELL, 43.
Bridges. M. E. *Johnson*. JOHN, 191.
Brussels. T. *Raworth*. CARR, 127.
Brussels (from: Third Residence). R. *Bly*. BLY, 63.
Burial In The East. A. *Flores*. FITT, 337.
Cristóbal Miranda. R. *Bly*. BOLD, 273.
Cristóbal Miranda. R. *Bly*. MILL, 309.
Cristóbal Miranda (from: Canto General). R. *Bly*. BLY,
   101.
Death Alone. A. *Flores*. FITT, 323.
Death Alone. J. L. *Grucci*. PELL, 30.
Discoverers Of Chile (from: Canto General). R. *Bly*. BLY,
   81.
Enigmas (from: Canto General). R. *Bly*. BLY, 131.
1. Entrance To The Wood [from: "Tres Cantos Materiales"
   (Three Material Songs)]. J. L. *Grucci*. PELL, 34.
Ercilla. J. M. *Cohen*. COH-2, 424.
Fable Of The Siren And The Drunkards. M. *Williams*. WILL-2,
   71.
Farewell. R. *Benson*. BENS, 81.
Fragments [from: "Canto General De Chile" (General Song of
   Chile)]. J. L. *Grucci*. PELL, 43.
Friends on the road (1921). R. *Bly* & J. *Wright*. BOLD, 284.
Friends On The Road (1921) (from: Canto General). R. *Bly* &
   J. *Wright*. BLY, 135.
Funeral In The East (from: Residence on Earth I and II).
   R. *Bly*. BLY, 35.
Furies and Sufferings (Excerpt). N. *Tarn*. CARP, 125.
Gentleman Without Company (from: Residence on Earth I and
   II). R. *Bly*. BLY, 37.
Horseman in the Rain. J. M. *Cohen*. COH-2, 425.
Hunger In The South (from: Canto General). R. *Bly*. BLY,
   89.

115

(NERUDA, PABLO)

Hymn And Return (1939) (from: <u>Canto General</u>). *R. Bly*. BLY, 97.

Hymn And Return [from: "Canto General De Chile" (General Song Of Chile)]. *J. L. Grucci*. PELL, 47.

"I remember you as you were that final autumn" (from: <u>Twenty Poems of Love and One Ode of Desperation</u>). *R. Bly*. <u>BLY</u>, 21.

I wish the wood-cutter would wake up. *R. Bly*. BOLD, 274.

I Wish The Woodcutter Would Wake Up (from: <u>Canto General</u>). *R. Bly*. BLY, 105.

In Spite of Anger. *R. Benson*. BENS, 103.

It Is Sure, My Love.... *J. L. Grucci*. PELL, 33.

"It Was The Grape's Autumn" (from: <u>Canto General</u>). *J. Wright & R. Bly*. BLY, 113.

"It was the grape's autumn." *R. Bly & J. Wright*. TRI-13, 297.

José Miguel Carrera. *R. Benson*. BENS, 107.

Larynx. *M. Williams*. WILL-2, 67.

Lautreamont regained (Excerpt). *B. Belitt*. TRI-13, 302.

Letter To Miguel Otero Silva, In Caracas (1948) (from: <u>Canto General</u>). *R. Bly*. BLY, 119.

Letter to Miguel Otero Silva, in Caracas (1948). *R. Bly*. BOLD, 278.

Lightless Suburb. *H. R. Hays*. HAYS, 243.

Liturgy Of My Legs. *D. Fitts*. FITT, 313.

Lone Gentleman. *D. Fitts*. FITT, 319.

Melancholy Inside Families (from: <u>Residence On Earth I and II</u>). *R. Bly & J. Wright*. BLY, 49.

Murderer's sleep. *M. J. Parr*. TRI-13, 299.

No. XVII. *H. R. Hays*. HAYS, 245.

Nocturnal Collection. *A. Flores*. FITT, 327.

Nothing But Death (from: <u>Residence on Earth I and II</u>). *R. Bly*. BLY, 25.

Nothing but Death. *R. Bly*. CARP, 121.

Nothing But Death (from: <u>Residencia En Tierra</u>). *R. Bly*. SIX64-7, 15.

November 7 Ode To A Day Of Victories. *D. Fitts*. FITT, 331.

Ocean [from: "Canto General De Chile" (General Song of Chile)]. *J. L. Grucci*. PELL, 46.

Ode Of The Sun To The People's Army. *H. R. Hays*. HAYS, 261.

Ode to a Girl Gardening. *R. Benson*. BENS, 131.

Ode to a Seagull. *R. Benson*. BENS, 123.

Ode To Barbed Wire. *C. Maurer*. CHI, 13.

Ode to broken things. *M. J. Parr*. TRI-13, 300.

Ode To My Socks (from: <u>Odas Elementales</u>). *R. Bly*. BLY, 141.

Ode To My Socks. *R. Bly*. MILL, 304.

Ode To Salt (from: <u>Odas Elementales</u>). *R. Bly*. BLY, 153.

Ode To The Magnolia. *J. M. Cohen*. COH-1, 31.

Ode to the Smell of Firewood. *R. Benson.* BENS, 117.
Ode To The Watermelon (from: <u>Odas Elementales</u>). *R. Bly.*
  BLY, 147.
Ode With A Lament. *H. R. Hays.* HAYS, 249.
Ode With a Lament. *W. S. Merwin.* CARP, 119.
Opium in the East. *B. Belitt.* TRI-13, 304.
Pastoral. *B. Belitt.* MILL, 314.
Poem 10. *J. L. Grucci.* PELL, 40.
Poem To Bolívar. *J. L. Grucci.* PELL, 27.
Poem 20. *D. J. Flakoll & C. Alegría.* BENE, 59.
Poem 20. *S. Resnick.* RES, 94.
Poemas de Amor No. 1. *W. K. Jones.* JONE-3, 130.
Poems of Love. *G. D. Craig.* CRAI, 227.
Religion in the East. *B. Belitt.* TRI-13, 306.
Savor. *H. R. Hays.* HAYS, 247.
Sexual Water (from: <u>Residence on Earth I and II</u>).
  J. Wright & R. Bly. BLY, 53.
Sexual Water. *H. R. Hays.* HAYS, 251.
Sixth Poem (from: <u>Twenty Poems of Love and One Ode of</u>
  <u>Desperation</u>). *R. Bly.* SIX64-7, 5.
Slow Lament. *J. L. Grucci.* PELL, 29.
Some Animals. *J. M. Cohen.* COH-1, 30.
Some Beasts (from: <u>Canto General</u>). *J. Wright.* BLY, 67.
Some beasts. *J. Wright.* BOLD, 267.
Some Beasts. *J. Wright.* MILL, 307.
Some Beasts (from: <u>Canto General</u>). *J. Wright.* SIX64-7, 11.
Sonata And Destructions (from: <u>Residence on Earth I and II</u>).
  R. Bly. BLY, 41.
Sonata And Destructions. *A. Flores.* FITT, 321.
Sonata: There's No Forgetting. *W. K. Jones.* JONE-3, 127.
3. Statute Of Wine [from: "Tres Cantos Materiales" (Three
  Material Songs)]. *J. L. Grucci.* PELL, 37.
Summits of Macchu Picchu, VI (Excerpt). *K. Flores.* CARP,
  129.
The Art Of Poetry (from: <u>Residence on Earth I and II</u>).
  R. Bly. BLY, 33.
The Dictators (from: <u>Canto General</u>). *R. Bly.* BLY, 93.
The dictators. *R. Bly.* BOLD, 273.
The Dictators (from: <u>Canto General</u>). *R. Bly.* SIX62-6, 11.
The enigmas. *R. Bly.* BOLD, 283.
The Head On The Pole (from <u>Canto General</u>). *R. Bly.* BLY, 73.
The head on the pole. *R. Bly.* BOLD, 269.
The Heights of Macchu Picchu. *T. Raworth.* CARA, 128.
The Heights Of Macchu Picchu, III (from: <u>Canto General</u>).
  J. Wright. BLY, 71.
The Heights of Macchu Picchu, III. *J. Wright.* BOLD, 268.
The heights of Macchu Picchu VI. *R. Benson.* BENS, 99.
The Phantom of the Cargo Ship. *R. Benson.* BENS, 93.
The Ruined Street (from: <u>Residence on Earth I and II</u>).
  R. Bly. BLY, 45.
The Sea Gulls of Antofagasta. *W. K. Jones.* JONE-3, 128.
The Ship. *W. K. Jones.* JONE-3, 131.

(NERUDA, PABLO)

The Strike (from: Canto General). *R. Bly.* BLY, 115.

The United Fruit Co. (from: Canto General). *R. Bly.* BLY, 85.

The United Fruit Co. *R. Bly.* BOLD, 271.

The United Fruit Co. *R. Bly.* MILL, 311.

The United Fruit Co. (from: Canto General). *R. Bly.* SIX64-7, 7.

There Is No Forgetfulness (from: Residence On Earth I and II). *R. Bly.* BLY, 57.

They Receive Instructions Against Chile (from: Canto General). *R. Bly.* BLY, 129.

They receive instructions against Chile. *R. Bly & J. Wright.* BOLD, 282.

They receive instructions against Chile. *R. Bly & J. Wright.* TRI-13, 298.

To The Foot From His Child. *M. Williams.* WILL-2, 47.

Toqui Caupolicán. *R. Benson.* BENS, 113.

Toussaint L'Ouverture (from: Canto General). *J. Wright.* BLY, 83.

Toussaint L'Ouverture. *J. Wright.* BOLD, 270.

Toussaint L'Ouverture. *J. Wright.* MILL, 313.

Walking Around. *T. Raworth.* CARA, 124.

Walking Around (from: Residence on Earth I and II). *R. Bly.* BLY, 29.

Walking Around. *H. R. Hays.* FITT, 311.

Walking Around. *M. E. Johnson.* JOHN, 193.

Walking Around. *J. L. Grucci.* PELL, 41.

Where Is Guillermina? *M. Williams.* WILL-2, 51.

Youth (from: Canto General). *R. Bly.* BLY, 91.

Other

The Lamb And The Pinecone (Interview). *R. Bly.* BLY, 156.

A Pine-Cone, a Toy Sheep.... *B. Belitt.* HOW-1, 146.

A Pinecone, A Toy Sheep... (Essay). *B. Belitt.* MILL, 316.

751   NERVO, AMADO   (1870-1919)   Mexico

Poetry

Allegro Vivace. *T. Walsh.* WALS, 633.

An Old Burden. *S. Beckett.* PAZ-1, 147.

And Thou, Expectant. *S. Beckett.* PAZ-1, 149.

As in a Dream. *G. D. Craig.* CRAI, 79.

At Peace. *G. D. Craig.* CRAI, 87.

Cowardice. *G. D. Craig.* CRAI, 77.

Cowardice. *S. Resnick.* RES, 54.

Death. *A. S. Blackwell.* BLAC, 58.

Deity. *A. S. Blackwell.* BLAC, 60.

Delicta Carnis. *G. D. Craig.* CRAI, 83.

Ecstasy. *A. S. Blackwell.* BLAC, 66.

Entreaty to the Cloud. *S. Beckett.* PAZ-1, 148.

Evocation. *A. S. Blackwell.* BLAC, 50.

Evocation. *S. Beckett.* PAZ-1, 148.

Fill It With Love. *M. E. Johnson.* JOHN, 101.
Grief Vanquished. *A. S. Blackwell.* BLAC, 62.
I Was Born Today. *A. S. Blackwell.* BLAC, 54.
If a Thorn Wounds Me. *A. S. Blackwell.* BLAC, 50.
If a Thorn Wounds Me. *A. S. Blackwell.* LIT-1, 35.
If a thorn wounds me. *A. S. Blackwell.* LIT-2, 39.
If Thou Say'st "Come." *G. D. Craig.* CRAI, 81.
If You Are Good. *M. E. Johnson.* JOHN, 95.
If You Are Good. *S. Resnick.* RES, 58.
Limpidity. *A. S. Blackwell.* BLAC, 52.
Limpidity. *A. S. Blackwell.* LIT-1, 16.
Limpidity. *A. S. Blackwell.* LIT-2, 26.
Los Mysticos. *E. W. Underwood.* UND, 60.
Mystical Poets. *T. Walsh.* WALS, 632.
Not All. *H. E. Fish.* JONE-3, 45.
Not All. *H. E. Fish.* TRAN, 230.
Not All Who Die.... *G. D. Craig.* CRAI, 81.
Old Burthen. *C. M. Hutchings.* JONE-3, 44.
Old Song. *E. W. Underwood.* UND, 64.
Purity. *B. G. Proske.* JONE-3, 43.
Purity. *B. G. Proske.* TRAN, 232.
Revenge. *A. S. Blackwell.* BLAC, 64.
Revenge. *A. S. Blackwell.* LIT-1, 16.
Revenge. *A. S. Blackwell.* LIT-2, 32.
Rondo Vago. *E. W. Underwood.* UND, 61.
Sister Water. *A. S. Blackwell.* BLAC, 34.
Sister Water. *A. S. Blackwell.* GOLD-2, 44.
Solidarity. *M. E. Johnson.* JOHN, 97.
Solidarity. *M. E. Johnson.* RES, 56.
The Buddha Of Basalt. *E. W. Underwood.* UND, 62.
The Chestnut Tree. *M. E. Johnson.* JOHN, 95.
The Cortège. *T. Walsh.* WALS, 631.
The Daisies. *A. S. Blackwell.* BLAC, 54.
The Dark Galley. *A. S. Blackwell.* BLAC, 62.
The Gift. *A. S. Blackwell.* BLAC, 64.
The Hail. *J. Wendell.* TRAN, 231.
The Mountain. *G. D. Craig.* CRAI, 85.
The Mountain. *E. W. Underwood.* UND, 63.
Thirst. *M. E. Johnson.* JOHN, 99.
To Leonora. *A. S. Blackwell.* BLAC, 56.
To the Cloud. *A. S. Blackwell.* BLAC, 58.
Translucency. *E. F. Lucas.* WALS, 626.
When Thou Lov'st Me. *G. D. Craig.* CRAI, 77.
Why Weep? No More! *M. E. Johnson.* JOHN, 97.
Fiction
Leah and Rachel. *W. K. Jones.* JONE-3, 338.
One Hope. *W. E. Colford.* COLF, 140.
Other
Puebla de los Angeles (Prose Miniature). *E. W. Underwood.*
  UND, 59.

752   NETTO, COELHO   (1864-?   )   Brazil
      Fiction
      The Pigeons.   *I. Goldberg.*   GOLD-1, 121.

753   NIETO, LUIS   (1910-   )   Peru
      Poetry
      Song.   *E. Dorn & G. Brotherston.*   DORN, n.p.

754   NIVAR DE PITTALUGA, AMADA   (   )   Dominican Republic
      Poetry
      The Son.   *F. E. Townsend.*   TOWN, 39.

755   NORIEGA, EDUARDO   (1853-?   )   Mexico
      Other
      Climatic Zones of Mexico (from: Geografía de Mexico).
      F. Starr.   STAR, 3.

756   NOVÁS-CALVO, LINO   (1905-   )   Cuba
      See also CALVO, LINO NOVÁS
      Fiction
      As I Am...As I Was.   *P. Bowles.*   HOW-1, 1959.
      That Night.   *Z. Nelken.*   TORR, 25.
      The Dark Night of Ramón Yendíe.   *R. Sayers.*   ONIS-2, 193.

757   NOVO, SALVADOR   (1904-   )   Mexico
      Poetry
      A Little Suite.   Brief Romance in Time of Absence I.
      E. W. Underwood.   UND, 188.
      Brief Romance in Time of Absence II.   *E. W. Underwood.*   UND,
      189.
      Brief Romance in Time of Absence III.   *E. W. Underwood.*
      UND, 190.
      Brief Romance in Time of Absence IV.   *E. W. Underwood.*   UND,
      191.
      Brief Romance in Time of Absence V.   *E. W. Underwood.*   UND,
      192.
      Elegy.   *M. González.*   CARA, 273.
      Epifania.   *J. M. Cohen.*   COH-2, 422.
      From the Remote Past (Fragment).   *S. J. Levine.*   PAZ-2, 141.
      Journey.   *H. R. Hays.*   FITT, 97.
      Poetry.   *D. D. Walsh.*   FITT, 99.
      Roberto, the Second Lieutenant.   *S. J. Levine.*   PAZ-2, 147.
      Shipwreck.   *E. W. Underwood.*   UND, 194.
      The Deluge.   *E. W. Underwood.*   UND, 195.
      The Departed Friend.   *L. Mallan.*   FITT, 97.

758   NUCETE SARDI, JOSÉ   (1897-   )   Venezuela
      Other
      Don Francisco Miranda In Russia (from: Caballero of Des-
      tiny).   *H. de Onís.*   ARC, 307.

759 NUNES, CASSIANO (   ) Brazil
     Poetry
     Blues Song. *J. R. Longland.* CHI, 97.
     Requiem. *J. R. Longland.* CHI, 95.

760 NÚÑEZ, ANA ROSA (   ) Cuba
     Poetry
     Black Haikus. *H. Ruiz del Vizo.* RUIZ, 70.

761 NÚÑEZ DEL PRADO, NILDA (   ) Bolivia
     Other
     Bolivian Dances. no tr. LIT-1, 7.

762 NUÑO, RUBÉN BONIFAZ (1923-   ) Mexico
     Poetry
     November Theme. *W. Eyster.* CRAN, 102.
     The Flower. *D. Flakoll & C. Alegría.* FLAK, 60.

763 OBLIGADO, PEDRO MIGUEL (1892-1967) Argentina
     Poetry
     A hero. *P. Gannon.* GAN, 39.

764 OBLIGADO, RAFAEL (1851-1920) Argentina
     Poetry
     Santos Vega. *A. S. Blackwell.* BLAC, 348.
     Santos Vega. *W. K. Jones.* JONE-2, 248.
     The Flower of the Silk-Cotton Tree. *A. Fife.* FIFE, 49.

765 OCAMPO, RICARDO (1928-   ) Bolivia
     Fiction
     The Indian Paulino. *H. Carpentier.* CARP, 292.

766 OCAMPO, SILVINA (1905?-   ) Argentina
     Poetry
     Palinurus Sleepless. *J. M. Cohen.* COH-2, 437.
     Persuasion Of Sleep. *W. Shand.* SHA, 56.
     Sleepless Palinurus. *D. Fitts.* FITT, 455.
     The Face. *W. Shand.* SHA, 57.

767 OCAMPO, VICTORIA (1893-   ) Argentina
     Other
     The Lakes Of The South (Essay). *H. de Onís.* ARC, 116.

768 OLAGUÍBEL, FRANCISCO MANUEL DE (1874-1924) Mexico
     Poetry
     Jesus. *E. W. Underwood.* UND, 108.
     Provenzal. *E. W. Underwood.* UND, 107.

769 O'LEARY, JUAN E. (1880-?) Paraguay
Poetry
The Savage. *W. K. Jones*. JONE-3, 135.
Other
Our Unsung Heroes (from: Libro de los Héroes). *H. de Onís*.
ARC, 498.

770 OLIVA, OSCAR (1938-) Mexico
Poetry
While Drinking a Cup of Coffee.... *W. S. Merwin*. PAZ-2, 39.

771 OLIVARES FIGUEROA, RAFAEL (1893-) Venezuela
Poetry
The Sower. *D. Fitts*. FITT, 159.

772 OLIVEIRA, MARLY DE ( ) Brazil
Poetry
Sonnet XVI. *F. P. Hebblethwaite*. YOU, 27.

773 ONETTI, JORGE (1931-) Argentina
Fiction
The Thunderbox. *G. Lawaetz*. LAWA, 103.

774 ONETTI, JUAN CARLOS (1909-) Uruguay
Fiction
A Dream Come True. *E. de Torres*. CARP, 190.
Dreaded Hell. *J. Franco*. COH-1, 34.
Jacob and the Other. *I. A. Langnas*. HOW-1, 182.
Jacob And The Other. *I. A. Langnas*. PRIZE, 319.
Santa Rosa. *H. Carpentier*. CHI, 103.
Welcome, Bob. *D. L. Shaw*. FRA-J, 85.
Welcome, Bob. *H. St. Martin*. MANC, 355.

775 OPPENHEIMER, FÉLIX FRANCO (1912-) Puerto Rico
Poetry
I Remember The Apostle. *B. Luby*. BABI, 274.

776 OQUENDO DE AMAT, CARLOS (1904-1936) Peru
Poetry
madhouse poem. *H. R. Hays*. CARP, 183.
Madhouse Poem. *H. R. Hays*. FITT, 353.
Mother. *H. R. Hays*. FITT, 355.
movie of the countryside. *J. Brof*. CARP, 186.
poem. *J. Brof*. CARP, 189.
Surrealist Poem Of The Elephant And The Song. *H. R. Hays*.
FITT, 353.
The Angel And The Rose. *H. R. Hays*. FITT, 355.

777 ORAÁ, FRANCISCO DE (1929-   ) Cuba
Poetry
All Mankind Is My Family. *R. Llopis*. BECK, 331.
From Now On. *R. Llopis*. BECK, 327.
The Bus in Which I Live. *R. Llopis*. BECK, 329.
The Makers of the Poem. *R. Llopis*. BECK, 337.

778 ORAÁ, PEDRO DE (1931-   ) Cuba
Poetry
April 17. *A. Boyer*. BECK, 479.
Baragaño Steps into the Mirror. *R. Llopis*. BECK, 487.
For Whom? *R. Llopis*. BECK, 491.
New Poetics. *A. Boyer*. BECK, 483.
New Poetics. *D. Gardner*. TARN, 65.
We'll Be. *A. Boyer*. BECK, 477.

779 ORCE REMIS, GUILLERMO (1917-   ) Argentina
Poetry
This Earthly Season. *W. Shand*. SHA, 128.
This Is How The Day Starts. *W. Shand*. SHA, 129.
We Are Despair. *W. Shand*. SHA, 129.

780 ORDÓÑEZ ARGÜELLO, ALBERTO (1914-   ) Nicaragua
Poetry
Song of Neztahualcoyotl. *D. Flakoll & C. Alegría*. FLAK, 43.

781 ORIBE, EMILIO (1893-   ) Uruguay
Poetry
Music. *J. Wendell*. TRAN, 259.
Song To The Glory Of The Sky Of America. *M. Lee*. FITT, 579.
The Power of Things. *M. González*. CARA, 369.
The Two Slopes Of Time. *M. Gonález*. CARA, 368.

782 OROZCO, OLGA (1920-   ) Argentina
Poetry
A Day For Not Being There. *W. Shand*. SHA, 154.
It Comes In Every Storm. *W. Shand*. SHA, 153.
The Grandmother. *W. Shand*. SHA, 155.

783 ORRILLO, WINSTON (1941-   ) Peru
Poetry
Amongst all the acid tastes. *C. A. de Lomellini & O. Bingham-Powell*. HAR67-4, 73.
The Town Loony. *C. A. de Lomellini & O. Bingham-Powell*. HAR67-4.

784 ORTA RUIZ, JESÚS (1923-   ) Cuba
[NABORÍ, INDIO pseud.]
Poetry
An Old Crust of Bread. *C. Beck*. BECK, 271.
April 18. *C. Beck*. BECK, 273.

(ORTA RUIZ, JESÚS)
Asphyxia. *C. Beck*. BECK, 281.
Even These. *C. Beck*. BECK, 265.
Exposure and a Way. *C. Beck*. BECK, 267.
For the 10th of October. *C. Beck*. BECK, 263.
Kings Day. *C. Beck*. BECK, 279.
Table of the Poor. *C. Beck*. BECK, 261.
The Last Rebuilding. *C. Beck*. BECK, 277.
The Old Clock. *C. Beck*. BECK, 275.
Two Rains. *C. Beck*. BECK, 269.

785 ORTEGA, JULIO (1942-   ) Peru
Poetry
Faces. *M. Shipman*. HAR67-2, 31.
Fishermen. *M. Ahern & D. Tipton*. AHER, 94.
Memory of Dust & Light. *D. Tipton*. AHER, 97.
My Country. *E. Hollis*. AHER, 105.
October. *D. Tipton*. AHER, 100.
Report for Isolda. *D. Tipton*. AHER, 103.
Report for Isolda. *D. Tipton*. TRI-13, 204.
Sound of Water. *D. Tipton*. AHER, 101.

786 ORTIZ, ADALBERTO (1914-   ) Ecuador
Poetry
The News. *D. Flakoll & C. Alegría*. FLAK, 82.

787 ORTÍZ, JUAN L. (1897-   ) Argentina
Poetry
A Transparent Ecstasy. *W. Shand*. SHA, 15.
It Was A Grey And Dry Afternoon.... *W. Shand*. SHA, 16.

788 ORTÍZ, LUIS G. (1896-   )
Poetry
My Fountain. *A. S. Blackwell*. WALS, 768.

789 ORTIZ DE MONTELLANO, BERNARDO (1899-1949) Mexico
Poetry
Second Dream. *T. Lamb, D. D. Walsh & D. Fitts*. FITT, 357.
Sketch. *E. W. Underwood*. UND, 165.
The Five Senses. *E. W. Underwood*. UND, 164.

790 OSORIO, MIGUEL ÁNGEL (1883-1942) Colombia
[Also wrote under JACOB, PORFIRIO BARBA and ARENALES,
RICARDO]
Poetry
Stanzas. *E. W. Underwood*. JONE-3, 92.
The Lament of October. *E. W. Underwood*. JONE-3, 91.

791   OTERO REICHE, RAÚL (1905-   ) Bolivia
Poetry
America. *D. D. Walsh.* FITT, 561.
Romanza Of The Guitarrist. *R. Humphries.* FITT, 557.
The Night Was Going....*R. Humphries.* FITT, 557.

792   OTERO SILVA, MIGUEL (1908-   ) Venezuela
Poetry
Sowing. *D. D. Walsh.* FITT, 295.

793   OTHÓN, MANUEL JOSÉ (1858-1906) Mexico
Poetry
A Steppe in the Nazas Country. *S. Beckett.* PAZ-1, 127.
A Steppe on the Nazas. *M. González.* CARA, 249.
Elegy. *S. Beckett.* PAZ-1, 127.
Envoy. *S. Beckett.* PAZ-1, 133.
"Look at the landscape: immensity below...." *J. M. Cohen.*
  COH-2, 328.
Sonnet Sequence I. *E. W. Underwood.* UND, 40.
Sonnet Sequence II. *E. W. Underwood.* UND, 40.
Sonnet Sequence III. *E. W. Underwood.* UND, 41.
The Bell. *A. S. Blackwell.* BLAC, 140.
The River. *A. S. Blackwell.* BLAC, 140.
The River. *A. S. Blackwell.* WALS, 549.
The Witches. *M. González.* CARA, 250.

794   OWEN, GILBERTO (1905-1952) Mexico
Poetry
Interior. *M. Strand.* PAZ-2, 139.
Interior. *E. W. Underwood.* UND, 211.
Poem In Which The Word Love Is Often Used. *E. W. Underwood.*
  UND, 212.

795   PACHECO, ARMANDO OSCAR (1901-   ) Dominican Republic
Poetry
The Crimson Path. *F. E. Townsend.* TOWN, 51.

796   PACHECO, JOSÉ EMILIO (1939-   ) Mexico
Poetry
An investigation of the bat. *A. Moncy.* TRI-13, 486.
Awakening Day (Fragment). no tr. YOU, 87.
Bounds. *E. Randall.* MU-69, 131.
Criticism Of Poetry. *A. Gullón.* CHI, 131.
El Ajusco. *T. Hoeksema.* CHI, 137.
For Some Time Now. *E. Randall.* MU-69, 129.
From Some Time to This Place. *P. Levine.* PAZ-2, 31.
Let's Say Amsterdam 1943. *E. Trejo.* CHI, 135.
Mosquitoes. *M. González.* CARA, 300.
Pompeii. *M. González.* CARA, 299.
The Acceleration of History. *M. González.* CARA, 298.

(PACHECO, JOSÉ EMILIO)
  The Climbing Vine. *P. Levine.* PAZ-2, 35.
  The Elements Of Night. *J. M. Cohen.* COH-1, 260.
  The fire waned (Fragments of the third part). *A. Moncy.*
    TRI-13, 480.
  The Mirror of the Enigmas: Monkeys. *M. González.* CARA,
    299.
  The Words of the Buddha. *P. Levine.* PAZ-2, 37.
  Venice. *A. Gullón.* CHI, 133.

797 PADILLA, HEBERTO (1932-   ) Cuba
  Poetry
  Anne Frank. *C. Beck.* BECK, 525.
  Anne Frank. *E. Randall.* TRI-13, 144.
  At the Tomb of Dylan Thomas. *C. Beck.* BECK, 539.
  Child's Play. *C. Beck.* BECK, 527.
  Cuban Poets No Longer Dream. *C. Beck.* BECK, 537.
  From Time to Time War Comes. *C. Beck.* BECK, 535.
  Girón Beach. *E. Randall.* TRI-13, 143.
  Like An Animal. *T. Raworth.* TARN, 71.
  Look at Her Lying There. *C. Beck.* BECK, 531.
  The Childhood of William Blake. *C. Beck.* BECK, 511.
  The Childhood of William Blake. *J. M. Cohen.* COH-3, 46.
  The Hour. *E. Randall.* TARN, 67.
  The Old Bards Say. *A. Kerrigan.* TARN, 71.
  Time of the Just and the Human. *C. Beck.* BECK, 529.

798 PADÍN, JOSÉ (1886-1963) Puerto Rico
  Fiction
  Military Justice. *B. Luby.* BABI, 117.

799 PADRÓN, JULIÁN (1910-1954) Venezuela
  Fiction
  Summer Fires. no tr. LIT-1, 94.

800 PAINE, ROBERTO (1916-   ) Argentina
  Poetry
  Elegies I. *W. Shand.* SHA, 126.
  Figure Of Death. *W. Shand.* SHA, 127.

801 PALACIOS, INOCENTE (   ) Venezuela
  Other
  Imagen de Caracas: A Unique Place. no tr. DR, 130.

  PALACIOS, PEDRO B. See [ALMAFUERTE pseud.].

802 PALÉS MATOS, LUIS (1898-1959) Puerto Rico
  Poetry
  Black Dance. *B. Luby.* BABI, 157.
  Clair De Lune. *D. D. Walsh.* FITT, 205.
  Doorway To Time In Three Voices. *R. Benson.* BENS, 173.

Elegy for the Duke of Marmalade. *R. Benson*. BENS, 153.
Elegy for the Duke of Marmelade. *D. de la Texera &*
  E. G. Matilla. MATI, 57.
Elegy Of The Duke Of Marmalade. *D. D. Walsh*. FITT, 207.
Equilibrium. *H. Ruiz del Vizo*. RUIZ, 87.
Festival Song to be Wept. *R. Benson*. BENS, 163.
Green Lizard. *W. K. Jones*. JONE-3, 81.
Hybridism Of The White Man. *H. Ruiz del Vizo*. RUIZ, 89.
Impressionistic Sketches. *E. G. Matilla*. MATI, 39.
Kalahari. *R. Benson*. BENS, 147.
Kalahari. *D. de la Texera*. MATI, 51.
Look Out For The Snake! *D. D. Walsh*. FITT, 209.
Merry Song for Tears (Excerpt). no tr. KAI, n.p.
Moonlight. *R. Benson*. BENS, 139.
Mulata-Antilla. *G. R. Coulthard*. COUL, 125.
Mulatta-Antilla. *M. González*. CARA, 351.
Ñam-Ñam. *R. Benson*. BENS, 151.
Ñam-ñam. *D. de la Texera*. MATI, 55.
Ñáñigo To Heaven. *D. Fitts*. FITT, 211.
Pueblo. *B. Luby*. BABI, 159.
Sounds of Stagnance and Monotony. *E. G. Matilla*. MATI, 43.
Spurious Song for a Baguiné. *R. Benson*. BENS, 157.
Spurious Song for a Baguiné. *R. Benson*. CARP, 79.
The Animals Within (Excerpt). *R. Benson*. CARP, 77.
The Animals Within, I. *R. Benson*. BENS, 141.
The Call. *B. Luby*. BABI, 160.
The Call. *E. G. Matilla*. MATI, 47.
The Unknown Pain. *M. González*. CARA, 354.
The Well. *D. D. Walsh*. FITT, 205.
The Well. *W. K. Jones*. JONE-3, 80.
The White Towers. *R. Benson*. BENS, 143.

803 PALMA, BENIGNO (1882-?   ) Panama
     Poetry
     To the Panama Canal. *A. S. Blackwell*. BLAC, 526.

804 PALOMARES, RAMÓN (1935-   ) Venezuela
     Poetry
     But your lustre and my splendor grow distant (from: The
       Soft Breeze Of Daybreak With Its First Fragrance).
       M. Savage. MU-73, 77.
     Elegy On The Death Of My Father. *M. Savage*. MU-73, 71.
     I seek a substance from the sky (from: The Soft Breeze of
       Daybreak With Its First Fragrance). *M. Savage*. MU-73,
       75.
     Night. *W. S. Merwin*. CARP, 383.

805 PALOMINO F., SALVADOR (1937-   ) Peru
     Poetry
     Weep Horn. *C. A. de Lomellini & G. Escobar*. HAR67-4, 4.

806   PANE, IGNACIO A. (1882-1920) Paraguay
      Poetry
      The Paraguayan Woman. *A. S. Blackwell*. BLAC, 470.

807   PAPASTAMATIU, BASILIA (   ) Argentina
      Fiction
      The shared thoughts, free prose, of Basilia Papastamatiu.
      R. Christ. TRI-13, 255.

   PARDOY-FARELO, ENRIQUE. See [TABLANCA, LUIS pseud.].

808   PARDOY GARCÍA, GERMÁN (1902-   ) Colombia
      Poetry
      Remoteness. *R. Humphries*. FITT, 463.
      The Moment. *R. Humphries*. FITT, 463.

809   PAREJA DÍEZ-CANSECO, ALFREDO (1908-   ) Ecuador
      Fiction
      Grubs. *Z. Nelken*. TORR, 159.

810   PARRA, MANUEL DE LA (1878-1930) Mexico
      Poetry
      A fable by Grimm. *E. W. Underwood*. UND, 95.
      The Cistern. *E. W. Underwood*. UND, 97.
      The Well. *S. Beckett*. PAZ-1, 171.

811   PARRA, NICANOR (1914-   ) Chile
      Poetry
      A Man. *W. Witherup & S. Echeverría*. TRI-13, 407.
      Disorder In Heaven. *T. Raworth*. CARA, 156.
      Everything Used to Look Good to Me. *W. S. Merwin*. CARP,
         255.
      Fame. *W. Barnstone*. MU-69, 67.
      I Jehovah Decree. *W. S. Merwin*. CARP, 249.
      I Move The Meeting Be Adjourned. *M. Williams*. WILL-2, 89.
      In The Graveyard. *M. Williams*. WILL-2, 91.
      Litany of the little bourgeois. *J. Laughlin*. BOLD, 362.
      Notice. *W. Barnstone*. MU-69, 67.
      Ode to Some Pigeons. *D. J. Flakoll & C. Alegría*. BENE, 73.
      Piano Solo. *W. S. Merwin*. COH-1, 139.
      Portrait Of The Author. *W. S. Merwin*. COH-1, 138.
      Rites. *M. Williams*. BOLD, 364.
      Saranguaco. *W. Barnstone*. MU-69, 65.
      Soliloquy of the Individual. *J. Hill*. CARA, 151.
      Soliloquy of the Individual. *D. J. Flakoll & C. Alegría*.
         FLAK, 216.
      Soliloquy Of The Individual. *R. Connally*. YOU, 32.
      The Imperfect Lover. *M. Williams*. WILL-2, 91.
      The Little Man. *M. Williams*. WILL-2, 83.
      The Pilgrim. *W. S. Merwin*. COH-1, 140.
      The Roller-Coaster. *T. Raworth*. CARA, 151.

The Trap. *W. S. Merwin*. CARP, 251.
The vices of the modern world. *W. S. Merwin*. BOLD, 359.
This Has To Be a Cemetery. *W. S. Merwin*. CARP, 257.
To the chicken guts. *W. Witherup & S. Echeverría*. TRI-13, 406.
Unpublished artifacts. *W. Witherup & S. Echeverría*. TRI-13, 408.
Young poets. *M. Williams*. BOLD, 365.
Zombies. *M. Williams*. WILL-2, 89.
Other
A Talk With Nicanor Parra. *M. Williams*. WILL-2, 75.

812   PARRA, PORFIRIO (1869-?   ) Mexico
      Fiction
      Pacotillas (Excerpt). *F. Starr*. STAR, 361.

813   PARRA, TERESA DE LA   (1895-1936) Venezuela
      Fiction
      Mama Blanca. no tr. LIT-2, 48.

814   PASEYRO, RICARDO   (1927-   ) Uruguay
      Other
      The dead word of Pablo Neruda (Essay). *C. Eshleman*. TRI-15, 203.

815   PASOS, JOAQUÍN   (1915-1947) Nicaragua
      Poetry
      Elegy of the Bird. *D. J. Flakoll & C. Alegría*. BENE, 77.
      Elegy of the Bird. *D. J. Flakoll & C. Alegría*. FLAK, 64.

816   PATO, BULHAO   (   ) Brazil
      Poetry
      The Two Mothers. *L. Elliott*. WALS, 697.

817   PAVÓN, LUIS (1930-   ) Cuba
      Poetry
      A Talk With Fausto Díaz. *R. Llopis*. BECK, 469.
      Cuba. no tr. BECK, 467.
      Of Things That Go Back to 1960. *R. Llopis*. BECK, 461.
      Sunday. *R. Llopis*. BECK, 465.
      The Havana Declaration. *R. Llopis*. BECK, 471.
      The Poet Asks for Stella. *R. Llopis*. BECK, 473.

818   PAYRÓ, ROBERTO J.   (1867-1928) Argentina
      Fiction
      Laucha's Marriage. *A. Brenner*. FRAN, 3.
      The Devil at Pago Chico. *H. de Onís*. ONIS-1, 193.
      The Devil in Pago Chico. *A. Brenner*. FRAN, 155.

819   PAZ, OCTAVIO (1914-   ) Mexico
       <u>Poetry</u>
       Altar of the sun. *S. Berg*. TRI-13, 167.
       Although the Snow May Fall. *R. Benson*. BENS, 195.
       Apparition. *C. Tomlinson*. DEL-68, 124.
       Beyond Love. *J. M. Cohen*. COH-2, 431.
       Blanco (1966). *C. Tomlinson & G. Aroul*. CARP, 212.
       Complementaries. *M. González*. CARA, 276.
       Dawn. *E. Weinberger*. PAZ-2, 123.
       Eve's Dream. *D. Flakoll & C. Alegría*. FLAK, 185.
       Fable of Two Gardens. *J. Hill*. CARA, 281.
       Here. *E. Weinberger*. PAZ-2, 125.
       Hurry. *E. Weinberger*. CHI, 19.
       Hymn Among Ruins. *R. Benson*. BENS, 205.
       Hymn Among Ruins. no tr. CRAN, 115.
       Hymn Among Ruins, 1948. *J. M. Cohen*. COH-1, 87.
       Hymn among ruins (1948). *J. M. Cohen*. COH-2, 433.
       Hymn Among the Ruins. *D. Levertov*. JONE-3, 50.
       Interior Star. *R. Benson*. BENS, 197.
       Lake. *R. Benson*. BENS, 181.
       Last Dawn. *M. González*. CARA, 277.
       Lightning in Repose. *R. Benson*. BENS, 189.
       Lightning, in repose. *T. Reynolds*. TRI-13, 332.
       Native Stone. *R. Benson*. BENS, 193.
       Night Water. *R. Benson*. BENS, 187.
       Nocturne. *D. J. Flakoll & C. Alegría*. BENE, 69.
       Nocturne. no tr. YOU, 82.
       Nocturno. *T. Reynolds*. TRI-13, 329.
       Oblivion. *D. Fitts*. FITT, 105.
       On Reading John Cage. *M. F. Wust & G. Aroul*. CARP, 205.
       One and the Same. *C. Tomlinson*. DEL-68, 122.
       Seeds for a Hymn. *R. Benson*. BENS, 201.
       Summer Night. *R. Benson*. BENS, 185.
       Tempest. *M. González*. CARA, 275.
       Testimonies. *J. M. Cohen*. COH-2, 429.
       The Besieged. *E. Weinberger*. CHI, 17.
       The Broken Water Jar. *L. Kemp*. EVER, 41.
       The Endless Instant. *D. Levertov*. CRAN, 112.
       The Mausoleum of Humayun. *C. Tomlinson*. DEL-68, 124.
       The return. *T. Reynolds*. TRI-13, 330.
       The River. *P. Blackburn*. EVER, 38.
       The Street. *W. K. Jones*. JONE-3, 53.
       The Wall. *D. Fitts*. FITT, 103.
       The written word. *T. Reynolds*. TRI-13, 328.
       There and Back. *M. González*. CARA, 280.
       Todos Santos, Dia de Muertos. *L. Kemp*. EVER, 22.
       Ustica. *M. González*. CARA, 277.
       Ustica. *C. Tomlinson & H. Gifford*. COH-1, 89.
       Village. *C. Tomlinson*. DEL-68, 122.
       Visitors. no tr. YOU, 83.
       Well-Spring. *R. Benson*. BENS, 191.

Wind From All Compass Points. *P. Blackburn.* COH-1, 91.
Wind From All Compass Points. *P. Blackburn.* MU-69, 51.
Wind from All Compass Points. *P. Blackburn.* PAZ-2, 127.
Works of the Poet. *E. Weinberger.* PAZ-2, 117.
Youth. *C. Tomlinson.* DEL-68, 124.
Fiction
My Life with the Wave. *E. Weinberger.* HOW-1, 273.
The Blue Bouquet. *L. Kemp.* MANC, 171.
Other
A literature of foundations (Essay). *L. Kemp.* TRI-13, 7.
What Does Poetry Mean? (Essay). *E. Randall.* MU-69, 10.

820 PEDREIRA, ANTONIO S. (1898-1939) Puerto Rico
Other
The Land And Its Meaning (from: Insularismo 1934). *B. Luby.*
BABI, 129.

821 PEDRONI, JOSÉ (1899-   ) Argentina
Poetry
The cradle. *H. Manning.* GAN, 51.

822 PEDROSO, REGINO (1896-   ) Cuba
Poetry
Five O'Clock Tea. *B. F. Carruthers.* JONE-3, 78.
Negro Brother. *H. Ruiz del Vizo.* RUIZ, 48.
Opinions Of The New Chinese Student. *L. Hughes.* HUGH, 372.
Opinions Of The New Student. *L. Hughes.* FITT, 247.
Tomorrow. *D. Fitts.* FITT, 245.

823 PELLEGRINI, ALDO (1903-   ) Argentina
Poetry
Morning. *W. Shand.* SHA, 60.
Variations On Travelling. *W. Shand.* SHA, 58.

824 PELLERANO CASTRO, ARTURO (1865-1916) Dominican Republic
Poetry
Creole Girl. *F. E. Townsend.* TOWN, 45.
In the Cemetery. *F. E. Townsend.* TOWN, 44.

825 PELLICER, CARLOS (1899-   ) Mexico
Poetry
Aurora. *Mary & C. V. Wicker.* PELL, 9.
Autumn Sonnets I, II, III. *Mary & C. V. Wicker.* PELL, 18.
Dawn. *E. W. Underwood.* UND, 156.
Desires. *Mary & C. V. Wicker.* PELL, 8.
Desires. *E. W. Underwood.* UND, 150.
Étude. *H. R. Hays.* FITT, 347.
Fire Song. *R. Benson.* BENS, 249.
Groups of Doves. *Mary & C. V. Wicker.* PELL, 12.
Harvester. *Mary & C. V. Wicker.* PELL, 17.

(PELLICER, CARLOS)
Memories of Iza (A Small Town of the Andes). *D. Justice.*
  PAZ-2, 171.
Nocturne III. *R. Benson.* BENS, 239.
Nocturne to My Mother. *R. Benson.* BENS, 229.
Prodigal Poem. *D. Justice.* PAZ-2, 177.
Remembrance. *Mary & C. V. Wicker.* PELL, 16.
Sketches for a Tropical Ode. *R. Benson.* BENS, 219.
Sketches For A Tropical Ode. *J. M. Cohen.* COH-1, 49.
Sketches For A Tropical Ode. *Mary & C. V. Wicker.* PELL, 21.
Snows of the Andes. *E. W. Underwood.* UND, 151.
Solar Flora. *R. Benson.* BENS, 241.
Sonnet. *M. González.* CARA, 266.
Studies. *R. Benson.* BENS, 213.
Studies. *D. Justice.* PAZ-2, 175.
Study. *R. Benson.* BENS, 237.
Study. *D. Justice.* PAZ-2, 169.
Study. *E. W. Underwood.* UND, 155.
Sunday. *D. Fitts.* FITT, 347.
Sunday. *Mary & C. V. Wicker.* PELL, 14.
The Reaper. *E. W. Underwood.* UND, 157.
Theme for a Nocturne. *R. Benson.* BENS, 235.
Theme for a Nocturne. no tr. CRAN, 111.
There Is No Time For Time. *R. Benson.* BENS, 215.
Third Time. *D. Fitts.* FITT, 349.
Third Time. *Mary & C. V. Wicker.* PELL, 11.
Three Etudes. *Mary & C. V. Wicker.* PELL, 5.
To Eduardo Villaseñor. *Mary & C. V. Wicker.* PELL, 15.
To José Manuel Puig Cassauranc. *E. W. Underwood.* UND, 150.
Uxmal. *E. W. Underwood.* UND, 152.
Wishes. *M. González.* CARA, 267.
Wishes. *D. Justice.* PAZ-2, 173.
You Are More Than My Sight. *R. Benson.* BENS, 227.

826 PEÑA BARRENECHEA, ENRIQUE (1904-   ) Peru
     Poetry
     Dead Poets. *M. B. Davis.* FITT, 541.
     Elegy For Bécquer. *M. B. Davis.* FITT, 539.
     Man's Road. *M. Lee.* FITT, 539.

827 PENNA E COSTA, MARÍLIA SÃO PAULO (1930-   ) Brazil
     Fiction
     The Happiest Couple in the World. *W. L. Grossman.* GRO,
       117.

828 PERALTA, ALEJANDRO (1899-   ) Peru
     Poetry
     Andean Crossing. *M. Lee.* FITT, 167.

829   PEREDA VALDÉS, ILDEFONSO (1899–   ) Uruguay
       Poetry
       Cradle Song To Put A Negro Baby To Sleep. *M. Lee.* FITT,
         483.
       The Guitar Of The Negroes. *H. Ruiz del Vizo.* RUIZ, 124.

830   PERÉS, RAMÓN DOMINGO (1863–?   ) Cuba
       Poetry
       The Aedian Harp. *T. Walsh.* WALS, 570.

831   PEREYRA, NICANDRO (1914–   ) Argentina
       Poetry
       Crossing The Pampa. *W. Shand.* SHA, 112.
       I Sing A Mournful Air. *W. Shand.* SHA, 111.

832   PÉREZ MARICEVICH, FRANCISCO (1937–   ) Paraguay
       Poetry
       Poem 8. *J. Upton.* TRI-13, 286.
       Still (Fragment). *J. Upton.* TRI-13, 285.

833   PÉREZ PERDOMO, FRANCISCO (1929–   ) Venezuela
       Poetry
       All Is Not A Dream. *H. P. Doezema.* MU-73, 51.
       Escape. *H. P. Doezema.* MU-73, 45.
       Lost Identity. *H. P. Doezema.* MU-73, 45.
       Only The Dream Reveals. *H. P. Doezema.* MU-73, 49.
       The Depravity Of The Stars (Excerpt). *H. P. Doezema.* MU-73,
         47.

834   PÉREZ PIERRET, ANTONIO (1885–1937) Puerto Rico
       Poetry
       My Pegasus. *T. Walsh.* WALS, 727.

835   PÉREZ SÓ, REYNALDO (1945–   ) Venezuela
       Poetry
       Tanmantra (Excerpt). *W. Barnstone.* MU-73, 89.
       To Die Of Another Dream (Excerpt). *W. Barnstone.* MU-73, 85.

836   PERÓN, EVA (1919–   ) Argentina
       Other
       My Mission in Life (Excerpts). *E. Cherry.* HAH, 91.

837   PESSOA, FERNANDO (1888–1935) Brazil
       Poetry
       After the Fair. *A. de Lacerda & D. Wevill.* DEL-70, 140.
       All love letters are.... *A. de Lacerda & D. Wevill.*
         DEL-70, 138.
       Everyday I discover.... *A. de Lacerda & D. Wevill.* DEL-70,
         142.
       Henry the Navigator. *A. de Lacerda & D. Wevill.* DEL-70,
         144.

(PESSOA, FERNANDO)
Ode. *A. de Lacerda & D. Wevill.* DEL-70, 144.
On a book abandoned on a journey. *A. de Lacerda & D. Wevill.*
DEL-70, 144.

838 PETIT DE MURAT, ULISES (1905-   ) Argentina
Poetry
The Gallery. *W. Shand.* SHA, 76.
The Tango. *W. Shand.* SHA, 77.
The Tavern. *W. Shand.* SHA, 78.

839 PEYROU, MANUEL (1902-   ) Argentina
Fiction
Juliet and the Magician. *D. Yates.* YATE, 31.

840 PEZOA VÉLIZ, CARLOS (1879-1908) Chile
Poetry
Afternoon in the Hospital. *G. D. Craig.* CRAI, 171.
Afternoon in the Hospital. *A. J. McVan.* TRAN, 198.
Age. *T. Walsh.* WALS, 702.
Nothing. *G. D. Craig.* CRAI, 169.

841 PIAZZA, LUIS GUILLERMO (1922-   ) Argentina
Other
There'll Always Be a Cordoba. no tr. LIT-1, 3.

842 PICCHIA, PAULO MENOTTI DEL (1892-   ) Brazil
Poetry
Bairro da Luz. *M. Cardozo.* NEI, 27.
The Mirror. *L. S. Downes.* DOWN, 26.
Thoughts in a Public Garden. *M. Cardozo.* NEI, 29.

843 PICHARDO MOYA, FELIPE (   ) Cuba
Poetry
The Carnival. *H. Ruiz del Vizo.* RUIZ, 20.

844 PICHÓN RIVIERE, MARCELO (   ) Argentina
Poetry
"friend soldier...." no tr. YOU, 12.
"your body has the delicacy of the dying...." no tr. YOU,
12.

845 PICO, PEDRO E. (1882-1945) Argentina
Drama
Common Clay (Excerpt). *W. K. Jones.* JONE-3, 393.
Common Clay. *W. K. Jones.* JONE-4, 55.

846 PICÓN-SALAS, MARIANO (1901-1965) Venezuela
Other
The Back Yard and the Geography of the Air (from: Viaje al
amanecer). *H. de Onís.* ONIS-1, 298.

847 PIERRA DE POO, MARTINA (   ) Cuba
     Poetry
     Love's Mirror. *J. I. C. Clarke.* WALS, 747.

848 PIETRI, PEDRO (1944-   ) Puerto Rico
     Poetry
     Puerto Rican Obituary. Originally Engl. BABI, 453.
     Puerto Rican Obituary. *D. Fernández Chericián & R. Márquez.*
        MARQ, 405.
     The Broken English Dream. *A. Matilla & E. G. Matilla.*
        MATI, 138.

849 PIGNATARI, DÉCIO (1927-   ) Brazil
     Poetry
     a/move/ment/. *H. de Campos.* WILL-1, n.p.
     beba coca cola. *H. de Campos.* WILL-1, n.p.
     earth. *H. de Campos.* WILL-1, n.p.
     earth/to possess/wanders/ploughs. no tr. BANN, 96.
     hombre. *H. de Campos.* WILL-1, n.p.
     LIFE. no tr. BANN, 85.
     LIFE. *H. de Campos.* WILL-1, n.p.
     man/hunger/woman. no tr. BANN, 97.
     'Organismo.' *H. de Campos.* WILL-1, n.p.

850 PIMENTEL, CYRO (1926-   ) Brazil
     Poetry
     Mirror Of Ashes. *L. S. Downes.* DOWN, 85.
     Poem No. 19. *L. S. Downes.* DOWN, 85.

851 PIMENTEL CORONEL, RAMÓN (1872-1909) Venezuela
     Poetry
     Jesus. *J. I. C. Clarke.* WALS, 648.

852 PINEDA, RAFAEL (1926-   ) Venezuela
     Poetry
     Chicha talking it up. *B. Belitt.* TRI-13, 435.
     For Maricastana, with a spray of immortelle. *B. Belitt.*
        TRI-13, 440.
     The commission. *B. Belitt.* TRI-13, 438.
     1926. *B. Belitt.* TRI-13, 436.

853 PIÑERA, VIRGILIO (1912-   ) Cuba
     Fiction
     The Dragée. *J. M. Cohen.* COH-3, 60.
     The philanthropist. no tr. CARZ, 19.

854 [PINO, ÁNGEL pseud.] (1875-1921) Chile
     DÍAZ GARCÉS, JOAQUÍN
     Other
     A Christening: Scenes from Domestic Life. no tr. JONE-3,
        359.

855 PINO, S. JOSÉ M. (   ) Mexico
Poetry
Rhyme. *A. S. Blackwell*. GOLD-2, 17.

856 PINO, WLADEMIR DIAS (1927-   ) Brazil
Poetry
solid. *H. de Campos*. WILL-1, n.p.

857 PINO SUÁREZ, JOSÉ MARÍA (1869-1913) Mexico
Poetry
Love's Language. *A. S. Blackwell*. BLAC, 174.

858 PIÑON, NÉLIDA (   ) Brazil
Fiction
Big-Bellied Cow. *G. Rabassa*. MU-70, 89.
Brief flower. *G. Rabassa*. TRI-13, 341.

859 PINTO, LUIZ ANGELO (1941-   ) Brazil
Poetry
lexical key. no tr. WILL-1, n.p.

860 PINTO DE MEDEIROS, ANTONIO (1920-   ) Brazil
Poetry
Act Of Faith. *L. S. Downes*. DOWN, 71.
Confession. *L. S. Downes*. DOWN, 72.

861 PIRES FERNANDES, LUIZ CARLOS (   )
Other
A Form of Dissent Now Threatened (Essay). *E. Brazil*. DR,
150.

862 PITA RODRÍGUEZ, FÉLIX (1909-   ) Cuba
Poetry
Ballad in Memory of a Dead Poet. *R. F. Hardy*. BECK, 81.
Because We Love Life. *L. Kearns*. TARN, 13.
Chronicle for a Future Poet. *C. Beck*. BECK, 79.
Chronicles of a New Dawn. *C. Beck*. BECK, 85.
Of Hard, Pure, Clear Stone. *R. F. Hardy*. BECK, 71.
Rifle Number 5767. *R. F. Hardy*. BECK, 75.
Fiction
The seed. no tr. CARZ, 11.
Tobias. *Z. Nelken*. TORR, 11.

863 PIZARNIK, ALEJANDRA (1937-   ) Argentina
Poetry
A Condition (Of Being). *G. McWhirter*. MU-69, 95.
A Dream Where Silence Is Made Of Gold. *G. McWhirter*.
MU-69, 97.
As Water Over A Stone. *G. McWhirter*. MU-69, 97.
Contemplation. *G. McWhirter*. MU-69, 95.
Poems. *W. Shand*. SHA, 267.

Rescue. *G. McWhirter.* MU-69, 97.
Rings Of Ashes. no tr. YOU, 9.
Sleep. *W. Shand.* SHA, 266.
The Absent One. *W. Shand.* SHA, 266.
Vertigo Or The Contemplation Of Something That Ends.
  G. McWhirter. MU-69, 95.

864 PLA, JOSEFINA (1909-   ) Paraguay
     Poetry
     Forever. *W. K. Jones.* JONE-3, 145.
     Triptych of Rebirth in Shadow. *W. K. Jones.* JONE-3, 143.

865 PODESTÁ, JOSÉ J. (1856-1937) Argentina
     (Joint author. See also GUTIÉRREZ, EDUARDO.)
     Drama
     Juan Moreira. *C. Escudero & W. K. Jones.* JONE-3, 371.

866 PONIATOWSKA, ELENA (1932-   ) Mexico
     Other
     Interview with Juan Soriano. *J. Rechy.* EVER, 141.

867 PORRAS BARRANECHEA, RAÚL (1897-   ) Peru
     Other
     Lima, Past And Present (from: Little Anthology). *H. de
       Onís.* ARC, 405.

868 PORTAL, MAGDA (1901-   ) Peru
     Fiction
     Women in the Party (from: La trampa). *F. G. Carrino &
       J. E. Hahner.* HAH, 85.
     Other
     Aprismo and the Woman (Excerpt). *F. G. Carrino &
       J. E. Hahner.* HAH, 84.

869 PORTOGALO, JOSÉ (1904-   ) Argentina
     Poetry
     Image Of Conscience. *W. Shand.* SHA, 71.
     Image Of Memories. *W. Shand.* SHA, 69.

870 POVEDA, JOSÉ MANUEL (1888-1926) Cuba
     Poetry
     Song Of The Creative Voice. *T. Walsh.* WALS, 743.
     The Manuscript. *T. Walsh.* WALS, 742.

871 POZAS A., RICARDO (   ) Mexico
     Other
     Juan Pérez Jolote (Part I of monograph). *L. Kemp.* EVER,
       91.

872   PRADO, PEDRO   (1886-1952)   Chile
      Poetry
      Lazarus. *A. S. Blackwell*. BLAC, 278.
      Lazarus. *G. D. Craig*. CRAI, 159.
      Our Mountain. *A. S. Blackwell*. BLAC, 286.
      The Birds of Passage. *G. D. Craig*. CRAI, 155.
      The hands of my beloved. *G. D. Craig*. CRAI, 157.
      Fiction
      Alsino (Excerpt). *R. Scott*. JONE-3, 334.

873   PRUD'HOMME, EMILIO   (1856-1932)   Dominican Republic
      Poetry
      Hymn to the Homeland. *F. E. Townsend*. TOWN, 49.

874   PUIG, MANUEL   (1932-   )   Argentina
      Fiction
      A Meeting. *S. J. Levine*. MANC, 435.

875   PUIGDOLLERS, CARMEN   (1924-   )   Puerto Rico
      Poetry
      A Whiteness Of Lily. *P. Vallés*. KAI, n.p.

876   QUEIROZ, DINAH SILVEIRA DE   (1911-   )   Brazil
      Fiction
      Guidance. *W. L. Grossman*. GRO, 100.
      Tarciso. *W. L. Grossman*. HOW-1, 235.

877   QUEIROZ, RACHEL DE   (1910-   )   Brazil
      Fiction
      Metonymy, or the Husband's Revenge. *W. L. Grossman*. GRO,
      27.

878   QUEREMEL, ÁNGEL MIGUEL   (1900-1939)   Venezuela
      Poetry
      Ballad Of Love And Blood. *R. Humphries*. FITT, 279.

879   QUERO CHIESA, LUIS   (1911-   )   Puerto Rico
      Fiction
      The Protest. *B. Luby*. BABI, 388.

880   QUINTERO ÁLVAREZ, ALBERTO   (1914-1944)   Mexico
      Poetry
      Facing the Sea. *J. M. Cohen*. COH-2, 436.

881   QUIROGA, HORACIO   (1878-1937)   Uruguay
      Fiction
      How the Flamingoes Got Their Stockings.   no tr.   MANC, 53.
      Justice. *Z. Nelken*. TORR, 55.
      The Alligator War. *A. Livingston*. HOW-1, 57.
      The Contract Workers. *W. E. Colford*. COLF, 108.
      The Fatherland. *H. Young*. ONIS-2, 126.

The Flamingos' Stockings. *W. P. Negron & W. K. Jones.*
JONE-3, 303.
The Fugitives. *D. de Kay.* FLOR-2, 398.
The Return of Anaconda. *A. Brenner.* FRAN, 239.
The Roof. no tr. FLOR-4, 179.
The Son. *L. Wilson & W. K. Jones.* JONE-3, 306.
The Son. *L. Wilson & W. K. Jones.* MILL, 331.
Three Letters...and a Footnote. *H. Kurz.* HAYDN, 934.

882 QUIRÓS, RODRIGO (1944-   ) Costa Rica
Poetry
Complete Apology From A Starry Sky. *A. Edwards.* YOU, 48.

QUÍSPEZ ASÍN, CÉSAR. See [MORO, CÉSAR pseud.].

883 RABASA, EMILIO (1856-1930) Mexico
Fiction
La Bola. *F. Starr.* STAR, 382.
The Day of the Battle. *F. Starr.* STAR, 375.
The Independent Press. *F. Starr.* STAR, 384.

884 RADAELLI, SIGFRIDO (1909-   ) Argentina
Poetry
The Silent Man. *W. Shand.* SHA, 94.
When A God Inhabits Us. *W. Shand.* SHA, 93.

885 RAMÍREZ DE ARELLANO, DIANA (1919-   ) Puerto Rico
Poetry
To A Poet. *B. Luby.* BABI, 307.

886 RAMÍREZ DE ARELLANO NOLLA, OLGA (1911-   ) Puerto Rico
Poetry
Island Of Childhood. *B. Luby.* BABI, 291.
The Puerto Rican Wild "Amapola." *B. Luby.* BABI, 292.

887 RAMOS, GRACILIANO (1892-1953) Brazil
Fiction
Caetés (Excerpt). *B. Guedes.* CHI, 71.
The Thief. *W. L. Grossman.* GRO, 41.

888 RAMOS, JOSÉ ANTONIO (1885-1946) Cuba
Drama
The Traitor (Excerpt). *W. K. Jones.* JONE-3, 447.
Traitor. *W. K. Jones.* JONE-4, 12.
When Love Dies. *I. Goldberg.* SHAY, 125.

889 RAMOS, PÉRICLES EUGÊNIO DA SILVA (1919-   ) Brazil
Poetry
Epitaph. *L. S. Downes.* DOWN, 69.
Future, 4. *M. Cardozo.* NEI, 163.
Poem Of The Sower. *M. Cardozo.* NEI, 161.

890 RAMPONI, JORGE ENRIQUE (1907–) Argentina
Poetry
Outline Of A Rainy Landscape. *W. Shand.* SHA, 88.
Top Of Flames. *W. Shand.* SHA, 89.

891 RATTI, HORACIO ESTEBAN (1903–) Argentina
Poetry
Joy Of The Song. *W. Shand.* SHA, 61.
Poem. *W. Shand.* SHA, 62.

892 [REBÊLO, MARQUES pseud.] (1907–) Brazil
CRUZ, EDDY DIAS DA
Fiction
The Beautiful Rabbits. *W. L. Grossman.* GRO, 33.

893 REBOLLEDO, EFRÉN (1877–1929) Mexico
Poetry
Insomnia. *E. W. Underwood.* UND, 94.
The Vampire. *S. Beckett.* PAZ-1, 171.
Voto. *E. W. Underwood.* UND, 93.

894 REGIS, EDSON (1923–) Brazil
Poetry
The Songs And Death. *L. S. Downes.* DOWN, 79.

895 REIS, MARCOS KONDER (1922–) Brazil
Poetry
Map. *M. Strand.* BISH, 167.
Parameter. *M. Strand.* BISH, 169.

896 RENDÓN, VÍCTOR M. (1859–1940) Ecuador
Drama
Lottery Ticket. *W. K. Jones.* JONE-4, 47.

897 REQUENA LEGARRETA, PEDRO (1893–1918) Mexico
Poetry
I Would Enfold Your Death And Mine. *T. Walsh.* WALS, 766.
Idyl. *G. Strange.* WALS, 763.

898 REQUENI, ANTONIO (1930–) Argentina
Poetry
A Man Sitting In A Plaza. *W. Shand.* SHA, 242.
Bough Of Grey Days. *W. Shand.* SHA, 243.
Light. *W. Shand.* SHA, 241.

899 REVILLA, MANUEL GUSTAVO ANTONIO (1863–?) Mexico
Other
Baltasar de Echave. *F. Starr.* STAR, 237.
Miguel Cabrera. *F. Starr.* STAR, 240.
The Fine Arts in Mexico (Essay). *F. Starr.* STAR, 230.
The Works of Tolsa. *F. Starr.* STAR, 235.

Tres Guerras and Tolsa. *F. Starr.* STAR, 232.
Wood Carving in Puebla (Essay). *F. Starr.* STAR, 233.

900 REYES, ALFONSO (1889-1959) Mexico
Poetry
A (from: <u>5 Casi Sonetos</u>). *E. W. Underwood.* UND, 126.
Comings and Goings of Santa Teresa. *J. M. Cohen.* COH-2, 362.
Face and Cross of the Cactus. *J. M. Cohen.* COH-2, 364.
Glosa de mi tierra. *E. W. Underwood.* UND, 123.
Gulf Of Mexico. *D. Fitts.* FITT, 51.
I (from: <u>5 Casi Sonetas</u>). *E. W. Underwood.* UND, 127.
La amenaza de la flor. *E. W. Underwood.* UND, 122.
Monterrey Sun. *S. Beckett.* PAZ-1, 194.
Nightmare. *M. González.* CARA, 264.
Quasi-Sonnet. *E. W. Underwood.* JONE-3, 54.
River of Oblivion. *S. Beckett.* PAZ-1, 191.
Scarcely.... *S. Beckett.* PAZ-1, 194.
Tarahumara Herbs. *S. Beckett.* PAZ-1, 188.
The Menace of the Flower. *S. Beckett.* PAZ-1, 187.
The Strength of Memory. *M. González.* CARA, 265.
To-and-Fro of Saint Theresa. *S. Beckett.* PAZ-1, 192.
Fiction
Major Aranda's Hand. *M. Johnson.* HOW-1, 82.
Drama
Eclogue of the Blind. *R. L. Maloney.* JONE-3, 54.
Other
Landscape of Mexico (from: <u>Vision of Anáhuac 1519</u>).
  E. W. Underwood. UND, 128.
Thoughts On The American Mind (Essay). *H. de Onís.* ARC, 225.
<u>Vision of Anáhuac 1519</u> (Excerpt). *H. de Onís.* ONIS-1, 335.

901 REYES, SALVADOR (1899-   ) Chile
Fiction
Vagabonds' Christmas Eve. *A. De Sola.* FLOR-2, 466.

902 REYES BERRÍOS, EDWIN (1944-   ) Puerto Rico
Poetry
high on me toward me.... *E. G. Matilla.* MATI, 193.
Inés the Wind.... *E. G. Matilla.* MATI, 189.
They Say That My Dark Hand.... *E. G. Matilla.* MATI, 191.

903 RIBERA CHEVREMONT, EVARISTO (1896-   ) Puerto Rico
Poetry
Red Christ. *M. Arrillaga.* MATI, 17.
Symphony of the Hammers. *M. Arrillaga.* MATI, 15.
The Castilian Language. *B. Luby.* BABI, 279.
The Wooden Wall. *B. Luby.* BABI, 278.

904 RICARDO, CASSIANO (1895-   ) Brazil
Poetry
Asking For A Favor From A High Government Official.
   M. Cardozo. NEI, 61.
Geography of Sleep. *P. Standish*. CARA, 71.
I Take Cognizance. *L. S. Downes*. DOWN, 31.
Last Will And Testament. *M. Cardozo*. NEI, 65.
Masochism. *J. Nist & Y. Leite*. NIST, 63.
M'Orpheus. *J. Nist & Y. Leite*. NIST, 59.
Nightfall. *B. Howes*. BISH, 27.
Pastoral Ode. *J. Nist & Y. Leite*. NIST, 67.
Rotation. *M. Cardozo*. NEI, 67.
Submarine Landscape. *P. Standish*. CARA, 70.
Tantalus. *J. Nist & Y. Leite*. NIST, 60.
The Banquet. *J. Nist & Y. Leite*. NIST, 66.
The Ex(orbit)ant Voyage. *M. Cardozo*. NEI, 69.
The Four Angels. *J. Nist & Y. Leite*. NIST, 60.
The Hidden Rose. *J. Nist & Y. Leite*. NIST, 62.
The Other Life. *J. Nist & Y. Leite*. NIST, 63.
The Song of the Wild Dove. *J. R. Longland*. BISH, 25.
Zoo. *J. Nist & Y. Leite*. NIST, 64.

905 RICHIEZ ACEVEDO, RAFAEL (1912-   ) Dominican Republic
Poetry
Agapito Javalera. *F. E. Townsend*. TOWN, 94.

906 RIGALI, ROLANDO (1941-   ) Cuba
Poetry
Likeness. *J. M. Cohen*. COH-3, 158.

907 RINALDINI, JULIO (1890-?   ) Argentina
Other
Buenos Aires (from: Quelques Regards sur l'Argentine)
   (Essay). *H. de Onís*. ARC, 382.

908 RIVAROLA MATTO, JOSÉ MARÍA (1917-   ) Paraguay
Drama
The End of Chipí González (Excerpt). *W. K. Jones*. JONE-3,
   454.
The Fate of Chipí González. *W. K. Jones*. JONE-1, 55.

909 RIVAS, ENRIQUE (   ) Mexico
Poetry
Possession. *L. R. Hayman*. CRAN, 96.

910 RIVAS, PEDRO GEOFFROY (1908-   ) Ecuador
Poetry
First Mystery (from: "The Four Mysteries of Creation" in
   Yulcuicat). no tr. YOU, 67.
Third Mystery (from: "The Four Mysteries of Creation" in
   Yulcuicat). no tr. YOU, 68.

911   RIVERA, BUENO DE (1914-   ) Brazil
      Poetry
      Dry Eyes. *L. S. Downes.* DOWN, 61.

912   RIVERA, ETNAIRIS (1949-   ) Puerto Rico
      Poetry
      Letter to Manuel. *D. Sánchez-Méndez.* MATI, 219.

913   RIVERA, JOSÉ EUSTACIO (1888-1928) Colombia
      Fiction
      The Vortex (Excerpt). *E. K. James.* ARC, 26.
      The Vortex (Excerpt). *E. K. James.* JONE-3, 209.

914   RIVERA, MIGDALIA (   ) Puerto Rico
      Poetry
      The Straight-Jacket. Originally Engl. BABI, 452.

915   RIVERO, ISEL (1941-   ) Cuba
      Poetry
      Newspaper Item. *A. Mitchell.* TARN, 105.

916   ROA BASTOS, AUGUSTO (1918-   ) Paraguay
      Poetry
      Triptych from the Four Elements. *W. K. Jones.* JONE-3, 146.
      Fiction
      Encounter with the Traitor. *N. T. di Giovanni.* HOW-1, 289.
      The Excavation. *D. Flakoll & C. Alegría.* FLAK, 85.
      The Living Tomb. *H. R. Hays.* CARP, 132.
      The Vacant Lot. *M. J. Wilkie.* MANC, 205.

917   ROCHA, GLAUBER (   )
      Other
      Beginning at Zero: Notes on Cinema and Society (Essay).
      J. Pottlitzer. DR, 144.

918   RODÓ, JOSÉ ENRIQUE (1871-1917) Uruguay
      Other
      Ariel (Excerpt). *W. K. Jones.* JONE-3, 327.
      Montalvo (Essay). *H. de Onís.* ARC, 355.

919   RODRÍGUEZ BETETA, VIRGILIO (1885-?) Guatemala
      Other
      The Discoverer of a New World in the New World. no tr.
      LIT-1, 52.

920   RODRÍGUEZ CERNA, JOSÉ (1889-1952) Guatemala
      Other
      Guatemalan Archaeology. no tr. LIT-2, 25.

921 RODRÍGUEZ CHARRO, FRANCISCO (   ) Dominican Republic
     Poetry
     Old Negro From The Port. *H. Ruiz del Vizo.* RUIZ, 113.

922 RODRÍGUEZ LARRETA, ENRIQUE (1875-1961) Argentina
     Fiction
     The Glory of Don Ramiro (Excerpt). *W. K. Jones.* JONE-3,
     254.

923 RODRÍGUEZ RIVERA, GUILLERMO (1943-   ) Cuba
     Poetry
     Among the Living. *R. F. Hardy.* BECK, 759.
     Discovery. *C. Beck.* BECK, 763.
     Next Day. *R. F. Hardy.* BECK, 761.
     To Hermann Hesse. *C. Beck.* BECK, 757.
     Vita Nuova. *N. Tarn.* TARN, 115.
     Working Hours. *C. Beck.* BECK, 765.

924 ROGELIO NOGUERAS, LUIS (1944-   ) Cuba
     Poetry
     The Brothers. *D. Gardner.* TARN, 129.
     The Same As Ever. *D. Gardner.* TARN, 127.

925 ROJAS, GONZALO (1917-   ) Chile
     Poetry
     Coal. *J. Upton.* TRI-13, 382.
     Love. *D. Flakoll & C. Alegría.* FLAK, 148.
     To silence. *J. Upton.* TRI-13, 381.

926 ROJAS, JACK (   ) Cuba
     Poetry
     "Tragic night of rumba." *H. Ruiz del Vizo.* RUIZ, 68.

927 ROJAS, MANUEL (1896-   ) Chile
     Fiction
     The Cub. *W. E. Colford.* COLF, 3.
     The Glass of Milk. *W. E. Colford.* COLF, 15.
     The Glass of Milk. *Z. Nelken.* TORR, 121.

928 ROJAS, RICARDO (1882-1957) Argentina
     Fiction
     The Incubus. *H. de Onís.* ONIS-1, 205.
     Other
     The Army Of The Andes (from: The Saint of the Sword).
     H. de Onís. ARC, 270.

929 [ROKHA, PABLO DE pseud.] (1894-   ) Chile
     DÍAZ LOYOLA, CARLOS
     Poetry
     Allegory Of Torment. *H. R. Hays.* FITT, 425.
     Elegy For All Ages. *H. R. Hays.* HAYS, 205.

Lament. *H. R. Hays.* HAYS, 199.
Seafaring Towns. *H. R. Hays.* HAYS, 197.
Subterranean Days And Nights. *H. R. Hays.* HAYS, 209.
The Pale Conquerors. *H. R. Hays.* HAYS, 199.
Tribal Lay. *H. R. Hays.* HAYS, 201.

930 [ROKHA, WINÉTT DE pseud.] (1896–1951) Chile
SANDERSON, LUISA ANABALÓN
Poetry
Song Of Thomas, Departed. *H. R. Hays.* FITT, 161.
Waltz In Yungay Square. *H. R. Hays.* FITT, 161.

931 ROMERO, ELVIO (1927-   ) Paraguay
Poetry
The Guitar of the People. *W. K. Jones.* JONE-3, 148.

932 ROMERO, JOSÉ RUBÉN (1892-1952) Mexico
Fiction
The Futile Life Of Pito Perez. *J. Coyne.* FLOR-2, 303.

933 ROSA NIEVES, CESÁREO (1901-   ) Puerto Rico
Poetry
I Am the Tropics. *W. K. Jones.* JONE-3, 84.
The Ensueñistas' "Ars Poetica." *W. K. Jones.* JONE-3, 83.

934 ROSADO VEGA, LUIS (1876-?) Mexico
Poetry
Nocturn of the Rain. *E. W. Underwood.* UND, 118.

935 ROSALES, CÉSAR (1910-   ) Argentina
Poetry
Autumn. *W. Shand.* SHA, 101.
The Vestige. *W. Shand.* SHA, 102.

936 ROSARIO QUÍLES, LUIS A. (1936-   ) Puerto Rico
Poetry
The Trial of Víctor Campolo (Fragments). *D. Sánchez-Méndez.*
  MATI, 111.

937 ROSE, JUAN GONZALO (1928-   ) Peru
Poetry
From the Liturgy. *D. Tipton.* AHER, 40.
From the liturgy. *D. Tipton.* TRI-13, 207.
The Beak of the Dove. *D. Tipton.* AHER, 40.
The Beak of the Dove. *R. Greenwell.* HAR67-2, 37.
The beak of the dove. *D. Tipton.* TRI-13, 208.

938 ROSS ZANET, JOSÉ GUILLERMO (1930-   ) Panama
Poetry
Poem of Contemporary Days and Love. *D. Flakoll & C. Alegría.*
  FLAK, 77.
"There are hunchbacks...." no tr. YOU, 101.
Without the Color of the Sky (Excerpt). no tr. YOU, 100.

939 ROSSLER, OSVALDO (1927-   ) Argentina
Poetry
The Myth Of Liberty. *W. Shand.* SHA, 216.
This Is The Place. *W. Shand.* SHA, 217.

940 ROTZAIT, PERLA (1923?-   ) Argentina
Poetry
Mutable Poem. *W. Shand.* SHA, 179.
Parable. *W. Shand.* SHA, 181.
The Penalty. *W. Shand.* SHA, 180.

941 ROZAS LARRAÍN, CARLOS (1910-   ) Chile
Fiction
The Black Ship. *L. Kemp.* PRIZE, 241.

942 RUBERTINO, MARÍA LUISA (1929-   ) Argentina
Poetry
Life. *W. Shand.* SHA, 233.
One Night. *W. Shand.* SHA, 232.

943 RUBIÃO, MURILO (1916-   ) Brazil
Fiction
Bárbara. *R. W. Horton.* COEL, 179.

944 RUBIO, ALBERTO (1928-   ) Chile
Poetry
Grandmother. *J. Upton.* TRI-13, 381.
Noble Ladies. *R. Connally.* YOU, 36.
Portrait Of A Girl. *M. Williams.* WILL-2, 97.
Portrait of a Little Girl. *D. Flakoll & C. Alegría.* FLAK,
  94.
The Grandmother. *M. Williams.* WILL-2, 95.
Winter. *J. Upton.* TRI-13, 380.

945 RUÍZ, RAÚL (1942-   ) Chile
Drama
The Cheater. *M. Williams.* WILL-2, 140.

946 RUÍZ ESPARZA, JUAN MANUEL (   ) Mexico
Poetry
C. *E. W. Underwood.* UND, 202.
E. *E. W. Underwood.* UND, 203.
I. *E. W. Underwood.* UND, 201.
U. *E. W. Underwood.* UND, 200.

947   RULFO, JUAN (1918-) Mexico
     Fiction
     Because We Are So Poor. L. Kemp. FLOR-3, 300.
     Macario. no tr. CRAN, 48.
     Macario. G. D. Schade. HOW-1, 295.
     No Dogs Bark. no tr. CRAN, 52.
     Pedro Páramo (Excerpt). L. Kemp. EVER, 45.
     Talpa. D. Flakoll & C. Alegría. FLAK, 32.
     Talpa. J. A. Chapman. FRA-J, 169.
     Talpa. G. D. Schade. MANC, 247.
     The Day of The Landslide. H. St. Martin. CARP, 223.
     They Gave Us The Land. J. Franco. COH-1, 174.

948   RUSCALLEDA BERDEDÓNIZ, JORGE MARÍA (1944-) Puerto Rico
     Poetry
     Advice. D. Sánchez-Méndez. MATI, 147.
     Poets Shouldn't Say.... D. Sánchez-Méndez. MATI, 151.

949   SABAT ERCASTY, CARLOS (1887-?) Uruguay
     Poetry
     The Diaphanous Shadows (Excerpt). M. González. CARA, 366.
     The Farewells (Excerpt). M. González. CARA, 365.

950   SÁBATO, ERNESTO (1911-) Argentina
     Fiction
     Report on the blind: Part III (from: Sobre héroes y tumbas). S. M. Gross. TRI-13, 95.

951   SABINES, JAIME (1926-) Mexico
     Poetry
     After All. P. Blackburn. CRAN, 105.
     As The Wounded Crab. M. Durán & G. Durán. MU-69, 85.
     Bach's Music Moves Curtains. P. Blackburn. EVER, 139.
     From the bodies.... W. S. Merwin. CARP, 331.
     Hallelujah! E. Trejo. CHI, 113.
     I Don't Know for Certain.... W. S. Merwin. PAZ-2, 71.
     I have eyes to see.... W. S. Merwin. CARP, 331.
     I Have Seen Them In The Pictures. J. M. Cohen. COH-1, 180.
     I Hear Pigeons. M. González. CARA, 294.
     I Hear Pigeons. E. Trejo. CHI, 109.
     I Put a Head. P. Levine. PAZ-2, 81.
     If Anyone Should Tell You That It Isn't So. M. González. CARA, 294.
     If Someone Tells You It's Not for Sure. P. Levine. PAZ-2, 79.
     In the House of the Day. P. Levine. PAZ-2, 75.
     In The Open Eyes Of The Dead. M. Durán & G. Durán. MU-69, 81.
     In What Corner. E. Trejo. CHI, 115.
     It Falls Over Your Eyes. E. Trejo. CHI, 111.

(SABINES, JAIME)
  Let's Sing. *P. Levine*. PAZ-2, 83.
  Like Crabs. *J. M. Cohen*. COH-1, 179.
  On Horseback. *P. Levine*. PAZ-2, 77.
  Smashed. *P. Blackburn*. EVER, 140.
  So Here We Are. *P. Levine*. PAZ-2, 85.
  Something on the Death of the Eldest Sabines. *P. Levine*.
    PAZ-2, 87.
  Surrounded By Butterflies. *M. Durán & G. Durán*. MU-69, 83.
  Tarumba (Excerpt). no tr. CRAN, 106.
  Tarumba. *W. S. Merwin*. PAZ-2, 73.
  The Lovers. *D. J. Flakoll & C. Alegría*. BENE, 103.
  The Signal (Excerpt). *W. S. Merwin*. CARP, 327.
  Weekly Journal (Excerpt). *W. S. Merwin*. CARP, 329.

952 SÁENZ, CARLOS LUIS (1899-   ) Costa Rica
    Poetry
    As a Petal. *E. du Gué Trapier*. TRAN, 213.

953 SÁENZ, DALMIRO J. (1926-   ) Argentina
    Fiction
    Far South. *D. Yates*. YATE, 113.

954 SÁENZ AZCORRO, FRANZ (   ) Mexico
    Poetry
    By the Dead Cities of Yucatán. *E. W. Underwood*. UND, 207.
    The Path. *E. W. Underwood*. UND, 206.
    Other
    November in Yucatán (Essay). *E. W. Underwood*. UND, 205.

955 SÁEZ BURGOS, JUAN (1943-   ) Puerto Rico
    Poetry
    Deliberately. *M. Arrillaga*. MATI, 135.
    Historic Tale in One Language Without a Moral.
      E. G. Matilla. MATI, 133.

956 SAINZ, GUSTAVO (1940-   ) Mexico
    Fiction
    Selfportrait with friends. *J. C. Murchison*. TRI-13, 117.

957 SALABERRY, ARABELLA (1946-   ) Costa Rica
    Poetry
    "The hours fall...." *A. Edwards*. YOU, 50.

958 SALADO ÁLBAREZ, VICTORIANO (1867-?) Mexico
    Fiction
    From Judicial Records (Excerpt). *F. Starr*. STAR, 290.
    Other
    Federico Gamboa (from: <u>From My Harvest</u>). *F. Starr*. STAR,
      297.

[SALARRUÉ pseud.]. See SALAZAR ARRUÉ, SALVADORE.

959   SALAS, HORACIO (1938-   ) Argentina
      Poetry
      Friends. *P. Morgan.* TRI-13, 234.
      Now That Death Surrounds You. *W. Shand.* SHA, 271.
      The Only Hope. *W. Shand.* SHA, 270.
      Those who are alone. *P. Morgan.* TRI-13, 233.

960   SALAZAR ARRUÉ, SALVADORE (1899-   ) El Salvador
      [SALARRUÉ pseud.]
      Fiction
      The Pot of Gold   *H. de Onís.* ONIS-1, 314.

961   SALAZAR BONDY, SEBASTIÁN (1924-1965) Peru
      Poetry
      Exiled from the Light. *E. Hollis & M. Ahern.* AHER, 17.
      Holographic Testament. *D. J. Flakoll & C. Alegría.* BENE,
        85.
      Interior Patio. *D. Tipton.* AHER, 19.
      Olographic Testament. *T. Reynolds.* CARP, 303.
      Question for the Lost Land. *T. Reynolds.* CARP, 305.
      Shades of Origin. *D. Tipton.* AHER, 14.
      Testament. *D. Tipton.* AHER, 13.
      Without Knowing Why. *E. Hollis & D. Tipton.* AHER, 15.
      Fiction
      I'm Sentimental. *D. Flakoll & C. Alegría.* FLAK, 178.
      Other
      Autobiographical Comment. *D. Tipton.* AHER, 123.

962   SALAZAR TAMARIZ, HUGO (1923-   ) Ecuador
      Poetry
      The Roots. *D. Flakoll & C. Alegría.* FLAK, 4.

963   SALAZAR VALDÉS, HUGO (   ) Colombia
      Poetry
      Black Dance. *H. Ruiz del Vizo.* RUIZ, 95.

964   SAMAYOA CHINCHILLA, CARLOS (1898-   ) Guatemala
      Other
      The Birth of Corn (Folklore). *H. de Onís.* ONIS-1, 310.

965   SAMPER ORTEGA, DANIEL (1895-1943) Colombia
      Fiction
      Storm In The Jungle (from: Zoraya). no tr. LIT-2, 14.

966   SANABIA, RAFAEL EMILIO (   ) Dominican Republic
      Poetry
      Ecstasy. *F. E. Townsend.* TOWN, 84.

967 SÁNCHEZ, FLORENCIO (1875-1910) Uruguay
Drama
Down the Gully. *W. K. Jones*. JONE-3, 387.
Down The Gully. *W. K. Jones*. SANCH, 122.
Evicted. *W. K. Jones*. SANCH, 199.
Midsummer Day Partners. *W. K. Jones*. JONE-4, 76.
Midsummer Day Partners. *W. K. Jones*. SANCH, 57.
My Son The Lawyer. *W. K. Jones*. SANCH, 15.
Our Children. *W. K. Jones*. SANCH, 287.
Phony Money. *W. K. Jones*. SANCH, 230.
The Family Circle. *W. K. Jones*. SANCH, 251.
The Foreign Girl. *W. K. Jones*. JONE-3, 381.
The Foreign Girl. *A. Coester*. PLAY, 1.
The Healing Hand. *W. K. Jones*. SANCH, 186.
The Immigrant Girl. *W. K. Jones*. SANCH, 77.
The Newspaper Boy. *W. K. Jones*. SANCH, 168.
The Tigress. *W. K. Jones*. SANCH, 212.

SÁNCHEZ, GUILLERMO. See [SOLARTE, TRISTÁN pseud.].

968 SÁNCHEZ, LUIS RAFAEL (1926-   ) Puerto Rico
Fiction
A Taste of Paradise. *C. M. Cutler*. MR, 249.

969 SÁNCHEZ BOUDY, JOSÉ (   ) Cuba
Poetry
Antillian Song. *H. Ruiz del Vizo*. RUIZ, 65.
Irregular Troilet. *H. Ruiz del Vizo*. RUIZ, 65.

970 SÁNCHEZ GARDEL, JULIO (1879-1937) Argentina
Drama
The Witches' Mountain. *J. Fassett*. BIER, 78.

971 SÁNCHEZ MAC GREGOR, JOAQUÍN (1932?-   ) Mexico
Poetry
Fallout shelter. *E. Randall*. TRI-13, 334.
Fallout Shelter. no tr. YOU, 84.
Polar ice. *E. Randall*. TRI-13, 334.
The Earth. no tr. YOU, 85.
The Lovers. no tr. YOU, 84.

972 SÁNCHEZ PELÁEZ, JUAN (1922-   ) Venezuela
Poetry
Animal By Habit (Excerpt). *A. McBride & M. McBride*.
   MU-73, 23.
I was crossing the black hills of an unknown land. (from:
   Elena And The Elements). *A. McBride & M. McBride*.
   MU-73, 21.
Less Objective Experiences. *A. McBride & M. McBride*.
   MU-73, 19.

One Stays Here. *A. McBride & M. McBride.* MU-73, 27.
Portrait Of The Unknown Beauty. *A. McBride & M. McBride.* MU-73, 19.
The Fleeing And The Permanent (Excerpts). *A. McBride & M. McBride.* MU-73, 23.

973 SÁNCHEZ QUELL, HIPÓLITO (1907-   ) Paraguay
Poetry
Praise Of Saccarello Street. *D. Fitts.* FITT, 163.

SANDERSON, LUISA ANABALÓN. See [ROKHA, WINÉTT DE pseud.].

974 SANÍN CANO, BALDOMERO (1861-?   ) Colombia
Other
The Transformation of America In Our Times (Essay). *H. de Onís.* ARC, 233.

975 SARDUY, SEVERO (1937-   ) Cuba
Fiction
From Cuba With A Song. *S. J. Levine.* FUEN, 231.

976 SAVIÑÓN, ALTAGRACIA (1886-1942) Dominican Republic
Poetry
My Vase of Green. *F. E. Townsend.* TOWN, 67.

977 SCHAPIRA FRIDMAN, FLOR (1935-   ) Argentina
Poetry
If You Were My Father. *W. Shand.* SHA, 265.
Only You Know How My Being Is Inhabited. *W. Shand.* SHA, 264.
We Have Fought. *W. Shand.* SHA, 264.

978 SCHINCA, MILTON (1926-   ) Uruguay
Poetry
CHILD(REN'S) BIOGRAPHY(IES). *R. Connally.* YOU, 113.

979 SCHMIDT, AUGUSTO FREDERICO (1906-1965) Brazil
Poetry
Birth of Sleep. *J. Nist & Y. Leite.* NIST, 108.
Destiny. *J. Nist & Y. Leite.* NIST, 111.
Farewell I. no tr. TRE, 20.
Genesis of Miracle. *J. Nist & Y. Leite.* NIST, 112.
I Have Seen the Sea. *J. Nist & Y. Leite.* NIST, 107.
Luciana. *P. Standish.* CARA, 91.
Morning Song. *P. Standish.* CARA, 90.
Not to Die. *J. Nist & Y. Leite.* NIST, 108.
One Day I Will Meet You. *J. Nist & Y. Leite.* NIST, 109.
Poem. *J. Nist & Y. Leite.* NIST, 110.
Preparation for Oblivion. *J. Nist & Y. Leite.* NIST, 109.
Search for Christmas. *J. Nist & Y. Leite.* NIST, 110.

(SCHMIDT, AUGUSTO FREDERICO)
Someone Is Sleeping in the Road.... *J. Nist & Y. Leite.*
NIST, 113.
Song of Night. *E. Brown.* LIT-1, 18.
Song of Night. *E. Brown.* LIT-2, 2.
The Princes. *L. S. Downes.* DOWN, 51.
The Princes. no tr. TRE, 18.
The Road of the Cold. *P. Standish.* CARA, 89.

980 SEABRA, BRUNO (   ) Brazil
Poetry
Theresa. *A. B. Poor.* POOR, 39.

981 SEGOVIA, TOMÁS (1927-   ) Mexico
Poetry
In These Clean Depths. *D. Demarest.* CRAN, 109.
The Day Has Eyes. *D. Demarest.* CRAN, 108.
The Distant Gardens. *D. Demarest.* CRAN, 108.
What Welcomes and Comforts. *M. Strand.* PAZ-2, 67.

982 SELVA, SALOMÓN DE LA (1893-1959) Nicaragua
Poetry
Elegy. *D. D. Walsh.* FITT, 535.
The Bullet. *N. Braymer & L. Lowenfels.* BRAY, 41.

983 SERPA, ENRIQUE (1899-   ) Cuba
Fiction
Against Regulations. *W. E. Colford.* COLF, 180.
Shark Fins. *G. R. Coulthard.* COUL, 101.

984 SHELLEY, JAIME AUGUSTO (1937-   ) Mexico
Poetry
Occidental Sax. no tr. YOU, 88.
The Birds. *W. S. Merwin.* PAZ-2, 45.
The Ring. *W. S. Merwin.* PAZ-2, 47.

985 SHIMOSE, PEDRO (1940-   ) Bolivia
Poetry
A Midsummer Night's Dream. *R. Márquez.* MARQ, 83.
A Petty-Bourgeois Suracademicrealistic Epigram. *R. Márquez.*
MARQ, 85.
Count Dracula on an Inspection Tour. *R. Márquez.* MARQ, 87.

986 SILÉN, IVÁN (1944-   ) Puerto Rico
Poetry
Christ - 1970. *E. G. Matilla.* MATI, 171.
I am going to write a poem. *R. Márquez.* MARQ, 431.
I am sometimes bored. *R. Márquez.* MARQ, 437.
I Sent For You. *R. Márquez.* MARQ, 427.
It's One-fifteen.... *E. G. Matilla.* MATI, 169.
The Offended Moon. *E. G. Matilla.* MATI, 183.
Woody Woodpecker. *E. G. Matilla.* MATI, 173.

987 SILVA, JOSÉ ASUNCIÓN (1865-1896) Colombia
     Poetry
     A Poem. *A. J. McVan*. TRAN, 207.
     A Poem. *T. Walsh*. WALS, 581.
     Art. *M. E. Johnson*. JOHN, 69.
     Avant-propos. *J. Hill*. CARA, 176.
     Equality. *G. D. Craig*. CRAI, 37.
     Her Two Tables   When Single When Married. *J. Hill*.
        CARA, 178.
     Mal-de-siècle   The Patient The Doctor. *J. Hill*. CARA,
        179.
     Nocturne. *J. Hill*. CARA, 173.
     Nocturne. *G. D. Craig*. CRAI, 33.
     Nocturne. *M. E. Johnson*. JOHN, 61.
     Nocturne. *A. J. McVan*. TRAN, 205.
     Nocturne. *T. Walsh*. WALS, 584.
     Nocturne III. *G. D. Craig*. RES, 44.
     Reality. *J. Hill*. CARA, 177.
     Seranade. *A. S. Blackwell*. BLAC, 402.
     Stars. *A. S. Blackwell*. BLAC, 402.
     Stars. *M. E. Johnson*. JOHN, 71.
     Stars. *A. S. Blackwell*. LIT-1, 101.
     Stars. *A. S. Blackwell*. LIT-2, 11.
     The Day of the Dead. *A. S. Blackwell*. BLAC, 404.
     The Day of the Dead. *A. S. Blackwell*. JONE-3, 88.
     The Firewood of St. John. *M. E. Johnson*. JOHN, 65.
     The Firewood of St. John. *M. E. Johnson*. RES, 42.
     The Response Of The Earth. *M. E. Johnson*. JOHN, 69.
     The Serenade. *A. S. Blackwell*. WALS, 587.
     The Third Nocturne. *M. Newman & P. T. Manchester*. JONE-3,
        86.

988 SILVA, MARGOT DE (   )
     Poetry
     Don Pablo Neruda. no tr. LOW, 3.

989 SILVA, VÍCTOR DOMINGO (1882-1960) Chile
     Poetry
     Ballad Of The Violin. *L. Elliott*. WALS, 723.
     Cain. *A. S. Blackwell*. BLAC, 292.
     Music in the Square. *A. S. Blackwell*. BLAC, 290.
     The Return. *T. Walsh*. WALS, 724.
     The Violin. *G. D. Craig*. CRAI, 173.

990 SILVA ESTRADA, ALFREDO (1933-   ) Venezuela
     Poetry
     Enunciations (Excerpt). *W. Barnstone*. MU-73, 69.
     Hardly (Excerpt). *W. Barnstone*. MU-73, 69.
     Over The Limit. *W. Barnstone*. MU-73, 65.

991 SILVA VALDÉS, FERNÁN (1887-?) Uruguay
     Poetry
     Ballad of the White Colt. *H. Fish.* TRAN, 256.
     The Gaucho Troubadour. *W. K. Jones.* JONE-3, 176.
     The Gaucho Troubadour. *W. K. Jones.* MILL, 362.
     The Indian. *W. K. Jones.* MILL, 365.
     The Indian. *W. K. Jones.* JONE-3, 178.

992 SILVEIRA, JOEL RIBEIRO (1918-) Brazil
     Fiction
     The Moon. *R. W. Horton.* COEL, 89.

993 SILVEIRA, TASSO DA (1895-1968) Brazil
     Poetry
     The Mirror. *L. S. Downes.* DOWN, 30.

994 SILVETTI PAZ, NORBERTO (1921-) Argentina
     Poetry
     Poem. *W. Shand.* SHA, 166.
     Song. *W. Shand.* SHA, 165.

995 SIMO, ANA MARÍA (1943-) Cuba
     Fiction
     A Deathly Sameness. *J. M. Cohen.* COH-3, 136.
     Aunt Albertina's last party. no tr. CARZ, 207.
     Growth of the Plant. *J. M. Cohen.* COH-3, 179.

996 SIMPSON, MÁXIMO (   ) Argentina
     Poetry
     Melancholy hotel. *P. Morgan.* TRI-13, 247.
     Michel. *P. Morgan.* TRI-13, 246.

997 [SINÁN, ROGELIO pseud.] (1904-) Panama
     DOMÍNGUEZ ALBA, BERNARDO
     Fiction
     They Came To A River. *J. Coyne.* FLOR-2, 409.

998 SKÁRMETA, ANTONIO (1940-) Chile
     Fiction
     First Comes The Sea. *C. Boisier.* WILL-2, 132.
     The Cartwheel. *J. C. Murchison.* CARP, 412.

999 SOLÁ, GRACIELA DE (1928-) Argentina
     Poetry
     Only Love. *W. Shand.* SHA, 224.
     The Face. *W. Shand.* SHA, 224.

1000 SOLANO, ARMANDO (1887- ?) Colombia
     Other
     Cartagena (from: Cities of Colombia). *H. de Onís.* ARC,
        421.

1001   [SOLARTE, TRISTÁN pseud.] (1924-   ) Panama
        SÁNCHEZ, GUILLERMO
        <u>Poetry</u>
        Poetic Approximation to Death. no tr. YOU, 93.

1002   SOLER, GUSTAVO (1932-   ) Argentina
        <u>Poetry</u>
        Definite Anathema And Psalm. *W. Shand.* SHA, 255.
        The Conditions For Silence. *W. Shand.* SHA, 256.

1003   SOLÓRZANO, CARLOS (1922-   ) Guatemala
        <u>Drama</u>
        Crossroads. *F. Colecchia & J. Matas.* COLE, 53.
        The Crucifixion. *G. Luzuriaga & R. Rudder.* LUZU, 141.

1004   SOMERS, ARMONÍA (1918-   ) Uruguay
        <u>Fiction</u>
        Madness. *S. Hertelendy.* HOW-1, 300.

1005   SORRENTINO, FERNANDO (1942-   ) Argentina
        <u>Fiction</u>
        There's A Man In The Habit Of Striking Me On The Head With
          An Umbrella. *N. T. di Giovanni & P. D. Cran.* MU-70, 51.

1006   SOSA LÓPEZ, EMILIO (1920-   ) Argentina
        <u>Poetry</u>
        Ariel. *W. Shand.* SHA, 167.
        Gardens. *W. Shand.* SHA, 168.

1007   SOTO, PEDRO JUAN (1928-   ) Puerto Rico
        <u>Fiction</u>
        Scribblings (Excerpt). *C. Connelly.* KAI, n.p.
        The Innocents. *P. J. Soto.* HOW-2, 262.
        The Innocents. *V. Ortiz.* MANC, 377.

1008   SOTO VÉLEZ, CLEMENTE (1905-   ) Puerto Rico
        <u>Poetry</u>
        The Promised Land. *B. Luby.* BABI, 308.

1009   SOUSA, ALFONSO FELIX DE (1925-   ) Brazil
        <u>Poetry</u>
        Lullaby. *L. S. Downes.* DOWN, 84.

1010   SOUSA, MILTON DE LIMA (1925-   ) Brazil
        <u>Poetry</u>
        The Living Peripheries. *L. S. Downes.* DOWN, 83.

1011   SOUTO ALABARCE, ARTURO (1930-   ) Mexico
        <u>Fiction</u>
        Coyote 13. *H. de Onís.* ONIS-2, 223.

1012   SQUIRRU, RAFAEL F. (1925-   ) Argentina
        Poetry
        The Illuminated Night. *W. Shand*. SHA, 200.
        War. *W. Shand*. SHA, 201.

1013   STEINER, STAN (   ) Puerto Rico
        Other
        The Odyssey Of A Jíbaro (from: The Islands: The Worlds of
            the Puerto Ricans). Originally Engl. BABI, 407.

1014   STORNI, ALFONSINA (1892-1938) Argentina
        Poetry
        A Lyric Letter to Another Woman. *G. D. Craig*. CRAI, 221.
        A Voice. *A. Fife*. FIFE, 57.
        Adolescent With Bear. *D. J. Flakoll & C. Alegría*. BENE, 35.
        Ancestral Burden. *R. O'Connell*. FITT, 519.
        Ancestral Weight. *M. E. Johnson*. JOHN, 153.
        Dear Little Man. *M. E. Johnson*. JOHN, 151.
        Dear Little Man. *S. Resnick*. RES, 88.
        Drizzle. *R. Benson*. BENS, 277.
        Epitaph for my Grave. *A. Fife*. FIFE, 59.
        Epitaph For My Tomb. *R. Humphries*. FITT, 519.
        Epitaph for my tomb. *H. Manning*. GAN, 43.
        I Am Going to Sleep. *R. Benson*. BENS, 281.
        I Am Going To Sleep. *W. K. Jones*. JONE-3, 160.
        I Am Going To Sleep. *W. K. Jones*. MILL, 338.
        Inheritance. *J. R. Wendell*. JONE-3, 158.
        Inheritance. *J. R. Wendell*. MILL, 336.
        Inheritance. *J. R. Wendell*. TRAN, 192.
        Lighthouse in the Night. *W. K. Jones*. JONE-3, 159.
        Little Man. *W. K. Jones*. JONE-3, 158.
        Me at the Bottom of the Sea. *R. Benson*. BENS, 271.
        Men in the City. *R. Benson*. BENS, 275.
        My Sister. *R. Benson*. BENS, 261.
        One. *R. Benson*. BENS, 267.
        Pain. *M. E. Johnson*. JOHN, 153.
        Sea Winds. *R. Benson*. BENS, 273.
        She Who Understands. *A. S. Blackwell*. BLAC, 390.
        She Who Understands. no tr. HAH, 173.
        She Who Understands. *A. S. Blackwell*. JONE-3, 159.
        She Who Understands. *A. S. Blackwell*. MILL, 335.
        Sierra. *R. Benson*. BENS, 265.
        Squares and Angles. *A. Fife*. FIFE, 57.
        Squares and Angles. *M. E. Johnson*. JOHN, 151.
        Squares and Angles. *W. K. Jones*. JONE-3, 157.
        Squares And Angles. *W. K. Jones*. MILL, 337.
        Squares and Angles. *S. Resnick*. RES, 86.
        The One Who Understands. *M. E. Johnson*. JOHN, 151.
        The Piety of the Cypress. *A. S. Blackwell*. BLAC, 390.
        The White Talon. *R. Benson*. BENS, 259.
        Tiny Man. no tr. HAH, 173.

World Of The Seven Wells. *D. D. Walsh*. FITT, 515.
You and I. *A. S. Blackwell*. BLAC, 386.
You Would Have Me White. *R. Benson*. BENS, 255.
Your Arrows. *A. J. McVan*. TRAN, 193.

1015 SUARDÍAZ, LUIS (1936-   ) Cuba
Poetry
Best Sellers. *A. Mitchell*. TARN, 91.
Close-Up. *C. Beck*. BECK, 673.
Farewell. *C. Beck*. BECK, 669.
Found. *A. Mitchell*. TARN, 91.
Song. *C. Beck*. BECK, 661.
The Heroes. *C. Beck*. BECK, 653.
The Seed. *C. Beck*. BECK, 665.
The Stag. *C. Beck*. BECK, 663.
Three Figures With Shadows. *C. Beck*. BECK, 655.
To Have Lived. *C. Beck*. BECK, 667.
Today, The Twelfth Of September, In Cordoba. *L. Kearns*.
    BECK, 651.
When They Invented God. *C. Beck*. BECK, 651.
Witness for the Prosecution. *C. Beck*. BECK, 657.

1016 SUASNAVAR, CONSTANTINO (1912-   ) Honduras
Poetry
Numbers IX. *M. Lee*. FITT, 239.
Numbers XVII. *D. Fitts*. FITT, 243.
Numbers XXI. *D. Fitts*. FITT, 241.
Numbers XXVI. *M. Lee*. FITT, 239.
Numbers XXX. *M. Lee*. FITT, 241.
Numbers XLIII. *D. Fitts*. FITT, 243.

1017 SUBERCASEAUX, BENJAMÍN (1902-   ) Chile
Fiction
The Salt Sea. *J. G. Underhill*. ONIS-2, 244.

1018 SURO, RUBÉN (1916-   ) Dominican Republic
(Rubén Suro García Godoy)
Poetry
Sonnet of Iodine and Salt. *F. E. Townsend*. TOWN, 30.

1019 SVANASCINI, OSVALDO (1920-   ) Argentina
Poetry
Bazaar (New Delhi). *W. Shand*. SHA, 156.
Pavilion Of The Pearl (Kyoto). *W. Shand*. SHA, 157.
The Green Buddha That Inhabits Bangkok. *W. Shand*. SHA,
    157.
The White Tomb (Taj). *W. Shand*. SHA, 156.

1020   TABLADA, JOSÉ JUAN   (1871-1945)   Mexico
        Poetry
        A la Watteau. *E. W. Underwood*. UND, 78.
        Alternate Nocturne. *J. Hill*. CARA, 259.
        Alternating Nocturne. *S. Beckett*. PAZ-1, 159.
        Alternating Nocturne. *E. Weinberger*. PAZ-2, 215.
        Alternating Nocturne. *E. W. Underwood*. UND, 77.
        Ballad of the Eyes. *E. W. Underwood*. UND, 79.
        Dawn in the Cockloft. *S. Beckett*. PAZ-1, 154.
        Dry Leaves. *W. S. Merwin*. PAZ-2, 207.
        Flying Fish. *J. Hill*. CARA, 258.
        Flying Fish. *W. S. Merwin*. PAZ-2, 213.
        Haikais. *L. Kemp*. CRAN, 95.
        Haiku of a day. *S. Beckett*. PAZ-1, 150.
        Haiku of the Flowerpot. *S. Beckett*. PAZ-1, 152.
        Heron. *E. W. Underwood*. UND, 82.
        Insomnia. *J. Hill*. CARA, 258.
        Night Moth. *H. St. Martin*. PAZ-2, 209.
        Onyx. *E. W. Underwood*. UND, 80.
        Panorama. *W. S. Merwin*. PAZ-2, 211.
        Peacock. *J. Hill*. CARA, 257.
        Pre-Raphaelitism. *T. Walsh*. GOLD-2, 59.
        Pre-Raphaelitism. *T. Walsh*. WALS, 644.
        Southern Cross. *H. St. Martin*. PAZ-2, 217.
        The Idol in the Porch. *S. Beckett*. PAZ-1, 155.
        The Monkey. *H. St. Martin*. PAZ-2, 209.
        The Morn. *E. W. Underwood*. UND, 82.
        The Parrot. *S. Beckett*. PAZ-1, 158.
        The Peacock. *H. St. Martin*. PAZ-2, 205.
        The Toads. *H. St. Martin*. PAZ-2, 207.
        The Willow. *E. W. Underwood*. UND, 82.
        Toads. *J. Hill*. CARA, 257.
        Tortoise. *J. Hill*. CARA, 257.
        Water-Melon. *J. Hill*. CARA, 258.

1021   [TABLANCA, LUIS pseud.]   (1883-?   )   Colombia
        PARDOY-FARELO, ENRIQUE
        Fiction
        Country Girl. *A. Malkus*. FLOR-2, 265.
        Country Girl. *A. Malkus*. MILL, 339.

1022   TALLET, JOSÉ ZACARÍAS   (1893-   )   Cuba
        Poetry
        The Rumba. *H. Ruiz del Vizo*. RUIZ, 36.

1023   TAMAYO, EVORA   (1940-   )   Cuba
        Fiction
        Sylvia. no tr. CARZ, 189.

1024   TAMAYO VARGAS, AUGUSTO (1914-   ) Peru
        Poetry
        Dreams Are Life. *M. A. de Maurer*. HAR68-5, 17.

1025   TAVARES DE SÁ, HERNANE (1911-   ) Brazil
        Other
        Brazileiros. no tr. LIT-1, 13.

1026   TEILLIER, JORGE (1935-   ) Chile
        Poetry
        A Tree Wakes Me Up. *M. Williams*. WILL-2, 111.
        End Of The World. *M. Williams*. WILL-2, 101.
        Leave-taking. *J. Upton*. TRI-13, 388.
        Renunciation. *M. Williams*. WILL-2, 109.
        Signals. *M. Williams*. WILL-2, 107.
        The lost dominions. *J. Upton*. TRI-13, 386.
        To A Boy In A Tree. *M. Williams*. WILL-2, 103.
        When Everyone Goes. *M. Williams*. WILL-2, 105.

1027   TEJADA GÓMEZ, ARMANDO (   ) Argentina
        Poetry
        Eternity. *P. Morgan*. TRI-13, 237.
        The fish dies by the mouth. *P. Morgan*. TRI-13, 239.
        The wind and the weathercock. *P. Morgan*. TRI-13, 238.

1028   TEJERA, NIVARIA (1930-   ) Cuba
        Poetry
        Fragments (from: La gruta). *D. Flakoll & C. Alegría*.
        FLAK, 91.

1029   TELES, LYGIA FAGUNDES (1922-   ) Brazil
        Fiction
        Happiness. *R. W. Horton*. COEL, 131.

1030   TÉLLEZ, HERNANDO (1908-1966) Colombia
        Fiction
        Ashes for the Wind. *H. de Onís*. ONIS-2, 238.
        Just Lather, That's All. *D. A. Yates*. FLOR-3, 254.
        Just Lather, That's All. *D. A. Yates*. MANC, 209.
        Just Lather, That's All. *D. A. Yates*. YATE, 143.

1031   TÉLLEZ, JOAQUÍN (   )
        Poetry
        Beside the Sea by Vera Cruz. *E. W. Underwood*. UND, 135.

1032   THENON, SUSANA (1937-   ) Argentina
        Poetry
        Circle. *W. Shand*. SHA, 268.
        I Only Know Of Platforms. *W. Shand*. SHA, 269.
        World. *W. Shand*. SHA, 268.

1033   THOMAS, PIRI (   ) Puerto Rico
        Fiction
        Puerto Rican Paradise (from: Down These Mean Streets).
           Originally Engl. BABI, 415.

1034   [TIEMPO, CÉSAR pseud.] (1906-   ) Argentina
        ZEITLIN, ISRAEL
        Poetry
        Daughter Of Saturday. *W. Shand.* SHA, 85.
        Harangue On The Death Of Chayim Nachman Bialik. *D. D. Walsh.*
           FITT, 253.
        Harangue on the Death of Chayim Nachman Bialik. *D. D. Walsh.*
           JONE-3, 164.
        Harangue On The Death Of Chayim Nachman Bialik. *D. D. Walsh.*
           MILL, 357.
        Israelite Graveyard. *R. Humphries, D. D. Walsh & D. Fitts.*
           FITT, 251.
        Prayer. *D. D. Walsh.* FITT, 259.
        Weeping And Singing. *D. D. Walsh.* FITT, 259.
        Weeping And Singing. *W. Shand.* SHA, 87.

1035   TOMAT-GUIDO, FRANCISCO (1923-   ) Argentina
        Poetry
        Earthly Olive Tree. *W. Shand.* SHA, 182.
        Flute Of The Blood. *W. Shand.* SHA, 182.

1036   TONDREAU, NARCISO (1861-1949) Chile
        Poetry
        Yesterday and To-Day. *A. B. Poor.* POOR, 46.

1037   TORRE NILSSON, LEOPOLDO (1924-   ) Argentina
        Fiction
        He who howls. *A. Moncy.* TRI-13, 489.

1038   TORRES BODET, JAIME (1902-   ) Mexico
        Poetry
        A Pit. *M. Lee.* JONE-3, 49.
        April. *B. L. Castellón.* FITT, 117.
        City. *R. Humphries.* FITT, 109.
        Core. *M. Lee.* FITT, 115.
        Dance. *R. Humphries.* FITT, 113.
        Dream. *E. W. Underwood.* UND, 176.
        Echo. *M. E. Johnson.* JOHN, 187.
        Love. *M. Lee.* FITT, 115.
        Midday. *D. Malcolm.* JONE-3, 49.
        Music. *M. E. Johnson.* JOHN, 189.
        Music. *E. W. Underwood.* UND, 173.
        Noon. *R. Humphries.* FITT, 111.
        Romance. *E. W. Underwood.* UND, 175.
        Song. *B. G. Proske.* TRAN, 236.
        The Cypress. *A. S. Blackwell.* BLAC, 166.

The House. *A. S. Blackwell*. BLAC, 164.
The Shadow. *E. W. Underwood*. UND, 174.
The Well. *A. S. Blackwell*. BLAC, 166.
Voyage. *B. G. Proske*. TRAN, 238.

1039 TORRES RÍOSECO, ARTURO (1897-   ) Chile
Poetry
Absence. *G. D. Craig*. CRAI, 215.
Bells By Night. *G. D. Craig*. CRAI, 207.
Prophetic Verses. *G. D. Craig*. CRAI, 209.
When I am dead.... *G. D. Craig*. CRAI, 207.

1040 TORRI, JULIO (1889-?) Mexico
Poetry
Circe. *M. Strand*. PAZ-2, 181.
La Gloriosa. no tr. CRAN, 83.
The Unknown Beloved. no tr. CRAN, 82.
Women. no tr. CRAN, 81.
Women. *M. Strand*. PAZ-2, 183.
Fiction
Some Reflections on Executions. *D. Demarest*. CRAN, 80.

1041 TOVAR, JUAN (1941-   ) Mexico
Fiction
Location Of The Heart. *M. S. Peden*. MU-70, 43.

1042 TREJO, MARIO (1926-   ) Argentina
Poetry
Panic In Valparaiso. *W. Shand*. SHA, 207.
Reasons For Surviving. *W. Shand*. SHA, 209.

1043 TREVISAN, DALTON (1925-   ) Brazil
Fiction
Good evening, sir. *G. Rabassa*. TRI-13, 292.
The Corpse In The Parlor. *J. E. Tomlins*. MU-70, 61.
The elephant's graveyard. *G. Rabassa*. TRI-13, 295.

1044 TRIANA, JOSÉ (1931-   ) Cuba
Drama
The Criminals. *P. A. Fernández & M. Kustow*. DR, 104.
The Criminals. *P. A. Fernández & M. Kustow*. WOOD, 240.

1045 TUNBERG, KARL A. (   )
Other
The New Cuban Theatre: A Report (Essay). no tr. DR, 43.

1046 TURCIOS, FROYLÁN (1875-1943) Honduras
Poetry
Blue Eyes. *A. S. Blackwell*. BLAC, 478.
Blue Eyes. *W. K. Jones*. JONE-3, 62.
Fiction
The Vampire (Excerpt). *R. A. Goldberg*. JONE-3, 314.

161

1047   UGARTE, MANUEL   (1878-1951)   Argentina
        Fiction
        The Healer (from: Tales of the Pampa). no tr. LIEB, 937.

1048   URBANEJA ACHELPOHL, LUIS MANUEL   (1874-1937)   Venezuela
        Fiction
        Ovejon. H. Kurz. HAYDN, 937.

1049   URBINA, LUIS G.   (1867-1934)   Mexico
        Poetry
        A Sunny Morning. A. S. Blackwell.   BLAC, 92.
        Alone. E. W. Underwood. UND, 85.
        And So.... A. Fife. FIFE, 55.
        Ascension. A. S. Blackwell. BLAC, 70.
        Ballad. E. W. Underwood. UND, 87.
        Birds. A. S. Blackwell. BLAC, 70.
        Dayspring. S. Beckett. PAZ-1, 144.
        First Romantic Interlude. E. W. Underwood. UND, 84.
        Noche Clara. E. W. Underwood. UND, 83.
        On the Lake. A. S. Blackwell. BLAC, 68.
        Our Lives Are Rivers. S. Beckett. PAZ-1, 145.
        Spare the Nests. A. S. Blackwell. BLAC, 74.
        The Ancient Tear. S. Beckett. PAZ-1, 142.
        The Centaur's Bath. S. Beckett. PAZ-1, 143.
        The Last Sunset. A. S. Blackwell. BLAC, 94.
        The Mass at Dawn. A. S. Blackwell. BLAC, 76.
        The Mass At Dawn. A. S. Blackwell. GOLD-2, 33.
        The Moonbeam. A. S. Blackwell. WALS, 614.
        The Silent Day. S. Beckett. PAZ-1, 144.
        The Triumph of the Blue. A. S. Blackwell. BLAC, 72.
        To a Friend Far Away. A. S. Blackwell. BLAC, 98.
        To Ricardo Castro. A. S. Blackwell. BLAC, 96.
        Witchcraft. A. S. Blackwell. BLAC, 68.

1050   UREÑA DE HENRÍQUEZ, SALOMÉ   (1850-1897)   Dominican Republic
        Poetry
        The Bird in the Nest. A. S. Blackwell. BLAC, 514.
        The Glory of Progress. A. S. Blackwell. BLAC, 508.

1051   URIBE, DIEGO   (1867-1921)   Colombia
        Poetry
        In Pursuit of the Dream. A. S. Blackwell. BLAC, 420.

1052   URIBE ARCE, ARMANDO   (1934-   )   Chile
        Poetry
        Poems. M. Williams. WILL-2, 115.

1053   URIBE DE ACOSTA, OFELIA   (   )   Colombia
        Other
        Una voz insurgente (Excerpt). F. G. Carrino & J. E. Hahner.
        HAH, 117.

1054   URIBE PIEDRAHITA, CÉSAR (1897-1951) Colombia
     Fiction
     The Anaconda Hunt (from: Toá). *L. Wilson.* JONE-3, 228.

1055   URONDO, FRANCISCO (1930-   ) Argentina
     Poetry
     End And Principles. *W. Shand.* SHA, 245.
     The Merry-Go-Round Bar. *W. Shand.* SHA, 244.
     To Love Her Is Difficult. *W. Shand.* SHA, 244.

1056   USIGLI, RODOLFO (1905-   ) Mexico
     Poetry
     Nocturn. *E. W. Underwood.* UND, 198.
     Drama
     Crown of Light. *T. Bledsoe.* USIG, 3.
     Crown of Shadows (Excerpt). *D. A. Flory.* JONE-3, 441.
     One of These Days.... *T. Bledsoe.* USIG, 111.

1057   USLAR PIETRI, ARTURO (1905-   ) Venezuela
     Fiction
     Ignis Fatuus. *H. de Onís.* ONIS-1, 292.
     Rain. *D. Conzelman.* FLOR-2, 435.
     The Drum Dance. *G. Alfred Mayer.* HOW-1, 169.
     The Voice. *W. E. Colford.* COLF, 120.

1058   VALDELOMAR, ABRAHAM (1888-1919) Peru
     Fiction
     The Good Knight Carmelo. *A. Flores.* FLOR-2, 448.

1059   VALDÉS, HERNÁN (   ) Chile
     Poetry
     I am as poor as a mouse.... *J. Upton.* TRI-13, 392.
     Oh King Achilles. *J. Upton.* TRI-13, 392.
     While. *J. Upton.* TRI-13, 391.

1060   VALENCIA, GUILLERMO (1873-1943) Colombia
     Poetry
     Reading Silva. *G. D. Craig.* CRAI, 113.
     She. *A. S. Blackwell.* BLAC, 414.
     Sursum. *T. Walsh.* JONE-3, 93.
     Sursum. *T. Walsh.* WALS, 652.
     The Camels. *G. D. Craig.* CRAI, 123.
     The Camels. *W. K. Jones.* JONE-3, 93.
     The Camels. *B. G. Proske.* TRAN, 209.
     The Two Beheadings. *T. Walsh.* WALS, 653.
     To Erasmus of Rotterdam. *J. Hill.* CARA, 181.
     To the Andes. *A. S. Blackwell.* BLAC, 412.
     To the Andes. *A. S. Blackwell.* LIT-1, 38.
     To The Andes. *A. S. Blackwell.* LIT-2, 15.

1061   VALENZUELA, JESÚS E.   (1856-1911)   Mexico
        Poetry
        A Song of Hands. *A. S. Blackwell.* BLAC, 122.
        A Song Of Hands. *A. S. Blackwell.* GOLD-2, 20.
        A Song of Hands. *A. S. Blackwell.* WALS, 541.
        Don Quixote. *A. S. Blackwell.* GOLD-2, 24.
        To Duque Job. *E. W. Underwood.* UND, 102.

1062   VALENZUELA, LUISA   (1938-   )   Argentina
        Fiction
        The Door. *N. T. di Giovanni.* MU-74, 120.

1063   VALLE, RAFAEL HELIODORO   (1891-1959)   Honduras
        Poetry
        Thirsting Amphora. *M. Lee.* FITT, 495.

1064   VALLEJO, CÉSAR   (1892-1938)   Peru
        Poetry
        A Catalogue of Bones. *N. Braymer & L. Lowenfels.* BRAY, 27.
        A Divine Falling Of Leaves. *J. Wright.* BLY, 187.
        "A man walks by...." *C. Eshleman.* HAR68-5, 2.
        'A man walks by with a loaf of bread on his shoulder.'
          C. Eshleman. BOLD, 154.
        Absent. *R. Benson.* BENS, 291.
        Agape. *J. Knoepfle.* CARP, 47.
        Agape (from: The Black Riders). *J. Knoepfle.* BLY, 195.
        Agape. *J. Knoepfle.* SIX64-7, 61.
        "And don't bother telling me anything" (from: Código Civil
          and Poemas Humanos). *R. Bly.* BLY, 257.
        "And so? The pale metalloid heals you?" (from: Código
          Civil and Poemas Humanos). *R. Bly.* BLY, 259.
        "And what if after so many words" (from: Código Civil and
          Poemas Humanos). *R. Bly & D. Lawder.* BLY, 263.
        Anger. *H. R. Hays.* HAYS, 285.
        Anger. no tr. MERT, 140.
        'Another touch of calm, comrade.' *C. Eshleman.* BOLD, 155.
        Aparta de mi este cáliz. *N. Braymer & L. Lowenfels.*
          BRAY, 34.
        As Like as Not I Am Another. *J. Hill.* CARA, 327.
        "At best I'm somebody else...." *S. Berg.* TRI-13, 94.
        Babble (from: The Black Riders). *J. Knoepfle.* BLY, 185.
        Beneath the Elms. *N. Braymer & L. Lowenfels.* BRAY, 7.
        "Between pain and pleasure...." *S. Berg.* TRI-13, 92.
        Black Stone Lying On A White Stone (from: Código Civil and
          Poemas Humanos). *R. Bly & J. Knoepfle.* BLY, 249.
        Black Stone Lying On A White Stone (from: Poemas Humanos).
          R. Bly & J. Knoepfle. SIX64-7, 71.
        Black Stone on a White Stone. *N. Braymer & L. Lowenfels.*
          BRAY, 23.
        Black Stone On Top Of A White Stone. no tr. MERT, 137.
        Black Stone On Top Of A White Stone. *T. Merton.* MILL, 367.

"But before all this lady runs out...." *C. Eshleman.*
TRI-13, 86.
Considerando en frío, imparcialmente. *N. Braymer &*
L. Lowenfels. BRAY, 16.
Cual mi explanación. *N. Braymer & L. Lowenfels.* BRAY, 11.
De puro calor tengo frío. *N. Braymer & L. Lowenfels.* BRAY,
22.
De todo esto yo soy el único que parte. *N. Braymer &*
L. Lowenfels. BRAY, 15.
Depth and Height. *N. Braymer & L. Lowenfels.* BRAY, 14.
Distant Footsteps. *H. R. Hays.* HAYS, 275.
Down To The Dregs (from: The Black Riders). *J. Wright.* BLY 191.
Dregs. *M. Lee.* FITT, 437.
Dregs. *M. Lee.* JONE-3, 112.
El alma que sufrió de ser su cuerpo. *N. Braymer &*
L. Lowenfels. BRAY, 24.
En el rincón aquel donde dormimos juntos. *N. Braymer &*
L. Lowenfels. BRAY, 12.
Estáis Muertos. no tr. MERT, 136.
Forbidden Love. *T. Raworth.* CARA, 322.
God (from: The Black Riders). *R. Bly.* BLY, 209.
Good Sense. *H. R. Hays.* SIX64-7, 67.
Hat, Coat, Gloves. *J. Hill.* CARA, 326.
Have You Anything To Say In Your Defense? (from: The Black
Riders). *J. Wright.* BLY, 217.
Hymn to the Volunteers of the Republic. *J. Hill.* CARA, 331.
I Am Cold from Sheer Heat. *R. Benson.* BENS, 317.
I am Going to Speak of Hope. *C. Eshleman.* CARP, 49.
I am Going To Talk About Hope (from: Código Civil and
Poemas Humanos). *R. Bly.* BLY, 241.
"I have a terrible fear of being an animal" (from: Código
Civil and Poemas Humanos). *R. Bly.* BLY, 261.
"I stayed here, warming the ink in which I drown," (from:
Código Civil and Poemas Humanos). *J. Wright & R. Bly.*
BLY, 245.
Ice Boat. *N. Braymer & L. Lowenfels.* BRAY, 10.
"If it rained tonight...." *J. M. Cohen.* COH-2, 374.
'If It Rained Tonight.' *D. D. Walsh.* FITT, 435.
Intensity and Elevation. *R. Benson.* BENS, 315.
Intensity and Height. *T. Raworth.* CARA, 325.
"It was Sunday...." *C. Eshleman.* TRI-13, 84.
Januariad. *R. Benson.* BENS, 299.
La colera que quiebra al hombre en niños. *N. Braymer &*
L. Lowenfels. BRAY, 30.
Lines. *T. Raworth.* CARA, 321.
Little Responsory For A Republican Hero. *H. R. Hays.* HAYS,
295.
Mass. *N. Braymer & L. Lowenfels.* BRAY, 31.
Masses (from: España, Aparta de Mí Este Cáliz). *R. Bly.*
BLY, 269.
Masses. *H. R. Hays.* HAYS, 297.

(VALLEJO, CÉSAR)
"One pillar holding up consolations," (from: Código Civil and Poemas Humanos). *J. Wright.* BLY, 255.
Otro poco de calma, camarada. *N. Braymer & L. Lowenfels.* BRAY, 28.
Our Daily Bread (from: The Black Riders). *J. Wright.* BLY, 199.
Pagan Woman (from: The Black Riders). *R. Bly.* BLY, 203.
Palms and Guitar. *C. Eshleman.* CARP, 53.
Palms And Guitars. *C. Eshleman.* HAR68-5, 3.
Peace, The Wasp.... no tr. MERT, 138.
Pedro Rojas. *H. R. Hays.* HAYS, 291.
Pilgrimage (from: The Black Riders). *J. Wright.* BLY, 183.
Poem To Be Read And Sung (from: Código Civil and Poemas Humanos). *J. Wright & R. Bly.* BLY, 247.
Quisiera hoy ser feliz de buena gana. *N. Braymer & L. Lowenfels.* BRAY, 18.
Solía escribir con su dedo grande en el aire. *N. Braymer & L. Lowenfels.* BRAY, 32.
Spain, Take From Me This Cup. *D. D. Walsh.* FITT, 439.
Spain, Take from Me This Cup. *D. D. Walsh.* JONE-3, 113.
Spain, Take This Chalice from Me. *T. Raworth.* CARA, 329.
Stumble between Two Stars. *R. Benson.* BENS, 309.
Stumble between Two Stars. *C. Eshleman.* CARP, 51.
Stumbling Between the Stars. *N. Braymer & L. Lowenfels.* BRAY, 20.
Tengo fe en ser fuerte. *N. Braymer & L. Lowenfels.* BRAY, 13.
"The Anger That Breaks A Man" (from: Poemas Humanos). *R. Bly.* SIX64-7, 65.
"The Anger That Breaks A Man Down Into Boys" (from: Código Civil and Poemas Humanos). *R. Bly.* BLY, 265.
"The anger that breaks man into children...." *C. Eshleman.* BOLD, 151.
The Black Cup (from: The Black Riders). *J. Wright & R. Bly.* BLY, 189.
The Black Messengers. *R. Benson.* BENS, 295.
The Black Messengers. *H. R. Hays.* HAYS, 271.
The Black Riders (from: The Black Riders). *R. Bly.* BLY, 179.
The Dark Messengers. *J. M. Cohen.* COH-2, 372.
The Distant Footsteps (from: The Black Riders). *J. Wright & J. Knoepfle.* BLY, 213.
The Eternal Dice. *R. Benson.* BENS, 293.
The Eternal Dice (from: The Black Riders). *J. Wright.* BLY, 205.
The Eternal Dice. *J. M. Cohen.* COH-2, 373.
The Eternal Dice. *J. Wright.* SIX64-7, 63.
'The Grown-Ups.' *D. D. Walsh.* FITT, 431.
The Last Steps. *S. Moss.* GARR, 271.
The Masses. *J. M. Cohen.* COH-2, 376.

The Miners. *H. R. Hays*. HAYS, 281.
The Mule Drivers (from: <u>The Black Riders</u>). *R. Bly*. BLY, 211.
The nine monsters. *C. Eshleman*. BOLD, 152.
The Nine Monsters. *H. R. Hays*. HAYS, 287.
"The one who will come...." *C. Eshleman*. TRI-13, 91.
"The point of the man...." *C. Eshleman*. TRI-13, 85.
The Rage That Shatters a Man into Children. *D. J. Flakoll & C. Alegría*. BENE, 41.
The Right Meaning (from: <u>Código Civil and Poemas Humanos</u>). *R. Bly*. BLY, 237.
The Rollcall Of Bones (from: <u>Código Civil and Poemas Humanos</u>). *R. Bly*. BLY, 251.
"The second of November tolls." *J. M. Cohen*. COH-2, 375.
'The Second Of November Tolls.' *D. D. Walsh*. FITT, 433.
The soul that suffered being its body. *S. Berg*. TRI-13, 92.
The Spider (from: <u>The Black Riders</u>). *R. Bly*. BLY, 181.
The Spider. *N. Braymer & L. Lowenfels*. BRAY, 9.
The Spider. *D. D. Walsh*. FITT, 435.
The Spider. *H. R. Hays*. HAYS, 273.
The Spider. *R. Bly*. SIX64-7, 59.
The Starving Man's Rack. *C. Eshleman*. HAR68-5, 1.
"The tennis-player in the instant he majestically" (from: <u>Código Civil and Poemas Humanos</u>). *R. Bly*. BLY, 253.
The Weary Circle (from: <u>The Black Riders</u>). *J. Knoepfle*. BLY, 207.
The Willows. *N. Braymer & L. Lowenfels*. BRAY, 8.
"The windows...." *C. Eshleman*. TRI-13, 88.
The wretched of the Earth. *C. Eshleman*. BOLD, 156.
The Wretched of the Earth. *C. Eshleman*. CARP, 57.
The Wretched Of The Earth. *C. Eshleman*. HAR68-5, 4.
To My Brother Miguel. *R. Benson*. BENS, 297.
To My Brother Miguel. *J. Knoepfle & J. Wright*. BLY, 215.
Today I Like Life Much Less. *R. Benson*. BENS, 313.
"Today I like life much less...." *C. Eshleman*. TRI-13, n.p.
<u>Trilce</u>.(Excerpt). *T. Raworth*. CARA, 323.
<u>TRILCE</u> (Excerpts). *C. Tomlinson & H. Gifford*. COH-1, 23.
Trilce XIV. *S. Moss*. GARR, 271.
Trilce XVIII. *R. Benson*. BENS, 303.
Trilce XXXIII. *S. Moss*. GARR, 275.
Trilce XLV. *R. Benson*. BENS, 305.
Trilce LXIII. *R. Benson*. BENS, 307.
Twilight (from: <u>The Black Riders</u>). *J. Knoepfle*. BLY, 193.
Un hombre está mirando a una mujer. *N. Braymer & L. Lowenfels*. BRAY, 19.
Un hombre pasa con un pan al hombro. *N. Braymer & L. Lowenfels*. BRAY, 36.
Village Poem. *R. Benson*. BENS, 287.
Wedding March. *N. Braymer & L. Lowenfels*. BRAY, 26.
White Rose (from: <u>The Black Riders</u>). *J. Wright*. BLY, 197.

(VALLEJO, CÉSAR)
III (from: Trilce). *J. Wright.* BLY, 223.
XV (from: Trilce). *J. Wright.* BLY, 227.
XVIII. *H. R. Hays.* HAYS, 277.
XXIV (from: Trilce). *J. Wright.* BLY, 229.
XXVIII. *H. R. Hays.* HAYS, 279.
XLIV. *H. R. Hays.* HAYS, 281.
XLV (from: Trilce). *J. Wright.* BLY, 231.
LXXVII (from: Trilce). *R. Bly.* BLY, 233.
Fiction
On the Other Side of Life and Death. *H. St. Martin &*
    R. Mezey. HOW-1, 88.

1065 VALLEJOS PÉREZ-GARAY, ROQUE (1943-   ) Paraguay
Poetry
7 (from: "The Drunken Archangels"). *J. Upton.* TRI-13, 291.
9 (from: "The Drunken Archangels"). *J. Upton.* TRI-13, 291.

1066 VARALLANOS, JOSÉ (1908-   ) Peru
Poetry
Mob Of Mountains. *M. Lee.* FITT, 165.

1067 VARELA, BLANCA (1926-   ) Peru
Poetry
Fountain. *D. A. Yates.* MU-69, 89.
In The Mirror. *D. A. Yates.* MU-69, 91.
Port Supe. *D. J. Flakoll & C. Alegría.* FLAK, 1.
The City. *D. A. Yates.* MU-69, 89.
The Observer. *D. A. Yates.* MU-69, 91.
The Things I Say Are True. *D. A. Yates.* MU-69, 87.

1068 VARGAS LLOSA, MARIO (1936-   ) Peru
Fiction
Amalia. *H. St. Martin.* LAWA, 61.
Sunday. *M. E. Ellsworth.* MANC, 411.
Sunday, Sunday. *A. Reid.* HOW-1, 387.
The Green House (Excerpt of Chapter One). *G. Rabassa.*
    TRI-13, 152.
Other
Fate and Mission of the Writer in Latin America (Speech).
    M. A. Maurer. HAR67-4, 56.
Literature is Fire (Epilogue). *M. Ahern de Maurer.* CARP,
    430.

1069 VASCONCELOS, JOSÉ (1882-1959) Mexico
Fiction
The Boar Hunt. *P. Waldorf.* CRAN, 64.
The Boar Hunt. *P. Waldorf.* MILL, 368.
Other
The Waterfalls Of South America (from: The Cosmic Race).
    H. de Onís. ARC, 140.

1070 VASCONCELOS MAIA, CARLOS (1923-   ) Brazil
      Fiction
      Sun. *W. L. Grossman*. GRO, 153.
      Sun. *R. P. Joscelyne*. COH-1, 219.

1071 VÁSQUEZ, EMILIO (1903-   ) Peru
      Poetry
      Indian Girl. *B. L. Castellón*. FITT, 479.

1072 VÁZQUEZ, MARÍA ESTHER (1933-   ) Argentina
      Poetry
      December. *W. Shand*. SHA, 258.
      Hot Dark January. *W. Shand*. SHA, 257.
      Other
      Everness: an approach to the poetry of Jorge Luis Borges
         (Essay). *R. Christ & P. Cantatore*. TRI-15, 245.

1073 VEGA, DANIEL DE LA (1892-1962) Chile
      Poetry
      In the Master's Footsteps. *A. S. Blackwell*. BLAC, 302.
      The Door. *L. Elliott*. WALS, 755.

1074 VEIRAVÉ, ALFREDO (1928-   ) Argentina
      Poetry
      Eternity. *W. Shand*. SHA, 226.
      The Iris Of The Eye. *W. Shand*. SHA, 225.

1075 VELA, RUBÉN (1928-   ) Argentina
      Poetry
      Poems With People. *W. Shand*. SHA, 227.
      Whilst The Bird Of Night Sings. *W. Shand*. SHA, 228.

1076 VELARDE, HÉCTOR (1898-   ) Peru
      Fiction
      Father's Day. *W. E. Colford*. COLF, 69.

1077 VELÁSQUEZ, PRIMO FELICIANO (1860-?   ) Mexico
      Other
      Andres de Olmos (Biography). *F. Starr*. STAR, 97.
      Antonio de Roa (Biography). *F. Starr*. STAR, 103.
      Diego Ordoñez (Biography). *F. Starr*. STAR, 101.
      Martyrs to the Faith (Biography). *F. Starr*. STAR, 98.
      The Tlaxcalan Settlements. *F. Starr*. STAR, 95.

1078 VELGAS, JUAN JOSÉ (   ) Chile
      Poetry
      The Asure Sky. *L. Elliott*. WALS, 757.

1079 VENTURINI, ROLANDO (   ) Argentina
      Fiction
      Sunday For An Architect. *I. A. Langnas*. PRIZE, 374.

1080 VERA, PEDRO J. (1915-   ) Ecuador
      Poetry
      Chile, the wretched beasts.... *C. Hayes*. LOW, 75.

1081 VERGARA, FRANCISCO (   ) Cuba
      Poetry
      I Told Caridá. *H. Ruiz del Vizo*. RUIZ, 63.

1082 VERISSIMO, ERICO (1905-   ) Brazil
      Other
      Sun, Sea, And Samba. Impressions of Rio de Janeiro (Essay).
      H. de Onís. ARC, 370.

1083 VIANA, FERNANDO MENDEZ (1933-   ) Brazil
      Poetry
      Circle. *F. P. Hebblethwaite*. YOU, 21.

1084 VIANA, JAVIER DE (1868-1926) Uruguay
      Fiction
      Gurí. *H. de Onís*. ONIS-1, 163.
      The Horse-Breaker. *W. E. Colford*. COLF, 99.

1085 VIANY, ALEX (   )
      Other
      The Old and the New In Brazilian Cinema (Essay).
      J. Pottlitzer. DR, 141.

1086 VICTORIA, MARCOS (1903-   ) Argentina
      Poetry
      To A Rusty Key. *W. Shand*. SHA, 63.

1087 VICUÑA CIFUENTES, JULIO (1865-1936) Chile
      Poetry
      Circumstances. *W. K. Jones*. JONE-3, 117.

1088 VIDIGAL, GERALDO (1921-   ) Brazil
      Poetry
      The Stone Faun. *L. S. Downes*. DOWN, 73.

1089 VIENTÓS GASTÓN, NILITA (1908-   ) Puerto Rico
      Other
      "Puertoricanists" and "Occidentalists" (Essay). *B. Luby*.
      BABI, 153.

1090 VIETA, EZEQUIAL (1922-   ) Cuba
      Fiction
      My friend Victor. no tr. CARZ, 137.

1091 VIGNALE, PEDRO JUAN (1903-   ) Argentina
      Poetry
      The Dead Grenadier. *D. D. Walsh*. FITT, 485.

1092   VIGNATI, ALEJANDRO (   ) Argentina
        Poetry
        Liberty Doesn't Push Itself (II). no tr. YOU, 6.

1093   VILARIÑO, IDEA (1920-   ) Uruguay
        Poetry
        Alone. *R. Connally*. YOU, 116.
        No Longer. *R. Connally*. YOU, 115.
        Return. *D. J. Flakoll & C. Alegría*. BENE, 81.
        To Pass By. *D. J. Flakoll & C. Alegría*. FLAK, 175.
        What Was Life. *M. González*. CARA, 371.

1094   [VILLA, ALVARO DE pseud.] (   ) Cuba
        ALVARES, ROLANDO
        Poetry
        Masquerade Of The Carnival. *H. Ruiz del Vizo*. RUIZ, 73.

1095   VILLAFAÑE, JAVIER (1910-   ) Argentina
        Poetry
        Fable Of The Poet. *W. Shand*. SHA, 104.
        The Prodigal Son. *W. Shand*. SHA, 105.

1096   VILLARINO, MARÍA DE (1905-   ) Argentina
        Poetry
        Gift Of Agonies. *W. Shand*. SHA, 79.

1097   VILLASEÑOR Y VILLASEÑOR, ALEJANDRO (1864-1912) Mexico
        Other
        Antón Lizardo. *F. Starr*. STAR, 170.
        The Policy of the United States. *F. Starr*. STAR, 173.

1098   VILLAURRUTIA, XAVIER (1903-1950) Mexico
        Poetry
        A Longing for Snow. *R. Benson*. BENS, 329.
        Air. *E. W. Underwood*. UND, 180.
        Amor condusse noi ad una Morte. *R. Benson*. BENS, 345.
        Amplifications. *R. Benson*. BENS, 321.
        Amplifications. *E. W. Underwood*. UND, 181.
        Angel-Nocturne. *D. Fitts*. FITT, 397.
        Boston Epigrams. *R. Benson*. BENS, 349.
        Cemetery in the Snow. *J. M. Cohen*. COH-2, 420.
        Cemetery in the Snow. *D. Justice*. PAZ-2, 159.
        Death in the Cold. *M. González*. CARA, 270.
        Eternal Nocturne. *R. Benson*. BENS, 341.
        Eternal Nocturne. *R. Benson*. PAZ-2, 151.
        Insomnia. *E. W. Underwood*. UND, 185.
        Los Angeles Nocturne. *R. Benson*. BENS, 335.
        Nocturne In Which Death Speaks. *D. Fitts*. FITT, 395.
        Nocturne of the Statue. *D. Justice*. PAZ-2, 149.
        Painting. *R. Benson*. BENS, 323.
        Phonographs. *E. W. Underwood*. UND, 183.

(VILLAURRUTIA, XAVIER)
  Picture. *E. W. Underwood.* UND, 184.
  Rose Nocturnal. *D. Justice.* PAZ-2, 155.
  Sleep Nocturne. *R. Benson.* BENS, 331.
  Solitude. *R. Benson.* BENS, 325.
  Streets. *R. Benson.* BENS, 327.
  Ten Stanzas to Death. *R. Benson.* BENS, 353.
  Village. *E. W. Underwood.* UND, 182.
  Fiction
  Night and Rain Over the City of Mexico. *E. W. Underwood.*
    UND, 179.
  Drama
  Incredible Though It Seems. *F. Colecchia & J. Matas.*
    COLE, 1.

1099 VITALE, IDA (1925-   ) Uruguay
  Poetry
  Answer Of The Dervish. *L. Bradford.* MU-74, 137.
  Canon. *D. J. Flakoll & C. Alegría.* FLAK, 223.

1100 VITIER, CINTIO (1921-   ) Cuba
  Poetry
  Each Time I Return To You. *E. Hollis.* MU-69, 73.
  Hand Over the Threshold. *C. Beck.* BECK, 243.
  Nicodemus Speaking. *N. Tarn.* TARN, 37.
  Spoken In The Soul. *E. Hollis.* MU-69, 75.
  Strangely, a Sort of Honor. *C. Beck.* BECK, 255.
  The Air. *C. Beck.* BECK, 257.
  The Bough. *C. Beck.* BECK, 251.
  The Dispossessed. *C. Beck.* BECK, 253.
  The Dispossessed. *T. Raworth.* TARN, 33.
  The Empty Place. *C. Beck.* BECK, 249.
  The Face. *C. Beck.* BECK, 237.
  The Light On Cayo Hueso. *N. Tarn.* TARN, 35.
  The Notice. *E. Arenal.* CARP, 233.
  The Word. *E. Arenal.* CARP, 231.
  The Word. *E. Hollis.* MU-69, 73.
  Words of the Prodigal Son. *D. J. Flakoll & C. Alegría.*
    FLAK, 106.

1101 VIVERO, DOMINGO DE (   ) Peru
  Poetry
  To Edison. *A. B. Poor.* POOR, 71.

1102 VOCOS LESCANO, JORGE (1924-   ) Argentina
  Poetry
  Time Is A Road. *W. Shand.* SHA, 187.

1103 VODÁNOVIC, SERGIO (1927-   ) Chile
  Drama
  Viña: Three Beach Plays. *W. I. Oliver.* OLIV, 257.

1104   WALSH, MARÍA ELENA (1930-   ) Argentina
      Poetry
      The Dead Horse. *W. Shand.* SHA, 246.
      The Forest of Agonies. *D. J. Flakoll & C. Alegría.* FLAK,
        211.
      The House. *W. Shand.* SHA, 248.
      Transit. *W. Shand.* SHA, 247.

1105   WALSH, RODOLFO J. (1927-   ) Argentina
      Fiction
      Gambler's Tale. *D. Yates.* YATE, 45.
      Shadow of a Bird. *D. Yates.* YATE, 185.

1106   WAST, HUGO (1883-?)
      Fiction
      The Missing Hand (Excerpt). no tr. JONE-3, 236.

1107   WEBER, DELIA (   ) Dominican Republic
      Poetry
      Errant Voice. *F. E. Townsend.* TOWN, 65.

1108   WESTPHALEN, EMILIO ADOLFO VON (1910-   ) Peru
      Poetry
      As Time Goes On. *H. R. Hays.* FITT, 417.

1109   WHITELOW, GUILLERMO (1923-   ) Argentina
      Poetry
      Island Within Me IX. *W. Shand.* SHA, 184.
      Island Within Me XXV. *W. Shand.* SHA, 184.
      Island Within Me XLIX. *W. Shand.* SHA, 185.

1110   WINDT LAVANDIER, JULIO DE (   ) Dominican Republic
      Poetry
      Mayo. *F. E. Townsend.* TOWN, 101.

1111   WYLD OSPINA, CARLOS (1891-1956) Guatemala
      Fiction
      The Honor of his House. *J. C. MacLean.* ONIS-2, 84.

1112   XAMMAR, LUIS FABIO (1911-1947) Peru
      Poetry
      The Spring. *M. Lee.* FITT, 481.

1113   XISTO, PEDRO (1900-   ) Brazil
      Poetry
      aboio cry of the Brazilian cowboy. no tr. BANN, 121.
      full/void. *H. de Campos.* WILL-1, n.p.
      Rock. no tr. BANN, 123.
      star/oyster. no tr. BANN, 119.
      stick/bread. no tr. BANN, 122.
      wind leaf. no tr. BANN, 124.

(XISTO, PEDRO)
  yarn. no tr. BANN, 120.
  ZEN. no tr. WILL-1, n.p.

1114   YÁÑEZ, AGUSTÍN (1904-) Mexico
    Fiction
    Aldo or Music Discovered. *Z. Nelken.* TORR, 137.

1115   YANOVER, HÉCTOR (1929-) Argentina
    Poetry
    I Want To Weep. *W. Shand.* SHA, 235.
    They Discuss Over My Chest. *W. Shand.* SHA, 234.

1116   ZABALA RUIZ, MANUEL (1933?-) Ecuador
    Poetry
    Humble Biography. *R. Connally.* YOU, 54.

1117   ZAID, GABRIEL (1934-) Mexico
    Poetry
    Accident. *S. Mondragón & S. Smith.* MU-69, 101.
    Birth of Venus. *D. Hoffman.* PAZ-2, 53.
    Final Splendor. *D. Hoffman.* PAZ-2, 59.
    Reverend Malthus On The Beach. *S. Mondragón & S. Smith.*
     MU-69, 101.
    Shepherd's Song. *D. Hoffman.* PAZ-2, 57.
    The Offering. *D. Hoffman.* PAZ-2, 55.
    Thousand And One Nights. *S. Mondragón & S. Smith.* MU-69,
     99.
    Window To The Sea. *S. Mondragón & S. Smith.* MU-69, 99.

1118   ZALAMEA, JORGE (1905-) Colombia
    Drama
    The Inn Of Bethlehem. *W. K. Jones.* JONE-4, 97.

1119   ZAMUDIO, ADELA (1854-1928) Bolivia
    Poetry
    To Be Born a Man. *F. G. Carrino & J. E. Hahner.* HAH, 60.

1120   ZAPATA ARIAS, IRENE ( ) Colombia
    Poetry
    Nigger Don't Die On The Streets. *W. Keller.* RUIZ, 107.

1121   ZAPATA OLIVELLI, JUAN ( ) Colombia
    Poetry
    Meridian Without Tears. *H. Ruiz del Vizo.* RUIZ, 103.

1122   ZAVALA, IRIS M. (1935-) Puerto Rico
    Poetry
    I'll never know your face. *R. Márquez.* MARQ, 445.
    Lament I. *R. Márquez.* MARQ, 443.
    Smile Lie Rockets.... *D. Sánchez-Méndez.* MATI, 109.

The Great Mammoth.... *D. Sánchez-Méndez*. MATI, 107.
Words words. *R. Márquez*. MARQ, 447.

1123   ZAVALETA, CARLOS E. (1928–   ) Peru
    Fiction
    Ernesto's Head. *M. A. de Maurer & C. A. de Lomellini*.
      HAR67–4, 13.

1124   ZEGARRA BALLÓN, ETHELBERTO (   ) Peru
    Poetry
    Sighs. *A. B. Poor*. POOR, 70.

1125   ZEGRI, ARMANDO (1891–   ) Chile
    Fiction
    Nights in Talca (from: Memorias del Ultimo Decadente).
      no tr. LIEB, 951.

  ZEITLIN, ISRAEL. See [TIEMPO, CÉSAR pseud.].

1126   ZOLEZZI, EMILIO (1905–   ) Argentina
    Poetry
    Fields Of The Heart. *W. Shand*. SHA, 81.
    The Tower. *W. Shand*. SHA, 82.

1127   ZORRILLA DE SAN MARTÍN, JUAN (1855–1931) Uruguay
    Poetry
    Does She Not Feel? *A. B. Poor*. POOR, 77.
    Tabaré. *W. K. Jones*. JONE–2, 280.
    The Mother's Farewell. *A. S. Blackwell*. BLAC, 444.
    The Mother's Farewell. *A. S. Blackwell*. LIT–2, 60.
    Thou and I. *A. B. Poor*. POOR, 76.
    Other
    The Idea of Patriotism. no tr. LIT–2, 45.

1128   ZUCCOLOTTO, AFRÂNIO (1914–   ) Brazil
    Poetry
    Niels Lyhne. *L. S. Downes*. DOWN, 56.

Translator Index

(Numbers refer to entries, not pages)

Aguilera, Francisco, 108
Ahern, Maureen, 118, 218, 256, 311, 492, 520, 538, 785, 961
Alegría, Claribel, 9, 52, 78, 118, 122, 205, 207, 231, 242, 278, 290, 296, 336, 475, 385, 387, 439, 460, 477, 486, 494, 542, 546, 560, 597, 602, 660, 684, 700, 710, 721, 722, 741, 750, 762, 780, 786, 811, 815, 819, 916, 925, 938, 944, 947, 961, 962, 1014, 1028, 1067, 1093, 1099, 1100, 1104
Alwan, Ameen, 242
Anderson, Ruth Matilda, 225, 296, 600
Arenal, Electra, 542, 1100
Aroul, Guy, 819
Arrillaga, María, 85, 158, 301, 601, 903, 955
Austin, Allison, 415

Babín, María Teresa, 95
Bailey, Wilber E., 5
Bain, Read, 468, 546
Baraona, Carlyn, 308
Barba-Martin, José, 157
Bardin, James C., 546
Barnstone, Willis, 358, 811, 835, 990
Bauman, Marilyn, 156
Beck, Claudia, 41, 42, 82, 325, 357, 380, 382, 383, 543, 595, 616, 661, 669, 697, 784, 797, 862, 923, 1015, 1100

Beckett, Samuel, 321, 467, 468, 505, 547, 618, 624, 751, 793, 810, 893, 900, 1020, 1049
Belitt, Ben, 78, 296, 738, 750, 852
Bell, Doreen, 296
Benson, Rachel, 475, 542, 750, 802, 819, 825, 1014, 1064, 1098
Berg, Stephen, 819, 1064
Beringer, Arthur, 523
Bernstein, J. S., 429
Bingham-Powell, Olga, 526, 783
Bishop, Elizabeth, 102, 148, 168, 210, 338, 606, 726
Bishop, John Peale, 468
Blackburn, Paul, 78, 178, 278, 342, 358, 392, 434, 494, 501, 520, 951
Blackwell, Alice Stone, 33, 43, 65, 70, 137, 143, 150, 151, 163, 170, 230, 254, 266, 269, 287, 296, 298, 309, 321, 341, 356, 373, 384, 397, 398, 404, 438, 441, 448, 462, 468, 484, 505, 532, 536, 537, 539, 546, 547, 559, 593, 630, 632, 639, 709, 710, 743, 751, 764, 788, 793, 803, 806, 855, 857, 872, 987, 989, 1014, 1038, 1046, 1049, 1050, 1051, 1060, 1073, 1127
Bledsoe, Thomas, 1056
Bly, Robert, 296, 468, 750, 1064
Boisier, Cecilia, 998

Booher, Kathy, 5
Borges, Jorge Luis, 142
Bové, Anthony, 594
Bowles, P., 756
Boyars, Arthur, 382
Boyer, Angela, 27, 88, 291, 320, 380, 387, 543, 661, 748, 778
Boyer, Mildred, 142
Bradford, Lisa, 330, 1099
Brand, Millen, 477
Braymer, Nan, 86, 199, 494, 726, 982, 1064
Brazil, E., 861
Brenner, Anita, 499, 630, 818, 881
Brinnin, John Malcolm, 217
Brof, Janet, 205, 273, 439, 776
Brotherston, Gordon, 236, 402, 474, 489, 490, 520, 741, 744, 753
Brotherston, J. G., 82, 171, 208, 228
Brown, Ashley, 168, 726
Brown, Elsie, 53, 979
Brown, Gerald, 122

C., K. G., 710
COFFLA (Common Front For Latin America), 32
Cabrera Infante, Guillermo, 171
Campos, Augusto de, 186
Campos, Haroldo de, 93, 145, 186, 189, 483, 849, 856, 1113
Cantatore, Paschal, 142, 1072
Cardozo, Manoel, 34, 48, 49, 61, 102, 117, 168, 222, 338, 379, 600, 683, 702, 706, 726, 842, 889, 904
Carpentier, Hortense, 354, 765, 774
Carranza, Sylvia, 27, 31, 41, 147, 291, 551, 631, 661, 697, 698, 729
Carrino, Frank G., 868, 1053, 1119
Carruthers, Ben F., 494, 822
Castellón, Blanca López, 1, 1038, 1071
Chapman, J. A., 947
Cherry, Ethel, 836
Christ, Ronald, 142, 807, 1072

Clarke, Joseph I. C., 619, 847, 851
Coester, Alfred, 532, 967
Cohen, John Michael, 12, 31, 41, 63, 142, 169, 217, 228, 231, 255, 296, 321, 323, 336, 367, 382, 387, 446, 468, 494, 536, 560, 597, 624, 661, 714, 722, 750, 757, 766, 793, 796, 797, 819, 825, 853, 880, 900, 906, 951, 995, 1064, 1098
Cohen, Robert, 502
Colbin, Annemarie, 234
Colecchia, Francesca, 50, 248, 319, 337, 437, 527, 541, 674, 1003, 1098
Colford, William E., 108, 126, 261, 296, 318, 440, 559, 598, 625, 679, 751, 881, 927, 983, 1057, 1076, 1084
Connally, Ron, 58, 73, 83, 106, 122, 146, 275, 290, 479, 557, 597, 681, 811, 944, 978, 1093, 1116
Connelly, Charles, 1007
Conzelman, Dorothy, 710, 1057
Cooper, J., 168
Costa, René De, 585
Cotton, Christine, 567
Coulthard, George Robert, 494, 802
Coulthard, R. E., 81, 659, 983
Coyne, Joan, 932, 997
Craig, George Dundas, 100, 142, 254, 296, 468, 507, 536, 542, 559, 630, 710, 750, 751, 840, 872, 987, 989, 1014, 1039, 1060
Cran, Patricia Davidson, 1005
Crow, John, 296
Cutler, Charles M., 968

Dana, Doris, 710
Davis, Darol, 5
Davis, Milton Ben, 445, 542, 745, 826
Davis, William M., 296
De Kay, Drake, 881
De la Texera, Diego, 802
De Sola, Alis, 79, 344, 646, 647, 901

Delgado, María Luisa Hurtado, 295, 297
Demarest, Donald, 46, 981, 1040
Di Giovanni, Norman Thomas, 74, 133, 142, 282, 342, 573, 737, 916, 1005, 1062
Dobzynski, Charles, 726
Doezema, Herman P., 833
Dorn, Edward, 236, 402, 474, 489, 490, 520, 744, 753
Downes, Leonard Stephen, 2, 34, 48, 49, 101, 102, 141, 145, 152, 168, 188, 192, 210, 213, 223, 224, 294, 331, 376, 485, 497, 508, 556, 600, 605, 612, 683, 689, 702, 704, 706, 708, 726, 728, 735, 736, 842, 850, 860, 889, 894, 904, 911, 979, 993, 1009, 1010, 1088, 1128
Durán, Gloria, 951
Durán, Manuel, 951

Eberhart, R., 48
Echeverría, Alfonso, 346
Echeverría, Serge, 597, 811
Edkins, Anthony, 407
Edwards, Alicia, 16, 23, 251, 306, 330, 957
Edwards, Faye, 544, 659, 882
Eichhorn, Douglas, 624
Elliott, Lilian E., 132, 599, 639, 816, 989, 1073, 1078
Ellsworth, Mary, 20, 1068
Emigh, Patricia, 86, 499
Escobar, Gabriel, 805
Escudero, Carlos, 503, 865
Eshleman, Clayton, 118, 814, 1064
Espinal, Marcia, 364
Eyster, Warren, 762

Fassett, Jacob S. Jr., 113, 650, 970
Fernández, Oscar, 315
Fernández, Pablo Armando, 1044
Fernández Cherician, David, 848
Fife, Austin A., 161, 296, 409, 617, 710, 764, 1014, 1049
Fish, Helen Eldredge, 131, 751, 991

Fitts, Dudley, 173, 201, 202, 217, 219, 243, 361, 472, 494, 504, 521, 535, 540, 542, 595, 654, 750, 766, 771, 789, 802, 819, 822, 825, 900, 973, 1016, 1034, 1098
Fitzgerald, Robert Stuart, 142
Flakoll, Darwin J., 9, 52, 78, 118, 122, 205, 207, 231, 242, 278, 290, 296, 336, 375, 385, 387, 439, 460, 477, 486, 494, 542, 546, 560, 597, 602, 660, 684, 700, 710, 721, 722, 741, 750, 762, 780, 786, 811, 815, 819, 916, 925, 938, 944, 947, 961, 962, 1014, 1028, 1067, 1093, 1099, 1100, 1104
Flores, Angel, 142, 299, 339, 406, 699, 750, 1058
Flores, Kate, 296, 710, 750
Flory, David A., 352, 1056
Francis, H. E., 38, 314, 525
Franco, Jean, 122, 214, 278, 429, 461, 609, 774, 947
Freeman, Lorraine O'Grady, 336

Gannon, Patricio, 80, 100, 142, 385, 583, 590, 630, 654, 763
Garafola, Lynn, 387
García, Edmund C., 693
Gardner, Donald, 27, 171, 205, 320, 383, 616, 661, 778, 924
Getsi, Lucia, 491
Gibson, John G., 382
Gifford, Henry, 1064
Gill, Roderick, 155, 225, 710, 719, 740
Godoy, Jorge, 225
Goldberg, Isaac, 6, 332, 356, 680, 752, 888
Goldberg, Robert Alan, 506, 1046
González, Eduardo, 205
González, Michael, 22, 134, 172, 205, 217, 296, 321, 414, 468, 475, 536, 610, 624, 722, 757, 781, 793, 802, 819, 825, 900, 949, 951, 1093, 1098
Green, Alden James, 337
Greenwell, Richard, 256, 311, 937
Gross, Stuart M., 950

Grossman, William L., 26, 48, 91,
    244, 284, 391, 498, 562, 606,
    636, 638, 827, 876, 877, 887,
    892, 1070
Grucci, Joseph Leonard, 494, 750
Guedes, Bernadette, 887
Guenther, Charles, 296
Gullón, Agnes, 796

Hagen, Carl, 560
Hahner, June E., 211, 329, 363,
    372, 615, 868, 1053, 1119
Hall, Donald, 536
Hardy, R. Frank, 105, 560, 862,
    923
Hasbrouck, Astrid S., 604
Hayes, Charles, 1080
Hayman, Lee Richard, 909
Hays, H. R., 1, 86, 142, 217,
    405, 406, 466, 475, 494, 542,
    617, 624, 695, 732, 733, 750,
    757, 776, 825, 916, 929, 930,
    1064, 1108
Hebblethwaite, Frank P., 249,
    292, 379, 413, 725, 772,
    1083
Hertelendy, Susana, 349, 1004
Hill, John, 7, 97, 209, 225, 382,
    387, 405, 480, 494, 542, 558,
    595, 663, 742, 811, 819, 987,
    1020, 1060, 1064
Hills, Elijah Clarence, 296
Hoeksema, Thomas 431, 576, 712,
    796
Hoffman, Daniel, 255, 1117
Hollander, John, 142
Hollis, Ena, 492, 785, 961, 1100
Honig, Edwin, 44
Honig, Margot, 44
Horton, Rod W., 3, 187, 191, 259,
    265, 401, 641, 943, 992, 1029
Howard, Richard, 142
Howes, Barbara, 904
Hughes, Langston, 494, 710, 822
Humphries, Rolfe, 546, 678, 791,
    808, 878, 1014, 1034, 1038
Hutchings, Chesley M., 142, 468,
    507, 751

Igo, John, 217

James, Earle K., 913
Jara, Joan, 561
Jesús, Salvador M. de, 564
Jodorowsky, Raquel, 567
Johnson, B. Jane, 65
Johnson, Mildred E., 22, 65, 80,
    100, 142, 225, 254, 296, 468,
    536, 546, 559, 624, 630, 663,
    750, 751, 900, 987, 1014,
    1038
Jones, Willis Knapp, 4, 17, 18, 51,
    65, 69, 100, 108, 142, 194,
    225, 254, 280, 295, 297, 321,
    360, 378, 398, 410, 425, 438,
    484, 494, 503, 505, 507, 546,
    548, 624, 630, 659, 663, 715,
    724, 746, 750, 751, 764, 769,
    802, 845, 864, 865, 881, 888,
    896, 908, 916, 918, 922, 931,
    933, 967, 991, 1014, 1046,
    1060, 1087, 1118, 1127
Jordan, J., 600
Joscelyne, R. P., 3, 498, 1070
Justice, Donald, 624, 825, 1098

Kaplan, L. C., 44
Karnezis, George, 677
Kearns, Lionel, 105, 862, 1015
Keller, Wilfred, 1120
Kemp, Lysander, 78, 144, 164,
    288, 296, 415, 437, 459, 594,
    711, 722, 819, 871, 941, 947,
    1020
Kerrigan, Anthony, 27, 227, 380,
    381, 616, 797
Kinnell, G., 168
Kittel, Muriel, 710
Knoepfle, John, 1064
Kociancich, Vlady, 573
Kurz, Harry, 243, 247, 274, 285,
    395, 529, 587, 613, 620, 634,
    881, 1048
Kustow, Michael, 1044

Lacerda, Alberto De, 837
Lamantia, Philip, 205
Lamb de Ortiz de Montellano,
    Thelma, 789
Langman, Ida, 626
Langnas, Izaak A., 455, 774,
    1079

Lasley, M. M., 198
Lauer, Mirko, 588
Laughlin, James, 811
Lawaetz, Gudie, 773
Lawder, Douglas, 1064
Lebovitz, Richard, 542
Lee de Muñoz Marín, Muna, 1, 7,
    65, 80, 114, 135, 137, 160,
    217, 254, 296, 397, 405, 409,
    448, 468, 536, 610, 630, 710,
    733, 739, 781, 826, 828, 829,
    1016, 1038, 1063, 1064, 1066,
    1112
Leite, Yolande, 48, 102, 140,
    168, 224, 338, 600, 683, 689,
    726, 904, 979
Levertov, Denise, 296, 819
Levine, Philip, 540, 796, 951
Levine, Suzanne Jill, 169, 336,
    415, 757, 874, 975
Levitin, Alexis, 102, 683
Livingston, Arthur, 881
Llopis, Rogelio, 31, 147, 291,
    382, 383, 551, 631, 697, 698,
    777, 778, 817
Llorente, Mariano Joaquín, 476
Lomellini, C. A. De, 252, 526,
    567, 723, 783, 805, 1123
Longland, Jean Rogers, 49, 102,
    137, 189, 338, 356, 501, 605,
    759
López Kelly, Maria Cristina, 153,
    427
Lowenfels, Lillian, 199, 494,
    982, 1064
Luby, Barry, 11, 24, 29, 60, 89,
    95, 98, 136, 149, 158, 197,
    241, 261, 264, 277, 302, 303,
    318, 326, 327, 411, 426, 438,
    459, 524, 528, 550, 568, 577,
    611, 623, 651, 657, 662, 666,
    676, 685, 686, 692, 701, 727,
    739, 740, 775, 798, 802, 820,
    879, 885, 886, 903, 1008,
    1089
Lucas, Ernest F., 751
Luzuriaga, Gerardo, 8, 157, 313,
    319, 337, 671, 696, 1003

McBride, Ann, 972
McBride, Mary, 972
McCord, Dora, 209
McCord, Howard, 209
Macdermott, Isabel K., 710
MacLean, Joan Coyne, 325, 420,
    1111
McMurray, David Arthur, 122, 387,
    494, 581, 687
MacShane, Frank, 86
McVan, Alice Jane, 80, 296, 321,
    547, 591, 617, 630, 633, 710,
    840, 987, 1014
McWhirter, George, 77, 415, 863
Mades, Leonard, 415
Malcolm, Donald, 1038
Malkus, Alida, 1021
Mallan, Lloyd, 52, 217, 545, 757
Malloy, Robert, 420
Maloney, R. L., 900
Manchester, Paul T., 546, 987
Manning, Hugo, 100, 127, 142,
    465, 646, 714, 745, 821,
    1014
Márquez, Robert, 9, 59, 103, 122,
    180, 205, 236, 270, 293, 383,
    387, 402, 439, 494, 520, 597,
    659, 687, 707, 712, 729, 985
    986, 1122
Matas, Julio, 50, 248, 319, 337,
    437, 527, 541, 674, 1003,
    1098
Matilla, Alfredo, 675, 848
Matilla, Ellen G., 675, 690, 802,
    848, 902, 955, 986
Matters, C. Virginia, 324
Maurer, Christopher, 142, 446,
    750
Maurer, Maureen Ahern, 118, 179,
    256, 311, 520, 716, 750,
    1024, 1068, 1123
Mayer, G. Alfred, 1057
Mendelsohn, G., 78
Merrill, James 683
Merton, Thomas, 217, 286, 1064
Merwin, W. S., 71, 78, 142, 168,
    434, 542, 572, 689, 716, 722,
    742, 770, 804, 811, 951, 984,
    1020
Mezey, Robert, 1064
Middleton, Christopher, 382

Mitchell, Adrian, 487, 560, 915, 1015
Molinari, George M., 420
Moncy, Agnes, 415, 796, 1037
Mondragón, Sergio, 205, 567, 572, 1117
Morgan, Edwin, 186, 189, 483
Morgan, Patrick, 112, 162, 439, 482, 654, 717, 959, 996, 1027
Moss, Stanley, 1064
Munguía Jr., E., 94
Murchison, John C., 349, 525, 670, 956, 998

Negron, W. P., 881
Nelken, Zoila, 28, 142, 214, 340, 515, 656, 756, 809, 862, 881, 927, 1114
Nelson, Naomi, 319
Newman, Mary, 987
Nieto, José, 610
Nist, John, 48, 102, 140, 168, 224, 338, 600, 683, 689, 726, 904, 979

O'Brien, Geoffrey, 542
O'Connell, Richard, 217, 361, 394, 405, 621, 1014
Oliphant, Dave, 597
Oliver, William I., 157, 204, 423, 527, 640, 1103
Onís, Harriet de, 28, 48, 62, 66, 109, 128, 136, 142, 144, 181, 216, 220, 229, 247, 289, 312, 328, 368, 420, 428, 440, 499, 506, 511, 533, 587, 603, 613, 620, 635, 648, 649, 656, 688, 710, 758, 767, 769, 818, 846, 867, 900, 907, 918, 928, 960, 964, 974, 1000, 1011, 1030, 1057, 1069, 1082, 1084
Ortiz, Gladys, 659
Ortiz, Victoria, 417, 1007
Ossman, David, 560

Pando, Georgina, 87, 173, 366
Paniagua, Lita, 349
Parr, Malcolm J., 750
Partridge, Frances, 214
Pax, Trudy, 687

Peden, Margaret Sayers, 176, 204, 415, 592, 1041
Perkins, Enid Eder, 17
Pettinella, Dora M., 542
Phibbs, Richard, 428
Pilditch, Charles, 659
Pollock, Seymour, 643
Pomposinni, Paola, 121
Pontiero, Giovanni, 606, 670
Poor, Dudley, 102, 223, 307, 338, 600
Poore, Agnes Blake, 287, 296, 326, 362, 443, 642, 652, 980, 1036, 1101, 1124, 1127
Pottlitzer, Joanne, 39, 138, 157, 319, 566, 917, 1085
Proske, Beatrice Gilman, 546, 630, 663, 751, 1038, 1060

Rabassa, Gregory, 86, 278, 429, 858, 1043, 1068
Randall, Elinor, 9, 59, 71, 103, 122, 172, 293, 325, 418, 439, 520, 595, 716, 796, 797, 971
Randall, Margaret, 105, 236, 382, 387, 502, 616
Randolph, Catherine, 659
Raphael, Lenox, 494
Raphael, Maryanne, 494
Raworth, Tom, 19, 100, 112, 118, 142, 254, 350, 359, 380, 381, 385, 430, 445, 446, 542, 559, 597, 630, 644, 668, 710, 712, 714, 750, 797, 811, 1064, 1100
Rechy, John, 204, 866
Reid, Alastair, 142, 1068
Rennert, Cesar, 142, 466, 566
Resnick, Seymour, 296, 546, 630, 663, 710, 750, 751, 1014
Reynolds, Tim, 236, 293, 325, 382, 387, 407, 417, 560, 595, 614, 729, 819, 961
Rice, John Pierrepont, 254, 296, 468
Roach, Eloïse, 464
Roberts, Louis E., 157
Rodeiro, José, 494
Rodríguez Feo, José, 595
Romeo, Anita Whitney, 470, 494, 748

Rose, R. Selden, 108
Rosenblatt, David, 494
Rothenberg, Jerome, 235, 256, 267, 542
Rowe, William, 256
Rubin, David, 670
Rudder, Robert, 8, 157, 313, 319, 337, 671, 696, 1003
Ruiz del Vizo, Hortensia, 76, 84, 97, 167, 174, 184, 185, 214, 253, 271, 338, 355, 365, 449, 454, 457, 458, 494, 500, 574, 600, 655, 760, 802, 822, 829, 843, 921, 926, 963, 969, 1022, 1081, 1094, 1121

St. Clair, David, 563
St. Martin, Hardie, 67, 86, 205, 214, 318, 349, 420, 439, 494, 548, 659, 774, 947, 1020, 1064, 1068
Sánchez-Méndez, Digna, 175, 277, 610, 676, 912, 936, 948, 1122
Saunders, Lillian, 377
Savage, Meredyth, 804
Sayers, Raymond, 756
Schade, George D., 78, 947
Schaefer, Elaine, 28, 137, 647
Schoijet, Mauricio, 435
Schulte, Rainer, 431, 567, 572
Schwartz, Stephen, 494, 614
Scott, Robert, 872
Senior-Ellis, Olive, 231
Serna-Maytorena, M. A., 491, 576
Servino, Alexander, 628
Shand, William, 19, 37, 57, 72, 75, 92, 96, 110, 120, 127, 130, 142, 154, 159, 162, 177, 196, 200, 203, 212, 221, 232, 233, 246, 258, 272, 304, 305, 347, 370, 386, 390, 396, 409, 419, 421, 433, 439, 442, 446, 465, 471, 478, 481, 493, 510, 522, 525, 553, 570, 572, 575, 586, 596, 608, 637, 645, 653, 654, 664, 673, 712, 714, 734, 741, 745, 766, 779, 782, 787, 800, 823, 831, 838, 863, 869, 884, 890, 891, 898, 935, 939, 940, 942, 959, 977, 994, 999,

(Shand, William)
1002, 1006, 1012, 1019, 1032, 1034, 1035, 1042, 1055, 1072, 1074, 1075, 1086, 1095, 1096, 1102, 1104, 1109, 1115, 1126
Shapiro, Norman R., 579
Shaw, Donald L., 774
Shelby, Barbara, 498
Shelby, Susan Louise, 625
Shepard, Isabel S., 254
Shipman, Matthew, 67, 538, 785
Simpson, L., 168
Smith, Sandra, 1117
Smith, William Jay, 710
Soto, Pedro Juan, 1007
Southern, Richard, 429
Stafford, William, 722
Standish, Peter, 48, 102, 132, 168, 338, 453, 496, 600, 683, 689, 726, 904, 979
Staples, Joseph, 542
Starr, Frederick, 14, 310, 424, 456, 488, 622, 713, 755, 812, 883, 899, 958, 1077, 1097
Steiner, Stan, 153
Stock, Robert, 338
Stolkowska, Stasia, 227
Strand, Mark, 245, 735, 794, 895, 981, 1040
Strange, Garret, 630, 639, 897
Suarez, Nico, 494

Tarn, Nathaniel, 325, 382, 387, 595, 644, 729, 750, 923, 1100
Taylor, Hallie D., 336
Temple, Helen, 142
Tercero, Dorothy M., 398
Texera, D. de la, 802
Tipton, David, 118, 179, 218, 256, 311, 492, 538, 553, 588, 672, 785, 937, 961
Todd, Ruthven, 142
Tomlins, Jack E., 1043
Tomlinson, Charles, 819, 1064
Torres, E. de, 774
Torres-Ríoseco, Rosalie, 139, 542
Townsend, Francis Edward, 15, 21, 114, 124, 167, 183, 268, 312, 317, 322, 335, 388, 397, 436,

(Townsend, Francis Edward)
444, 447, 450, 516, 517, 518,
531, 534, 552, 565, 580, 589,
703, 730, 731, 754, 795, 824,
873, 905, 966, 976, 1018,
1107, 1110
Toye, Shiela, 65
Trapier, Elizabeth du Gué, 100,
468, 546, 952
Trejo, Ernesto, 796, 951
Troupe, Quincy, 205
Turner, Elizabeth, 66

Ulyatt, Philomena, 278
Underhill, John G., 1017
Underwood, Edna Worthley, 64, 68,
107, 182, 193, 226, 260, 296,
309, 310, 321, 368, 384, 412,
464, 468, 469, 475, 505, 547,
571, 582, 618, 624, 627, 653,
682, 720, 751, 757, 768, 789,
790, 793, 794, 810, 825, 893,
900, 934, 946, 954, 1020,
1031, 1038, 1049, 1056, 1061,
1098
Updike, John, 142
Upton, John, 55, 83, 104, 106,
165, 300, 334, 393, 452, 509,
705, 712, 722, 832, 925, 944,
1026, 1059, 1065

Valencia, Marisa, 67
Valentine, Jean, 168
Vallés, Patricia, 116, 136, 399,
875
Vandemoer, Nick, 116, 318, 718
Veltfort, Lenore, 166, 371
Volland, Anita, 296

Waldorf, Paul, 1069
Wallace, Elizabeth, 281
Walsh, Donald Devenish, 44, 86,
115, 202, 205, 209, 215, 217,
350, 368, 369, 405, 475, 542,
545, 584, 595, 617, 691, 694,
710, 757, 789, 791, 792, 802,
982, 1014, 1034, 1064, 1091,
Walsh, Thomas, 225, 266, 296,
298, 303, 404, 451, 505, 536,
555, 617, 739, 751, 830, 834,
840, 870, 897, 987, 989,
1020, 1060
Weeks, Ramona, 238
Weinberger, Eliot, 71, 542, 819,
1020
Wendell, Jessie Read, 254, 505,
751, 781, 1014
Wevill, David, 837
Wicker, C. V., 51, 825
Wicker, Mary, 51, 825
Wiezell, Richard John, 659, 825
Wilbur, R., 102, 726
Wilkie, Mary Jane, 74, 916
Williams, Miller, 83, 106, 206,
569, 597, 750, 811, 944, 945,
1025, 1052
Williams, William Carlos, 255
Williams, William G., 65, 495,
617
Wilson, Linda, 881, 1054
Witherup, William, 597, 811
Woodruff, Gregory, 122, 133, 296
Wright, James, 168, 750, 1064
Wust, Monique Fong, 819

Yates, Donald A., 47, 90, 125,
142, 333, 348, 353, 389, 513,
554, 625, 667, 839, 953,
1030, 1067, 1105
Yglesias, Luis Ellicott, 432
Young, Howard, 881

Zitron, Abraham, 749

Geographic Index

(Numbers refer to entries, not pages.)

ARGENTINA

8, 19, 33, 37, 38, 40, 47,
57, 72, 74, 75, 80, 90, 92,
96, 100, 110, 112, 113, 120,
123, 127, 130, 131, 133, 142,
150, 154, 159, 162, 177, 196,
198, 200, 201, 203, 212, 221,
230, 232, 233, 234, 235, 246,
258, 267, 272, 278, 282, 283,
295, 297, 299, 304, 305, 313,
314, 333, 337, 344, 345, 347,
352, 353, 370, 375, 385, 386,
389, 390, 396, 409, 419, 421,
423, 432, 433, 439, 440, 441,
442, 443, 445, 446, 465, 471,
476, 478, 481, 482, 490, 493,
499, 501, 503, 510, 522, 525,
553, 570, 572, 573, 575, 583,
586, 590, 591, 596, 608, 621,
630, 634, 637, 645, 646, 650,
654, 664, 668, 673, 693, 712,
714, 717, 734, 737, 741, 745,
763, 764, 766, 767, 773, 779,
782, 787, 807, 818, 821, 823,
831, 836, 838, 839, 841, 844,
845, 863, 865, 869, 874, 884,
890, 891, 898, 907, 922, 928,
935, 939, 940, 942, 950, 953,
959, 970, 977, 994, 996, 999,
1002, 1005, 1006, 1012, 1014,
1019, 1027, 1032, 1034, 1035,
1037, 1042, 1047, 1055, 1062,
1072, 1074, 1075, 1079, 1086,
1091, 1092, 1095, 1096, 1102,
1104, 1105, 1109, 1115, 1126

BOLIVIA

66, 115, 132, 247, 281, 341,
400, 559, 761, 765, 791, 985,
1119

BRAZIL

2, 3, 26, 34, 35, 44, 48, 49,
53, 61, 91, 93, 99, 101, 102,
109, 117, 138, 140, 141, 145,
148, 152, 168, 186, 187, 188,
189, 191, 192, 210, 211, 213,
222, 223, 224, 244, 249, 259,
265, 284, 289, 292, 294, 307,
315, 329, 331, 332, 338, 372,
376, 379, 391, 401, 413, 453,
483, 485, 496, 497, 498, 508,
511, 556, 562, 563, 600, 603,
605, 606, 612, 613, 615, 628,
636, 638, 641, 652, 680, 683,
687, 688, 689, 702, 704, 706,
708, 725, 726, 728, 735,
736, 752, 759, 772, 816, 827,
837, 842, 849, 850, 856, 858,
859, 860, 876, 877, 887, 889,
892, 894, 895, 904, 911, 943,
979, 980, 992, 993, 1009,
1010, 1025, 1029, 1043, 1070,
1082, 1083, 1088, 1113, 1128

CHILE

5, 18, 32, 52, 79, 83, 106,
108, 139, 156, 166, 206, 243,
266, 269, 280, 308, 319, 336,
346, 348, 349, 351, 362, 410,
435, 462, 507, 509, 539, 542,
554, 561, 566, 567, 569, 579,
581, 585, 587, 597, 598, 599,

(CHILE)
626, 639, 647, 656, 705, 710, 719, 724, 749, 750, 811, 840, 854, 872, 901, 925, 927, 929, 930, 941, 944, 945, 989, 998, 1017, 1026, 1036, 1039, 1052, 1059, 1073, 1078, 1087, 1103, 1125

COLOMBIA
43, 50, 62, 64, 84, 157, 215, 216, 229, 242, 274, 358, 360, 364, 429, 448, 451, 454, 480, 555, 558, 576, 617, 649, 678, 742, 790, 808, 913, 965, 974, 987, 1000, 1021, 1030, 1051, 1053, 1054, 1060, 1118, 1120, 1121

COSTA RICA
16, 23, 151, 207, 251, 306, 330, 369, 473, 537, 544, 604, 633, 635, 882, 952, 957

CUBA
10, 12, 27, 31, 36, 41, 42, 54, 56, 63, 76, 82, 88, 97, 105, 143, 147, 155, 163, 169, 171, 174, 181, 184, 185, 195, 199, 208, 214, 225, 227, 228, 239, 253, 262, 271, 276, 291, 316, 320, 323, 325, 357, 359, 363, 365, 367, 380, 381, 382, 383, 387, 392, 405, 416, 417, 418, 430, 449, 455, 457, 458, 461, 463, 470, 487, 489, 494, 500, 529, 532, 541, 543, 551, 560, 595, 607, 609, 614, 616, 619, 631, 644, 648, 661, 663, 669, 674, 679, 697, 698, 718, 729, 732, 733, 748, 756, 760, 777, 778, 784, 797, 817, 822, 830, 843, 847, 853, 862, 870, 888, 906, 915, 923, 924, 926, 969, 975, 983, 995, 1015, 1022, 1023, 1028, 1044, 1081, 1090, 1094, 1100.

DOMINICAN REPUBLIC
15, 21, 114, 124, 144, 167, 183, 268, 312, 317, 322, 335, 388, 397, 436, 444, 447, 450, 516, 517, 518, 519, 531, 534, 552, 565, 580, 589, 703, 707, 730,

(DOMINICAN REPUBLIC)
731, 754, 795, 824, 873, 905, 921, 966, 976, 1018, 1050, 1107, 1110

ECUADOR
9, 17, 51, 58, 73, 190, 217, 219, 220, 275, 285, 361, 371, 479, 548, 557, 671, 747, 786, 809, 896, 910, 962, 1080, 1116

EL SALVADOR
45, 240, 293, 472, 486, 584, 602, 696, 960

GUATEMALA
65, 86, 209, 236, 402, 460, 533, 691, 721, 919, 920, 964, 1003, 1111

HONDURAS
495, 512, 1016, 1046, 1063

MEXICO
6, 14, 20, 46, 68, 71, 78, 94, 103, 107, 119, 125, 126, 161, 164, 170, 178, 182, 193, 202, 204, 226, 231, 237, 245, 255, 260, 287, 288, 298, 309, 310, 321, 340, 343, 354, 356, 368, 377, 384, 395, 407, 412, 415, 424, 425, 434, 437, 456, 464, 467, 468, 469, 475, 488, 504, 505, 506, 513, 515, 527, 540, 547, 571, 582, 592, 593, 594, 618, 622, 624, 625, 627, 653, 667, 682, 709, 711, 713, 716, 720, 722, 743, 746, 751, 755, 757, 762, 768, 770, 789, 793, 794, 796, 810, 812, 819, 825, 855, 857, 866, 871, 880, 883, 893, 897, 899, 900, 909, 932, 934, 946, 947, 951, 954, 956, 958, 971, 981, 984, 1011, 1020, 1038, 1040, 1041, 1049, 1056, 1061, 1069, 1077, 1097, 1098, 1114, 1117

NICARAGUA
69, 70, 205, 273, 279, 286, 296, 474, 684, 744, 780, 815, 982

PANAMA
30, 250, 373, 374, 408, 535, 549, 574, 665, 803, 938, 997, 1001

Geographic Index

PARAGUAY
25, 55, 104, 165, 194, 300,
334, 378, 393, 452, 484, 715,
769, 806, 832, 864, 908, 916,
931, 973, 1065

PERU
1, 7, 28, 67, 111, 118, 121,
160, 179, 180, 218, 252, 254,
256, 270, 311, 328, 350, 422,
428, 492, 514, 520, 526, 538,
588, 620, 642, 672, 677, 694,
700, 723, 753, 776, 783, 785,
826, 828, 867, 868, 937, 961,
1024, 1058, 1064, 1066, 1067,
1068, 1071, 1076, 1101, 1108,
1112, 1123, 1124

PUERTO RICO
11, 13, 24, 29, 60, 81, 85,
87, 89, 95, 98, 116, 129,
135, 136, 149, 153, 158, 173,
175, 197, 241, 257, 261, 263,
264, 277, 301, 302, 303, 318,
324, 326, 327, 366, 399, 403,
411, 426, 427, 438, 459, 524,
528, 530, 550, 564, 568, 577,
578, 601, 610, 611, 623, 629,
643, 651, 655, 657, 658, 659,
662, 666, 675, 676, 685, 686,
690, 692, 701, 727, 739, 740,
775, 820, 834, 848, 875, 879,
885, 886, 902, 903, 912, 914,
933, 936, 948, 955, 968, 986,
1007, 1008, 1013, 1033, 1089,
1122

URUGUAY
4, 22, 77, 122, 128, 146,
290, 398, 414, 502, 523, 536,
545, 546, 632, 640, 670, 681,
774, 781, 814, 829, 881, 918,
949, 967, 978, 991, 1004,
1084, 1093, 1099, 1127

VENEZUELA
39, 59, 134, 137, 172, 248,
339, 342, 355, 394, 406, 420,
431, 466, 477, 491, 521, 660,
699, 738, 758, 771, 792, 804,
813, 833, 835, 846, 851, 852,
878, 972, 990, 1048, 1057

Further Reading: Selected References

This selective, annotated reference list of literary and cultural histories, essays, bibliographies, interviews, editorials, reviews, etc.--mostly written during the last decade--bears witness to the increasing interest in and recognition of Latin American literature in the United States. The reader is reminded that some of the most important and incisive critical essays on the topic have appeared in the form of prefaces or introductions to the anthologies included in this Index. We have highlighted this feature, when appropriate, in our "Annotated Bibliography of Anthologies and Anthology Code."

HISTORIES, ESSAYS, CRITICISM

ANDERSON-IMBERT, ENRIQUE. Spanish-American Literature. A History. 2nd ed. Revised and updated by Elaine Malley. Detroit: Wayne State University Press, 1969. Volume I (1492-1910), Volume II (1910-1963). Paperback.
   Excellent survey of Spanish-American literature between 1492 and 1963. Both volumes of the 1969 paperback edition include a bibliography to "...commence [the] study of Spanish-American literature..." and a most useful Index of Authors, which identifies pseudonyms, country of origin, and dates. Every chapter is preceded by an "historical framework," "cultural tendencies," and a discussion of general characteristics, first, of verse, followed by prose (novel, short story, essay) and theater.

ARCINIEGAS, GERMÁN. Latin America: A Cultural History. Translated from the Spanish by Joan MacLean. New York: Alfred A. Knopf, 1967. 594p.
   A brilliantly written cultural history of Latin America: treats ideas and their influence, customs, arts, literature, and so on.

CARRERA ANDRADE, JORGE. Reflections on Spanish-American Poetry. Translated by Don C. Bliss and Gabriela de C. Bliss. Albany: State University of New York Press, 1973.
   The Ecuadorian writer presented the following essays at different U. S. colleges and universities during 1970 and 1971:

(CARRERA ANDRADE, JORGE)
"Spanish-American Originality," "Poetry and Society in Spanish-America," "Trends in Spanish-American Poetry (Twentieth Century)," "Decade of My Poetry," "Poetry of Reality and Utopia."

EZQUENAZI-MAYO, ROBERTO and MEYER, MICHAEL C., eds. Latin American Scholarship Since World War II: Trends in History, Political Science, Literature, Geography and Economics. Lincoln, Nebraska: University of Nebraska, 1971. 335p.
Nineteen scholars analyze Latin American studies, with emphasis on history and political science, but there are four essays on literature, and one each on geography and economics.

FOSTER, DAVID WILLIAM and FOSTER, VIRGINIA RAMOS. Modern Latin American Literature. 2 Volumes. Compiled and edited by David W. Foster and Virginia Ramos Foster. New York: Frederick Ungar Publishing Co., 1975. Volume I: 539p.; Volume II: 508p.
Critical reviews and evaluations of 137 Latin American writers, "...culled from critical excerpts from Spanish, Portuguese, French, German, Italian, and Swedish sources..." Both volumes give a list of authors by country and a useful list of works mentioned in each one of the critical portraits. Volume II also contains a Cross-Reference Index to Authors (pp.483-488) and an Index to Critics (pp.489-508).

FRANCO, JEAN. An Introduction to Spanish-American Literature. New York: Cambridge University Press, 1969. 390p.
"She gives an intellectually and artistically exciting review about Spanish-American literature." Brief treatment of the colonial period, with emphasis on independence and national periods.

_____. The Modern Culture of Latin America: Society and the Artist. New York: Praeger, 1967. 339p.
Perceptive essays which cover a large number of specialized topics concerning the contemporary Latin American artist and his relationship to his socio-political and cultural environment.

GALLAGHER, D. P. Modern Latin American Literature. New York: Oxford University Press, 1973. 197p.
A discussion of 19th century Latin American literature (pp. 1-10), the "regionalist novel" (pp. 82-86), and Latin American fiction since 1940 (pp. 87-93). Essays include literal translations of excerpts from works by César Vallejo (Peru), Pablo Neruda (Chile), Octavio Paz (Mexico), Jorge Luis Borges (Argentina), Mario Vargas Llosa (Peru), Gabriel García Márquez (Colombia), and Guillermo Cabrera Infante (Cuba).

Further Reading: Essays, Criticism

GUIBERT, RITA. Seven Latin American Writers Talk to Rita Guibert.
Translated from the Spanish by Frances Partridge. Introduction
by Emir Rodríguez Monegal. New York: Alfred A. Knopf, 1973.
436p.
"Rita Guibert, an Argentine and former LIFE en Español report-
er, confronts the fact that though Latin American literature is
now often acclaimed as perhaps the richest and most original in
the world it simply has not caught on with U. S. readers."
(Philip Herrera, Time, April 2, 1973.) The book focuses on Pablo
Neruda (Chile), Jorge Luis Borges (Argentina), Miguel Ángel Asturias (Guatemala), Octavio Paz (Mexico), Julio Cortázar (Argentina), Gabriel García Márquez (Colombia), Guillermo Cabrera Infante (Cuba). The book includes photographs of each author.

HARSS, LUIS and DOHMANN, BARBARA. Into the Mainstream. Conversa-
tions with Latin-American Writers. New York: Harper & Row,
1967. 385p.
Readable essays on ten contemporary Latin American writers, "a
psychobiographic approach" to Alejo Carpentier (Cuba), Miguel
Ángel Asturias (Guatemala), Jorge Luis Borges (Argentina), João
Guimarães Rosa (Brazil), Juan Carlos Onetti (Uruguay), Julio
Cortázar (Argentina), Juan Rulfo (Mexico), Carlos Fuentes (Mexi-
co), Gabriel García Márquez (Colombia), and Mario Vargas Llosa
(Peru).

HENRÍQUEZ-UREÑA, PEDRO. A Concise History of Latin American Culture.
Gilbert Chase, translator. New York: Praeger, 1966. 214p.
Paperback.
"Traces the origins of Spanish-American culture from colonial
times to the present, pointing out also the important pre-Colom-
bian influences on Latin America's cultural heritage."

_____. Literary Currents in Hispanic America. New York: Russell
and Russell, 1963. 345p.
An excellent synthesis of the cultural history of Spanish and
Portuguese America.

MENTON, SEYMOUR. Prose Fiction of the Cuban Revolution. Austin,
Texas: University of Texas Press, 1975.
An important contribution for the understanding of contemporary
Cuban narrative. Critical survey of twenty-two novels, one volume of short stories, and one other of short stories written by
non-Cubans about the Revolution. The book includes a "Chronology
of Novels and Short Stories" written between 1959 and 1973
(pp. 277-285), an excellent bibliography divided into seven main
sections, one of which is an "Annotated Bibliography of Anthologies of the Cuban Short Story" (pp. 294-299), and a useful
author-title-subject index.

RODMAN, SELDEN. South America of the Poets. Illustrations by Bill
Negrón. New York: Hawthorn Books, 1970. 270p. Paperback.
Interviews of major literary figures in South America and a
traveler's observations of the following countries: Argentina,
Uruguay, Paraguay, Peru, Bolivia, Brazil, Guyana, Venezuela, Co-
lombia, Ecuador, and Chile.

RODRÍGUEZ MONEGAL, EMIR. El "boom" de la novela latinoamericana.
Ensayo. Caracas, Venezuela: Editorial Tiempo Nuevo, 1973.
119p.
A lucid essay on the so-called "boom of the Latin American
novel," by the Uruguayan teacher, writer and critic, E. Rodríguez
Monegal. Includes a bibliography (pp. 105-114).

SCHWARTZ, KESSEL. A New History of Spanish American Fiction. Coral
Gables, Fla.: University of Miami Press, 1972. 2 volumes.
"It includes the evaluations not merely of major novels but of
numerous little-known works spanning nearly 400 years...." Good
discussions on such contemporary Latin American writers as
Fuentes, García Márquez, Mallea, Borges, Agustín Yáñez, Alejo
Carpentier, José María Arguedas, and others. Bibliography and
indices of authors and works. It does not replace but updates
Anderson-Imbert's Spanish-American Literature. A History.

BIBLIOGRAPHIES, DICTIONARIES, ENCYCLOPEDIAS

"Checklist of Translations of Spanish American Plays." In W. K.
Jones' Men and Angels. Three South American Plays. Carbondale:
Southern Illinois University Press, 1970.
This checklist is arranged alphabetically by country and by
name of dramatist and identifies sources for translations, most
of them not published but filed in manuscript form in several re-
positories. Countries represented are: Argentina, Boliva,
Chile, Colombia, Cuba, Ecuador, Guatemala, Mexico, Nicaragua,
Peru, Puerto Rico, Uruguay, Venezuela, Philippines, and the state
of New Mexico.

CHRISTENSEN, GEORGE K. "A Bibliography of Latin American Plays in
English Translation." Latin American Theatre Review, 6:29-39
(Spring 1973).
"This bibliography is an attempt to list both the published and
the manuscript copies for the benefit of scholars, future trans-
lators and theatre directors." It contains materials relating to
Argentina, Brazil, Colombia, Cuba, Nicaragua, Panama, Paraguay,
Peru, Puerto Rico, and Venezuela.

COLL, EDNA. Indice informativo de la novela hispanoamericana. Las
Antillas. Tomo I. Universidad de Puerto Rico, Editorial Uni-
versitaria, 1974. (Printed in Spain.) 418p. [plus 6 more]
Although in Spanish, a useful compilation of novelists in Puerto
Rico, the Dominican Republic and Cuba. For each country, an au-
thor index is provided.

FURTHER READING: ESSAYS, CRITICISM

Diccionario de la literatura latinoamericana. Washington, D. C.:
Unión Panamericana, Secretaría General, Organización de los Esta-
dos Americanos, 1956-1963.
Five volumes of this critical dictionary on Latin American literature have appeared to date: I. Bolivia, II. Chile, III. Colombia, IV. Argentina (2 volumes in one), V. Ecuador and América
Central (2 volumes in one). Written in Spanish, and still in
progress, this work presents a vast panoramic overview of Latin
American literary evolution from colonial times to the present.

ENGBER, MARJORIE. Caribbean Fiction and Poetry. Compiled by Marjorie
Engber. New York: Center for Inter-American Relations, 1970.
86p. Paperback.
Bibliography of fiction and poetry by Caribbean authors published in the United States and Great Britain, from 1900 through
September of 1970. The works from French, Dutch, and the Spanish-
speaking areas are included only if they have been translated into English. Of the 472 volumes, divided into anthologies, poetry,
short stories, and novels, 52 contain writings by Spanish Ameri-
cans. This bibliography identifies 58 anthologies, some of which
duplicate titles in Levine's Latin American Fiction and Poetry in
Translation.

FLORES, ANGEL. Bibliografía de escritores hispanoamericanos, 1609-
1974. New York: Gordian Press, 1975. 318p.
An important bibliography of Spanish-American writers. Includes
index.

FOSTER, DAVID W. The 20th Century Spanish American Novel: A Bibliographical Guide. Metuchen, N. J.: Scarecrow Press, 1975. 234p.
Bibliography of the criticism pertaining to 56 well-known
Spanish-American novelists. For each author, nationality and
dates are followed by citations to books, bibliographies, and essays. The majority of the items are in Spanish, culled from
periodicals.

GROPP, ARTHUR E. A Bibliography of Latin American Bibliographies.
Compiled by Arthur E. Gropp. Metuchen, N. J.: The Scarecrow
Press, Inc., 1968. Supplement. 1971.
Gropp updates the second edition of Cecil Knight Jones' (1872-
1945) Bibliography of Latin American Bibliographies. Jones or-
ganized his bibliography by countries, whereas Gropp arranged
them by subjects and within subjects, by countries. The Supplement (1971) includes bibliographies published as monographs during
1965-1969. It also includes bibliographies not recorded in the
1968 edition and references to 64 bibliographical journals which
do not duplicate those cited in previous editions. A new supplement to Gropp, sponsored by the Seminar on the Acquisition of
Latin American Library Materials (SALALM), under the general ed-
itorship of Daniel Raposo Cordeiro will be published by Scarecrow
Press, in 1977. It will include periodical articles since 1966
and books from 1969 on.

GROPP, ARTHUR E. A Bibliography of Latin American Bibliographies
Published in Periodicals. Volume I: A - D; Volume II: E - Z.
Metuchen, N. J.: The Scarecrow Press, 1976. 1102p.
970 references culled from more than 1000 periodicals covering
materials prior to and through 1965.

Handbook of Latin American Studies. Gainesville: University of
Florida Press, 1936-
Prepared by a number of contributors for the Latin American,
Portuguese, and Spanish Divisions of the Library of Congress. An
essential research tool, particularly in the humanities and the
social sciences, which broadly surveys the bibliographical output
of Latin America "ensuring regular and timely receipt of materials
intended for review." Annotations are brief but useful. Abbre-
viations, acronyms, title list of journals indexed, and subject
and author indices included.

HULET, CLAUDE L. Latin American Poetry in English Translation. A
Bibliography. Compiled by Claude L. Hulet. Washington, D. C.:
Pan American Union, 1965. 192p.
Represented in this bibliography are 19 Spanish-speaking na-
tions, Brazil, and Haiti. Inclusions through August 1, 1962.
Also contains: "Anthologies, Collections and Miscellaneous Works
Containing Poetry," "Periodicals Frequently Used in this Bibliog-
raphy," "Appendix," and "Author Index."

_____. Latin American Prose in English Translation. A Bibliography.
Compiled by Claude L. Hulet. Washington, D. C.: Pan American
Union, 1964. 191p. (Basic Bibliographies, I).
Includes materials on 19 Spanish-speaking countries, Brazil,
and Haiti, through August 1, 1962: biography, drama, essay, literary criticism, novel, philosophy, short story, anthropology,
archaeology, sociology and related subjects, anthologies and
other works containing translations, periodicals frequently used
in the bibliography, a bibliography of bibliographies of translations, author index. Foreword and introduction by Claude L. Hulet, pp. xiv-xvii.

LEVINE, SUZANNE JILL. Latin America. Fiction & Poetry in Translation. Compiled by Suzanne Jill Levine. New York: Center for
Inter-American Relations, 1970. 72p.
List of contemporary fiction and poetry by authors from Spanish
and Portuguese-speaking countries of the Western Hemisphere, published in English, in the United States through December 1970.
This bibliography identifies 33 anthologies.

MATLAW, MYRON. Modern World Drama. An Encyclopedia. New York:
E. P. Dutton & Co. Inc., 1972. 960p.
Has brief but up-to-date discussions of drama in Latin America.
Includes bibliographies.

Further Reading: Essays, Criticism

PARISEAU, EARL J., ed. Latin America: An Acquisition Guide for Colleges and Public Libraries. Consortium of Latin American Studies, Publication No. 7, 1975. 754p.

An impressive guide "to assist the reference and acquisitions librarian at smaller colleges, universities, and public libraries to build basic collections of Latin American library materials. The Guide contains approximately 2,600 references concerning Mexico, Central America, the Caribbean, and South America. Emphasis is on works in English but important foreign language materials are also included. The English, Dutch, French, and Spanish-speaking Caribbean are all represented, as well as the Commonwealth of Puerto Rico and the U. S. Virgin Islands." Contents: General Reference Works and Bibliographies, Art, Economics, Education, Geography, Government and Politics, History, Indigenous Peoples, Law, Literature, Music, Philosophy, Society, appendices and an author index.

Puerto Rican Literature: Translations into English. Literatura Puertorriqueña: Traducciones al Inglés. Compiled by the staff of the Biblioteca José M. Lázaro. Recinto de Río Piedras, Universidad de Puerto Rico, 1974. 38p. (Mimeographed).

This bibliography is limited to Puerto Rican authors in the holdings of the Puerto Rican Collection of the Biblioteca José M. Lázaro. "The number of sources consulted to compile this edition was very limited due to time limitations, but we plan to expand it in future editions." This guide includes short stories, essays, novels, poetry, drama, anthologies, newspapers indexed, plus author, Spanish title, and English title indices.

SHAW, BRADLEY A. Latin American Literature in Translation: An Annotated Bibliography. New York: New York University Press, 1976.

This bibliography of anthologies and individual works on Latin American literature in English translation is "...a guide for professors who wish to select books for courses of literature in translation, and for students and other interested readers who wish to begin their study of the literature." This work, which partially updates the bibliographies of Hulet, Levine, and Engber, is limited to fiction, poetry and drama, and selected literary essays in English translation. No references are made to works published after December 31, 1974. It is divided in three sections: Spanish American literature, Brazilian literature, and the literature of the Caribbean islands and the Guyanas (mostly French). Two appendixes are also added: a selected, annotated list of the Spanish chronicles of the New World, and Indian literature of Latin America in English translation. Author, English titles, original titles, and country indices provided.

WILGUS, KARNA S. Latin American Books. An Annotated Bibliography.
Compiled and edited by Karna S. Wilgus. New York: Center for
Inter-American Relations, 1974. 80p.
A useful "selection of books for students and teachers, which
covers the area from Mexico and the Caribbean southward to Chile
and Argentina--its history, cultural and geographical diversity,
people, problems and its relations to the United States." Part I,
Section 4, includes an annotated list of Latin American novels,
short stories, poetry, essays, plays, history and criticism.

WOODYARD, GEORGE W. and LYDAY, LEON F. "Studies on the Latin American Theatre 1960-1969." Theatre Documentation, Volume 2, Number 1 & 2 (Fall 1969/Spring 1970), pp. 49-84.
694 "...references to studies published between 1960 and 1969
on the Latin American theatre, including critical references from
scholarly and specialized journals, book-length studies, Ph.D.
dissertations, and reviews of books cited." Provides a useful
supplement to the PMLA annual bibliography. "Primary sources are
not included, except in those cases in which an anthology or collection contains a valuable introduction or prologue." Includes
an index to 117 dramatists.

ARTICLES, REVIEWS

ALEGRÍA, FERNANDO. "The Most Significant Decade in Latin American
Fiction." Publishers Weekly 200:166-168 (September 27, 1971).
"Some of our young novelists and critics seem to feel that they
have invented the 20th Century novel...They are only guilty of
honest ignorance, or playful vanity." Alegría makes one mistake
in this article. He declares that Miguel Ángel Asturias is "the
first Latin American novelist ever to win..." the Nobel Prize.
The Chilean Gabriela Mistral received the Nobel Prize for Literature in 1945.

BLACKBURN, SARA. "Translator Supreme." The New York Review of Books
(September 15, 1974), pp. 40-42.
A paean in honor of Gregory Rabassa, Professor of Romance Lan-
guages at Queens College and the Graduate School, C.U.N.Y., con-
sidered one of the few great contemporary translators. "Since
1963, he has been offering English-speaking readers the best of
an extraordinary flowering of Latin American fiction: Julio
Cortázar's 'Hopscotch,' Gabriel García Márquez's 'One Hundred
Years of Solitude,' José Lezama Lima's rich intensely sensuel
'Paradiso,' Mario Vargas Llosa's 'The Green House'..., etc."

Books Abroad. An International Literary Quarterly. Sponsored by the
University of Oklahoma, 1927-
Particularly during the 70's, several issues of Books Abroad
have been devoted to a critical survey of Latin American prose
and poetry. Of particular interest are the following volumes:

FURTHER READING: ESSAYS, CRITICISM

Volume 44, Number 1, Winter 1970. Includes the important essay by Mario Vargas Llosa entitled "The Latin American Novel Today" (pp. 7-45), and contributions by Donald A. Yates, Marta Morello-Frosh, Wolfgang Lucting, Gregory Rabassa, Klaus Müller-Bergh, Frank Dauster, Emir Rodríguez Monegal. Also contains photographs of José Lezama Lima (Cuba), Mario Vargas Llosa (Peru), Julio Cortázar (Argentina), and Gabriel García Márquez (Colombia).

Volume 45, Number 2, Spring 1970. H. Ernest Lewald's "Argentine Literature: National or European?"

Volume 45, Number 3, Summer 1971. "The Cardinal Points of Borges: A Symposium." (pp. 383-469). 14 articles, including Thomas E. Lyon's "Jorge Luis Borges: Selected Bibliography," a photograph of Borges (1964) and a facsimile page from "Nota sobre the Purple Land."

Volume 46, Number 4, Autumn 1972. "Symposium on Octavio Paz." (pp. 543-613). 12 articles, four photos of Paz, and a facsimile of his poem "Pasado en claro."

Volume 47, Number 1, Winter 1973. "Introducing Two 1972 Laureates." Essays on Gabriel García Márquez (Colombia) and Octavio Paz (Mexico). Includes "A Selection of Spanish American Fiction 1935-1970."

Volume 47, Number 3, Summer 1973. 10 articles devoted to Gabriel García Márquez (pp. 444-505), on the occasion of his acceptance of the Newstadt International Prize for Literature. Photo of G. García Márquez.

Volume 50, Number 3, Summer 1973. A volume devoted entirely to Julio Cortázar, includes one short story, essays, criticism, bibliography and numerous photographs.

CHRIST, RONALD. "Translators Arise!" The New York Times Book Review (September 8, 1974), p. 47.
Ronald Christ, teacher of English, translator, and editor, makes a dramatic plea for translators "to raise their own consciousness ...you have nothing to gain but your royalties and your royalty." "...Translation of Latin American literature has reached an unequaled level of achievement...American translations...are among the best in the world."

DAVIS, DEBORAH LARRABEE. "Will 1973 Be the Year for Latin Writers?" Publishers Weekly, 203:40-43 (February 19, 1973).
An informative article which focuses on the current U. S. publishing interest in Latin American fiction and provides interesting insights on the publishing industry, translators, critics, editors, non-profit organizations and the Latin American authors themselves. The article is enhanced by eleven photographs of contemporary Latin American writers.

FUENTES, CARLOS. "Remembering Pablo Neruda." The New York Times Book Review (November 11, 1973), pp. 55, 51.
Homage to Pablo Neruda, Nobel Prize for Literature in 1971, "a teen-age poet, flanked by Rimbaud and Whitman at 20, [who] revo-

(FUENTES, CARLOS).
lutionized the poetry written in the Spanish language...All of
Spanish America was resurrected in his tongue...Our novels were
written under the sign of Neruda..."

HONIG, EDWIN. "A Conversation with Octavio Paz." New Boston Review,
Volume I, Number 4, (Spring 1976), pp. 3-6.
The Mexican poet Octavio Paz speaks about the art of transla-
tion.

LEVINE, SUZANNE JILL. "Last Battle for a Free Press in Uruguay."
The New York Times Book Review (May 12, 1974), p. 47.
A bitter article which decries the brutality of the police
against such Uruguayan writers and publishers as Juan Carlos
Onetti, Nelson Marra, Mercedes Rein, Hugo R. Alfaro, and others.

_____. "A Massive Novel of Peruvian Realities." Review of Conversa-
tions in the Cathedral, by Mario Vargas Llosa. Translated from
the Spanish by Gregory Rabassa. The New York Review of Books
(March 23, 1975), p. 1.
"It would be a pity if the enormous but not unsurmountable difficulties of reading this massive novel prevent readers from be-
coming acquainted with a book that reveals, as few others have,
some of the ugly complexities of the real Latin America."

LOTTMAN, HERBERT R. "Gabriel García Márquez, an Interview." Publishers Weekly, 205:8-9 (May 13, 1974).
The Colombian author of One Hundred Years of Solitude is letting
his new novel cool while he plunges into films and journalism.
He asserts that "Novelists are crows, feeding on the garbage of
society."

REVIEW. Published since 1968 by the Center of Inter-American Relations, Inc., New York. (Annual: 1968, 1969, 1970; twice a year:
1971, 1972; three times a year since 1973.)
Essays, interviews, critical analysis and excerpts from poems,
novels, short stories, illustrations, and reviews by well-known
Spanish-speaking and English authors, critics, artists. An in-
dispensable journal for the understanding of contemporary Latin
American literature.

RODRÍQUEZ MONEGAL, EMIR. "The New Latin American Novelists."
TriQuarterly 13/14:13-32 (Fall/Winter 1968/69).
An excellent survey of the contemporary Latin American novel.
The entire theme of this issue of TriQuarterly focuses on Latin
American literature.

Saturday Review. "World Literary Survey." April 19, 1975,
pp. 19-31.
Brief but excellent overview of some lesser-known authors, includes Gregory Rabassa's essay on the contemporary literature of
Brazil (pp. 19-20) and Luis A. Diez's essay on Latin America
(pp. 27-29).

		ORDER CARD MESSAGE AREA						
		SELECTION LIST		QUANTITY ORDERED		ORDER LIST PRICE		QTY
TR. CODE	LIBRARY OF CONGRESS NUMBER	NUMBER	SYMBOLS					
		AGENCY	P	R/C	QTY	AGENCY	P	R/C	QTY
33	Ref Z 1609 T7 F74							

AGENCY	P	R/C	QTY	AGENCY	P	R/C	QTY	AGENCY	P	R/C	QTY
50	C001										

Further Reading: Essays, Criticism

SHEPPARD, R. Z. "Caged Condor." Review of <u>Conversations in the Cathedral</u>, by Mario Vargas Llosa. Translated by Gregory Rabassa. <u>Time</u> (February 17, 1975), p. 82.

In this review, Sheppard compares the Colombian Gabriel García Márquez with Faulkner and the Peruvian Mario Vargas Llosa with Dreiser. "Throughout Central and South America, writers still seem willing to tackle the long, complex novel of politics, society and class."

VARGAS LLOSA, MARIO. "The Latin American Novel Today: Introduction." <u>Books Abroad</u>, 44:7-16 (Winter 1970).

Probably the finest and most perceptive essay on the present state-of-the-art of the Latin American novel. Although there is a definitive emphasis on the novel, Vargas Llosa's impeccable style transcends the boundaries of the narrative to encompass all literary genres. He asserts that "...the maturity of the Latin American novel signifies the achievement of aesthetic independence...the Latin American novelist no longer imitates: he assimilates, he adapts, he modifies, he discriminates and puts to use those imported models that are most consistent with his own literary objectives. Communication has replaced subordination, mutual exchange has replaced dependence. For the first time, literary influences do not operate in only one direction: it is no longer surprising to detect in the works of young European writers a resemblance to the work of Cortázar, or to discover in the pages of <u>Tel Quel</u> of Paris that a French essayist repeats as his own the literary opinions that Borges formulated ten years ago." (pp. 10-11).

WHITE, EDMUND. "Four Ways to Read a Masterpiece." Review of José Lezama Lima's <u>Paradiso</u>. Translated from the Spanish by Gregory Rabassa. <u>The New York Times Book Review</u> (April 21, 1974), pp. 27-28.

"...the stated intention of <u>Paradiso</u> is to portray as closely as possible the daily life of a Cuban man and his family."

WOOD, MICHAEL. "The Poetry of Neruda." Review of <u>Residence on Earth</u>, <u>Extravagaria</u>, and <u>Five Decades: A Selection (Poems: 1925-1970)</u>. <u>The New York Review of Books</u> (October 3, 1974), pp. 8-11.

A critical review and penetrating analysis of these translations makes it clear that in general "...translators [refuse] to leave him alone, a reluctance to say what he says, a perverse, elaborate flight from the tone of the original."